We Believe

Living in the Light of God's Truth

JAMES T. DRAPER JR.

LEARNING ACTIVITIES AND LEADER GUIDE BY TERRY HADAWAY

LifeWay Press®
Nashville, Tennessee

ISBN 0-6330-9129-4

This book is the text for course CG-0958 in the subject area Biblical Studies in the Christian
Growth Study Plan.

Dewey Decimal Classification Number: 230.6
Subject Headings: BAPTISTS—DOCTRINES \ BAPTISTS—HERITAGE \ SOUTHERN BAPTISTS

Unless otherwise noted, all Scripture quotations are from the *Holman Christian Standard Bible®,*
copyright 1999, 2000, 2002, 2003 by Holman Bible Publishers. Used by permission.

Scripture quotations marked NKJV are from the *New King James Version.*
Copyright © 1979, 1980, 1982, Thomas Nelson, Inc., Publishers.

Scripture quotations marked KJV are from the *King James Version.*

We believe that the Bible has God for its author; salvation for its end; and truth, without
any mixture of error, for its matter and that all Scripture is totally true and trustworthy.

To order additional copies of this resource, write to LifeWay Church Resources Customer Service;
One LifeWay Plaza; Nashville, TN 37234-0113; fax (615) 251-5933;
phone toll free (800) 458-2772; e-mail *customerservice@lifeway.com;*
order online at *www.lifeway.com;* or visit the LifeWay Christian Store serving you.

Printed in the United States of America

Leadership and Adult Publishing
LifeWay Church Resources
One LifeWay Plaza
Nashville, TN 37234-0175

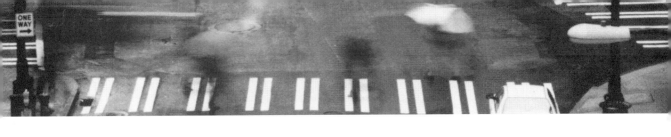

Contents

The Author

JAMES T. DRAPER JR. is the president and chief executive officer of LifeWay Christian Resources of the Southern Baptist Convention in Nashville, Tennessee. Prior to coming to LifeWay in 1991, he pastored a number of churches in Texas, Oklahoma, and Missouri, including First Baptist Church in Euless, Texas. Draper has traveled in 32 countries around the world, leading evangelistic services, teaching conferences, and meeting with missionaries and nationals.

A graduate of Baylor University, Draper received a master of divinity degree from Southwestern Baptist Theological Seminary. He holds doctor of divinity degrees from Howard Payne University, Campbell University, and California Baptist University and a doctor of humanities degree from Dallas Baptist University.

Draper has served on the boards of trustees for a number of Southern Baptist schools and agencies. He served as the president of the Southern Baptist Convention from 1982 to 1984.

Draper is the author of more than 20 books, including *The Church Christ Approves; Say, Neighbor, Your House Is on Fire;* and *Authority: The Critical Issue for the Body of Christ.* His writings include studies of Old Testament books, such as Amos, Proverbs, Jonah, Job, and Psalms, and New Testament books, such as Philippians, Colossians, 1 and 2 Timothy, James, and Hebrews.

Draper and his wife, Carol Ann, have three grown children and six grandchildren.

Introduction

The 21st century has revealed the most chaotic and disoriented culture in the history of our world. Although the roots of today's problems can be traced to earlier times and cultures, it seems that the depth and pervasiveness of spiritual and moral confusion are greater today than ever before. What should we believe? Why should we believe anything at all? How do we know what is true or whether anything is true?

Our culture tells us that many different belief systems exist, each offering an equally valid view of truth. What works for one person may not work for another, but whatever works is true and right. This distorted way of thinking denies the existence of absolute truth, so nothing can be said to be true or false at all times and places. Therefore, every standard of truth is challenged or rejected. We are told that we must accept all ideas and values without passing judgment on any that differ from our own. Without an objective standard of truth, we must never pass judgment on someone's actions or ideas. Whatever someone believes or does must be accepted. Tolerance of all thoughts, ideas, and behaviors is the rule of our day.

At the same time, the spiritual and moral foundation of our nation is crumbling. The standards that cultivated human dignity and respect in America are the values revealed in the Bible. Yet today the Christian faith is ridiculed as bigoted, and biblical values are relentlessly attacked as outmoded and coercive. Immorality abounds. The family as God designed it is disappearing. Biblical Christianity is being rejected for false forms of spirituality. And the emptiness of the human heart is only increasing.

Why should we study what we believe? Because only Christianity offers a viable alternative to the crisis of belief in our culture today. Believers have no question about the existence of absolute truth. God's word is truth (see John 17:17), and Jesus Himself is "the way, the truth, and the life" (John 14:6). Through obedience to the word of Christ, we can know the truth that sets us free (see John 8:32). Knowing that truth, we are compelled to share it with others and to transform our culture through the love of Christ. This study will help you develop a biblical belief system and commit to share the truth with others. In addition, you will be better equipped to contend for your faith in a society that is increasingly hostile to the message of Jesus Christ (see Jude 3).

Why should we study what we believe? Because our beliefs determine our values and our actions. God has a purpose for our lives. God has put us here to reflect His presence, to reveal His truth, and to carry out His unique will for our lives. Therefore, it is vital for us to know what God's Word says about Himself, His world, His ways, and His purposes. This study will lead you to discover these truths. You will know what you believe about key biblical beliefs, and you will be able to explain the basis of your belief system.

Why should we study what we believe? Because Jesus promised an abundant life (see John 10:10), not a life of confusion and chaos. By understanding and living according to biblical beliefs, we can have meaning in life, invest in the things that matter to God, and meet the challenges of life in the 21st century. We must learn to think and live by biblical values to see life as God intended. This study will help you build a meaningful life on God's truth through the indwelling presence of God's Son and in the power of God's Spirit.

Our study of biblical beliefs will be organized around these questions:

• What is God like, and how do we know?
• Who are we, and how can we know God personally?
• Why did God establish the church, and what is our role in it?
• What is our purpose in life?
• Should Christians try to shape society?
• Where is this world headed?
• How can we participate in God's plan?

By discovering biblical answers to these questions, you will learn how to know and live by God's truth. I pray that you will be blessed and your Christian life enriched through this journey.

CHAPTER 1

What Is God like, and How Do We Know?

We live in a day of great spiritual confusion and deception. In our society many competing voices claim to know the truth about who God is and what His purpose is for our lives. Muslims believe that God is the unknowable, capricious ruler of the universe who demands adherence to his laws. Hindus and New Age followers believe that all things and all people are part of their impersonal concept of God. And in our increasingly secular society many people do not even believe that God exists.

Write the way you would respond if someone asked you this question: What is God like? Limit your answer to 25 or fewer words.

_____

_____

_____

_____

The questions of who God is and what He is like are important for every individual to answer. Your belief about God determines not only your priorities and purposes for your life on earth but also your eternal destiny. Your answers to these questions must be based on the truth, not on myths and misconceptions.

The Christian faith is founded on a clear understanding of who God is and what God is like. People can know God because He has chosen to reveal Himself to us. His revelation comes through two primary sources—nature and the Bible. Theologians sometimes refer to these sources as natural and supernatural revelation, respectively. In reality, both forms of revelation are supernatural because God is supernatural.

My understanding of God came very early in my life. My father and grandfather were Baptist preachers. What they knew about God came from their study of the Bible. Some of my earliest memories are of my parents teaching me biblical truths about God. I accepted Jesus as my Savior when I was six years old, so I have been a believer most of my life. Through these many years the Bible has been the primary source of my understanding of what God is like.

I recall one experience when my appreciation of the Bible as the source of truth became very real to me. The summer before my sophomore year in college, I preached many times in youth revivals. My grandfather was dying of cancer when I visited him for the last time. One morning he looked at me with a twinkle in his eye and asked, "Little Jimmy, would you like to know where you could find a good sermon?" "Of course," I said. Clutching his Bible the way a mother would cradle a newborn baby, he said, "From Genesis to Revelation!" He died a few weeks after that, and his counsel sealed my commitment to the Bible as the measure of all truth and the foundation of all valid messages from God.

Join me in discovering why the Bible is our clearest source of information about God. Then we will examine what the Bible tells us about God's nature and His will for all people.

What Do We Believe About the Scriptures?

The best and most accurate commentary on the Bible is the Bible itself. Look with me at two statements from the Bible about its origin. The first is 2 Timothy 3:16-17. Stop and read those verses in the margin. The word *inspiration* literally means *God-breathed*. God breathed truth into His chosen writers, and the words they wrote were His words. However, they were not taking dictation, with their minds in neutral, acting like puppets on strings. God used each writer's understanding and personality, but He directed the message that was recorded. *Inspiration* means that God directly revealed His truth through the writer's words.

"All Scripture is inspired by God and is profitable for teaching, for rebuking, for correcting, for training in righteousness, so that the man of God may be complete, equipped for every good work" (2 Tim. 3:16-17).

"No prophecy of Scripture comes from one's own interpretation, because no prophecy ever came by the will of man; instead, moved by the Holy Spirit, men spoke from God" (2 Pet. 1:20-21).

Check the correct answer. The Bible is inspired because—
☐ it has been relied on for years and years;
☐ it contains stories about God and Jesus;
☐ it is God-breathed;
☐ it has been proved to be inspired.

We gain further insight about the nature of the Bible from 2 Peter 1:20-21, which is printed in the margin. Peter declared that the biblical prophets "spoke from God" because they were "moved by the Holy Spirit." The word *moved* means *carried along*. The Greek word translated *Spirit* is *pneuma*, which means *breath, spirit,* or *wind*. As Peter wrote these words, he may have recalled his experiences as a fisherman on the Sea of Galilee. His small boat depended on the wind to fill the sail and carry the craft along. Peter's understanding of the way God's prophets spoke His truth was that the Holy Spirit (*breath of God—pneuma*) carried their thoughts along the same way the wind (*pneuma*) carries a boat.

When God supernaturally directed the writers of Scripture, He did not suspend their personalities, literary styles, or emotions. But He communicated His truth by guiding their thoughts, guarding them from error, and producing a totally reliable message. Thus, every word of the original manuscripts bears the authority of divine authorship. This means that the Bible is accurate in all it says, and it does not deceive its readers theologically, historically, chronologically, geographically, or scientifically.

When the Bible and modern science differ in regard to a specific belief, which do you believe?
☐ Modern science   ☐ The Bible

Why? _____

_____

_____

The Bible contains approximations on some subjects and uses figures of speech and the common language of particular cultures and periods of time; but whatever it says, the Bible says it accurately. God's Word is not a textbook on science or history. It is not even a textbook on theology. However, what the Scriptures reveal about any of these areas of thought is correct, and no one will be deceived or led into error by believing what the Bible says. Though written by more than 50 authors over a period of 1,500 years, this amazing Library of 66 books has one unifying theme—the revelation of the one true God and His plan of redemption.

True and Trustworthy

Several terms emphasize the reliability of the Bible:
- *Inerrancy*—without error
- *Infallibility*—cannot fail
- *Plenary, verbal inspiration*— all the words of the Bible are inspired, not just the concepts. One book of the Bible is just as inspired as another.

These terms affirm what *The Baptist Faith and Message* states about the Bible: "The Holy Bible was written by men divinely inspired and is God's revelation of Himself to man. It is a perfect treasure of divine instruction. It has God for its author, salvation for its end, and truth, without any mixture of error, for its matter. Therefore, all Scripture is totally true and trustworthy."[1]

The Authority of the Bible

God's inspiration of Scripture is the basis for its authority. We can be certain about the truths revealed in the Bible because God is its author. Not everyone holds to this view of ultimate authority. Look at these three basic approaches to understanding truth:

1. *Rationalism* maintains that humans have the intrinsic ability to gather facts and arrive at valid conclusions. In its expanded form *rationalism* means that truth can be determined by experimentation—by human senses and observation of phenomena. Whatever a person is able to comprehend and state as truth is true, according to this view. Such reasoning makes the human mind the ultimate authority, whether by natural ability, mystical infiltration, experimentation, or sensory experience. All of these processes ultimately bring the human mind to the forefront as the ultimate source of authority.

2. *Ecclesiastical authority* holds that the church stands in the position of ultimate authority. Whatever the church determines to be true must be accepted without question. The classic model of ecclesiastical authority is the historical position of the Roman Catholic Church, which places itself and its decrees above any other source of knowledge, including the Bible.

3. *Divine revelation* includes both God's general revelation in creation and His special revelation, which is the Bible. We can observe certain fundamental truths about God's existence, wisdom, and sovereignty through nature. However, the Bible alone reveals His character, attributes, laws, purpose for humankind, and acts of redemption. Evangelical Christians look to this inspired Book as the ultimate revelation of truth and therefore the final authority in all matters of belief and behavior.

Divinely Inspired

These quotations represent past Baptist leaders' commitment to the authority of Scripture.

- "The holy scriptures ... are given by Divine inspiration and in their first donation were without error, most perfect and therefore Canonical."[2]—John Smyth, the leader of the first Baptist church, Amsterdam, 1609

- "The Authority of the Holy Scripture for which it ought to be believed dependeth not upon the testimony of any man or Church; but wholly upon God (who is truth itself) the Author thereof; therefore it is to be received, because it is the Word of God."[3] —The Second London Confession (1688–89), an influential Baptist statement of faith

- "It [the Bible] must come with authority, claiming and proving its claim to be the word of God ... that man may with confidence believe and trust the promises and hopes of pardon and peace it may hold out."[4]—James P. Boyce, a founding professor, The Southern Baptist Theological Seminary

- "It has always been a matter of profound surprise to me that anybody should ever question the verbal inspiration of the Bible."[5]—B. H. Carroll, founder, Southwestern Baptist Theological Seminary

Historically, Baptists have held to the position of divine revelation as the sole basis of our knowledge of truth. Read in the box on page 10 several statements made by Baptist leaders from the past. These confirm the historic Baptist belief in the authority and integrity of the Scriptures. Baptists' historic, orthodox position is, and always has been, that the Bible is accurate in all it says and, when properly interpreted, does not deceive its readers in any way or mislead them in any area of truth.

Match each term with its meaning.

___ 1. Rationalism   a. The church is the ultimate authority.

___ 2. Ecclesiastical authority   b. God reveals Himself through nature and the Bible.

___ 3. Divine revelation   c. Humans can gather facts and arrive at valid conclusions.

The Purpose of the Bible

Why has God so deliberately and persistently inspired chosen writers to record His Word? Again, let the Bible speak for itself. The clearest purpose statement for the Bible occurs in John 20:30-31. Stop and read John's words in the margin.

> "Jesus performed many other signs in the presence of His disciples that are not written in this book. But these are written so that you may believe Jesus is the Messiah, the Son of God, and by believing you may have life in His name" (John 20:30-31).

The Bible is the Book of life—it comes from the Source of all life, describes the true meaning of life, and reveals the way to abundant and everlasting life. That way to life is Jesus Christ. All who believe and receive Him have His life—eternal life. John affirmed this truth in his first epistle: "God has given us eternal life, and this life is in His Son. The one who has the Son has life. The one who doesn't have the Son of God does not have life. I have written these things to you who believe in the name of the Son of God, so that you may know that you have eternal life" (1 John 5:11-13).

One dominant theme gives unity to the entire Bible. This theme is Jesus Christ, who is identified as the Word of God (see John 1:1,14). When certain Jews became enraged and sought to kill Jesus because He healed a man on the Sabbath, He challenged them by saying, " 'You pore over the Scriptures because you think you have eternal life in them, yet they testify about Me' " (John 5:39). On the day of His resurrection Jesus appeared to two believers on their way to Emmaus. Listen to this description of their conversation: "Beginning with Moses and all the Prophets, He interpreted for them in all the Scriptures the things concerning Himself" (Luke 24:27). Later that evening Jesus appeared in Jerusalem to His disciples and said, " 'These are My words that I spoke to you while I was still with you, that everything written about Me in the Law of Moses, the Prophets, and the Psalms must be fulfilled' " (Luke 24:44). In each of these statements Jesus pointed to Himself as the primary subject of all the Scriptures. What an amazing testimony to the divine authorship of the Bible! Most of the biblical writers had no personal knowledge of Jesus; yet they were all inspired to write about Him. There is no human explanation for such a remarkable phenomenon.

We are indebted to the Scriptures for all we know about Jesus, and that testimony about Him is confirmed by our personal experience with Him. We do not measure our understanding of Jesus Christ by our experience; rather, our understanding of Him is confirmed by Scripture. We can be certain that none of our God-given experiences will contradict what the Bible declares about Christ.

Some leaders claim that Jesus Christ is the criterion for our understanding of Scripture. That is true as long as the Jesus they refer to is the same Jesus presented in the Bible. We cannot properly interpret the Scripture as a result of mystical experience. Any authentic revelation of Christ comes through the written Word of God. Experience must always be evaluated in the light of this final authority.

Some critics discount certain Scriptures, claiming that Jesus did not say or do certain things. However, Jesus clearly affirmed all Scripture as reliable. Any attempt to place Him in opposition to the record of the Holy Word denies the truth. The life and work of Jesus constitute the basic subject matter of the Bible. And all we read there about Him is as reliable as the nature of God—the One who inspired this sacred Book. *The Baptist Faith and Message* affirms this fact: "The Holy Bible was written by men divinely inspired and is God's revelation of Himself to man. It is a perfect treasure of divine instruction. It has God for its author, salvation for its end, and truth, without any mixture of error, for its matter. Therefore, all Scripture is totally true and trustworthy. ... All Scripture is a testimony to Christ, who is Himself the focus of divine revelation."[6]

The Proof of the Bible

Is there evidence beyond the claim of Scripture for its reliability? Is there a means of actually testing the truthfulness of the Bible? Josh McDowell is a Christian apologist who has done extensive research on the claim that the Bible is the totally reliable and trustworthy Word of God. In his interesting book *Evidence That Demands a Verdict* McDowell cites many types of evidence proving the Bible to be true. One of these is the evidence of fulfilled prophecies. For example, McDowell states that "the Old Testament contains over 300 references to the Messiah that were fulfilled in Jesus." He presents a list of 61 of these prophecies along with biblical statements of their fulfillment. A total of 29 prophecies were made about Jesus' betrayal, trial, death, and burial. Although various biblical writers made these 29 predictions over a period of several hundred years, they were all fulfilled during one 24-hour period of time. McDowell goes on to record numerous other prophecies that came to completion in the person of Jesus.[7] Such amazing evidence goes far beyond the possibility of chance or random occurrences. Here is undeniable proof of the divine authorship of Scripture!

Another type of evidence can be offered for the reliability of Scripture: the ultimate test of Scripture is the evidence of the transformed lives of those who believe its teachings. The writer of Hebrews declared, "The word of God is living and effective" (Heb. 4:12). The Bible is a living Book because it is the message of the only true and living God, who imparts His life to those who believe what He promises. And the Bible is effective in the sense of effectively producing significant change in believers.

How does your daily life show evidence that the Bible is reliable? _____

_____

_____

_____

How Reliable Are the Biblical Documents?

Both the quantity and the quality of the manuscripts of the Scriptures give us confidence in the Bible's accuracy. Although no original manuscripts of Old Testament books exist, scribes took painstaking efforts to preserve the Old Testament books by copying them by hand. One valuable library of copies was made by the Masoretes around A.D. 600 to 950. They devised complex methods to safeguard the accuracy of their copies of Old Testament manuscripts.

The Dead Sea Scrolls, discovered in 1947, provided us a Hebrew text dating from the second century B.C. Including all Old Testament books except Esther, the Dead Sea Scrolls confirm the reliability of the Masoretic text and other ancient manuscript copies of the Old Testament.

Another important discovery was the pre-Christian Greek version of the Old Testament called the Septuagint, produced from about 285 to 270 B.C. This version is frequently quoted in the New Testament because it served as the Bible of Greek-speaking Christians in the apostolic period. Scholars have also used this text to confirm the accuracy of Hebrew versions of the Old Testament.[8]

No book in ancient literature can compare with the New Testament in documentary support. About 24,000 manuscripts exist—5,664 in Greek; 8,000 to 10,000 in Latin; and 8,000 in Ethiopic, Slavic, and Armenian. In contrast, we have only 7 ancient copies of Plato's writings, 5 of Aristotle's, and 643 of Homer's.

The New Testament manuscripts are not only numerous but also very early. Approximately 75 papyri fragments date from the early second to the mid-eighth century A.D., covering 25 of the 27 New Testament books. One fragment of the Book of John has been dated as early as 100 A.D.

We therefore possess New Testament manuscripts dating within a couple of generations after the originals were written. In contrast, the oldest existing manuscripts of most nonbiblical books date from 8 or 10 centuries after the original works were written. For example, the oldest manuscript of Caesar's *Gallic War*, composed between 58 and 56 B.C., dates from about 900 years after Caesar's day.[9]

The quality of the New Testament manuscripts is without parallel. Because of the great reverence the early Christians had for the Scriptures, they exercised extreme caution in accurately copying and preserving the authentic text. No discrepancies among texts call into question a major doctrine or factual teaching.[10]

Readers today can be confident that English versions of both the Old and New Testaments are trustworthy translations of reliable Hebrew and Greek texts.[11]

The following testimony is one example of the millions of people who have experienced what may be a less dramatic, but nonetheless real, personal transformation. This story begins with a young boy named Johnny Lee Clary, who grew up in Del City, Oklahoma. His father taught him to dislike all African-Americans. Although Johnny became acquainted with Christian truth through Carter Park Baptist Church, his home environment prevented him from continuing in his childhood faith. As a teenager he was sent to live with his sister in California, where conditions were so bad that he considered ending his own life. One day at age 14 Johnny watched a TV program featuring David Duke, a grand wizard of the Ku Klux Klan. This leader declared the same hatred for blacks that Johnny had learned from his father. After Johnny sent for the information being offered, a Klansman visited him and enlisted him in that organization. Within 16 years Johnny had worked his way to the top position of national grand wizard.

A second life enters this story in the person of Wade Watts, who was also a leader. However, his organization was the NAACP—the National Organization for the Advancement of Colored People. These two men met during a debate on an Oklahoma City radio station in the 1970s. At that time Watts was a target of the Klan, and Clary admits that he called Watts "every name in the book." But Watts always responded with "God bless you, Son; Jesus loves you." Later Clary began to realize that something was missing in his life. In desperation he began reading the Bible. The first passage he noticed was Luke 15, the parable of the Prodigal Son. After reading this account of repentance and returning to God, Clary began a new path of life. He resigned from the Klan in 1989 and, to his own amazement, sensed God's call to preach the very message that had changed his heart.

Johnny Lee Clary called Wade Watts to ask if he remembered him. Watts replied, "Remember you, Son? I've been praying for you for years." Clary's first sermon was in the all-black church where Watts was the pastor. In that service four of Watts's children were saved! This father exclaimed, "Who would have ever believed that God would take an old Ku Klux Klansman, have me pray for him all these years, and use him to come down here and lead my unsaved kids to the Lord?" That day a friendship began between two men who recognized that they were brothers in the Lord. Watts is now in heaven, and Clary is serving the Lord as a full-time evangelist.

"All flesh is like grass,
and all its glory like a flower
of the grass.
The grass withers, and the flower
drops off,
but the word of the Lord endures
forever" (1 Pet. 1:24-25).

This story illustrates what the Bible means when it states, "If anyone is in Christ, there is a new creation; old things have passed away, and look, new things have come" (2 Cor. 5:17). There is no other reasonable explanation for such a miracle except the power of the inspired, totally reliable Word of the living God. We believe that this Bible is the ultimate authority for all matters of faith.

How reassuring to know that in this world of uncertainty we have one changeless, enduring source of truth. Jesus referred to the permanence of God's Word when He said, " 'Heaven and earth will pass away, but My words will never pass away' " (Matt. 24:35). And Peter echoed this truth in 1 Peter 1:24-25 when he quoted the words of Isaiah. Those verses appear in the margin.

God has given us the Bible to be the solid foundation for our faith. In this single volume we find the absolutes so essential to a life of fulfillment and security.

I hope that we can agree on the reliability of the Bible as the inspired revelation of God's truth. Now let's consider what this special Book reveals about its Author.

What Do We Believe About God?

Genesis begins with the fact of God: "In the beginning God" (Gen. 1:1). The Bible does not attempt to prove God's existence. God *is!* And the good news of the Bible is that God has chosen to make Himself known to His creation! From Genesis 1:1 to the end of Revelation, God reveals Himself to people.

The Nature of God as Trinity

Perhaps the most challenging truth about God for us to understand is the fact that in the Bible God reveals Himself as Father, Son, and Holy Spirit. Each is a distinct person with specific roles; yet all three have the same essence, nature, and characteristics—they are the same God. God is therefore one God in three persons. Such a reality is beyond our ability to comprehend. However, we accept many mysteries in life as true even though we cannot explain them. Don't let Satan deceive you into assuming that the Trinity is not true just because you cannot understand how this wondrous truth can be.

Rather than struggle with trying to "unscrew the inscrutable" mystery of the triune nature of God, join me in looking at what the Bible teaches us. Although the term *Trinity* does not appear in the Scriptures, Bible interpreters use that word to describe the threefold nature of God. One theologian suggests that *Tri-unity* would be a more accurate term. Both words refer to the truth that God appears in Scripture as Father, Son, and Holy Spirit. There are no division, no competition, and no limitation among these three. Each is fully God, and each has meaning only in relation to the others. Let's briefly explore the identity of each member of the Trinity.

God the Father. God the Father is the source and origin of all things. He is first revealed in Scripture as the Creator. Beyond that, His love and grace moved Him to provide salvation within Himself, since human beings are powerless to save themselves from sin. God accomplished this by sending His Son to be the Revealer of truth and the Redeemer of lost humankind. God then sent His Spirit to bear witness of Christ, convict the world of sin, and live inside all believers. The Father is worthy of all human adoration and worship because of His perfect holiness and righteousness. He hears and answers our prayers, makes provision for all our needs, and is continuously present with us. After our lives on earth have ended, believers will live with our Father in heaven forever.

Jesus' favorite word for *God* was *Father.* In every sermon and every prayer Jesus spoke of God as Father. One Bible student counted 275 of these references in the New Testament. We owe a large debt to Jesus for teaching us that God is His Father and an even greater debt for making it possible for us to become children of God so that we too can know Him as our Father.

When Jesus stood before Pilate to answer the charges made against Him, He declared, " 'I have come into the world for this: to testify to the truth. Everyone who is of the truth listens to My voice' " (John 18:37).

Jesus said that everyone who is of the truth listens to His voice. Use the following continuum to rate your listening. Place an *X* at the point that represents the degree to which you listen to Jesus.

●——●

Is Jesus speaking to me?   I listen and do everything Jesus says.

Now place an *O* at the place on the continuum that best represents the degree to which you want to listen to Jesus.

What are three things you can do to move from where you are to where you want to be?

1. _____

2. _____

3. _____

God the Son. Another mystery about the Trinity is the dual nature of God the Son. Jesus was both fully human and fully divine. Jesus' humanity is undisputed, for His biography is found in the four Gospels. Like other people, Jesus was born to a woman and had normal human experiences like growth, subjection to parents, hunger, thirst, temptation, suffering, and death. However, the Bible tells us that Jesus was conceived by the Holy Spirit (see Matt. 1:20). Jesus' unique virgin birth revealed His supernatural nature as the Son of God. In Jesus, God came to earth in the flesh. Therefore, unlike any other human, Jesus lived without sin as perfect humanity and perfect divinity.

Jesus' life on earth was a perfect model of what God intended humanity to be. His sinless life qualified Him to be the adequate sacrifice for the sins of all humankind. His death was a penal, substitutionary death. Therefore, Jesus' death is sufficient to secure salvation for all who receive Him by faith. As He died on the cross, He cried, " 'It is finished!' " (John 19:30). The debt of sin was paid in full, and our redemption was completed. This is the central message of the Bible: God came in the person of Jesus Christ and provided the means of salvation for every person. Jesus rose from the dead and ascended to heaven, where He now intercedes for all believers at the throne of God. He also dwells within believers as our Lord. And as *The Baptist Faith and Message* states, one day Jesus will "return in power and glory to judge the world and to consummate His redemptive mission."[12] All of His redeemed will live and rule with Him forever.

Penal: Jesus took on Himself God's judgment for sin. *Substitutionary:* Jesus died in our place, paying the price for our sins.

God the Holy Spirit. The Bible opens and closes with clear references to the Spirit of God (see Gen. 1:2; Rev. 22:17). And throughout its pages we find many more statements that reveal the Holy Spirit as God. Like the Father and the Son, the Spirit is a person. Notice this description given by Jesus: " 'When the Spirit of truth comes, He will guide you into all the truth. For He will not speak on His own, but He will speak whatever He hears' " (John 16:13). The Holy Spirit teaches (see Luke 12:12), speaks (see Acts 13:2), helps (see Rom. 8:26), grieves (see Eph. 4:30), guides (see John 16:13), and performs other functions that reveal His personhood.

Scripture identifies the Holy Spirit as God.

Read the following passages and summarize what each passage says about the Holy Spirit.

Acts 5:3-4: _____

_____

1 Corinthians 3:16: _____

_____

2 Corinthians 3:17: _____

_____

The Holy Spirit has the attributes of God, such as life (see Rom. 8:2), truth (see John 16:13), love (see Rom. 15:30), holiness (see Eph. 4:30), eternity (see Heb. 9:14), and omnipresence (see Ps. 139:7). He does the works that only God can do, such as creating (see Gen. 1:1), casting out demons (see Matt. 12:28), producing spiritual regeneration (see John 3:8), and raising the dead (see Rom. 8:11). The Holy Spirit's specific ministries include inspiring Scripture (see 2 Pet. 1:20-21), revealing Christ's truth and glorification (see John 16:13-15), convicting people of sin (see John 16:8-11), interceding for those who pray (see Rom. 8:26), distributing spiritual gifts (see 1 Cor. 12:7-11), sealing believers (see Eph. 1:13), guiding believers into truth (see John 16:13), producing Christ's character in believers (see Gal. 5:22-23), and many more.

> "The fruit of the Spirit is love, joy, peace, patience, kindness, goodness, faith, gentleness, self-control" (Gal. 5:22-23).

The prominent role of the Holy Spirit in a Christian's life is reflected in the fact that believers are born of the Spirit, sealed by the Spirit, led by the Spirit, and can walk in the Spirit. One of the most important commands for Christians is "Be filled with the Spirit" (Eph. 5:18). It admonishes believers to submit to the guidance of the Holy Spirit. Such surrender enables the Holy Spirit to produce His fruit—the life and character of Christ—in a person's life (see Gal. 5:22-23).

Some people argue that the Bible makes no reference to the Trinity. Read Matthew 28:19-20 and 2 Corinthians 13:13. Then write a statement in response to someone who might doubt biblical evidence of the Trinity. Use these Scriptures to support your statement.

_____

_____

_____

Several biblical statements include all three persons of the Trinity. One of these is the Great Commission (see Matt. 28:19-20). Another is Paul's benediction in 2 Corinthians 13:13. Notice the terms used there to identify the ministry of each member of the Trinity: "The grace of the Lord Jesus Christ, and the love of God, and the fellowship of the Holy Spirit be with all of you." Here is a clear revelation of God's ministry, through His threefold nature, to meet all our needs. Because the Father is love, He extends grace through the Son and produces fellowship by the Holy Spirit. Viewed through the lens of biblical truth, the Trinity is not an insurmountable mystery but an all-encompassing ministry.

The Essential Nature of God

God is so great that any attempt to condense His nature and attributes into human language will fall far short of being complete. However, we can identify five qualities that help us understand more about what God is like.

Spirituality. God is a spiritual being. In John 4:24 Jesus said, " 'God is Spirit.' " This fact has four significant implications that illuminate our understanding of God's nature.

God's Nature
Spirituality
Self-existence
Immensity
Eternity
Unity

1. Spirituality means that God is immaterial and incorporeal. That is, He is not made of physical substance; He does not have a physical body as humans do. When Jesus appeared to His disciples after His resurrection, He said, " 'Look at My hands and My feet, that it is I Myself! Touch Me and see, because a ghost [spirit] does not have flesh and bones as you can see I have' " (Luke 24:39). Jesus was demonstrating that He was corporeal, that He had a real body. In contrast, God in the persons of the Father and the Holy Spirit does not have a material body.

2. Spirituality means that God is invisible. Several Bible references speak of God as invisible (see Rom. 1:20; Col. 1:15; 1 Tim. 1:17). In Deuteronomy 4:15-19 Moses reminded the Israelites of their encounter with God at Mount Sinai: " 'You saw no form of any kind the day the Lord spoke to you at Horeb out of the fire' " (v. 15). Moses went on to warn them not to make any image to represent God. Israel's neighbors were idol worshipers, tempting Israel to create a visible form to represent God. The second of the Ten Commandments prohibited making any type of visible representation of God so that these idols would not become objects of worship.

In the introduction to his Gospel, John stated, "No one has ever seen God" (John 1:18), affirming God's invisibility. Other statements in Scripture, however, seem to contradict this. For example, after Jacob's encounter with God he declared, " 'I saw God face to face' " (Gen. 32:30). At the burning bush Moses "hid his face, because he was afraid to look at God" (Ex. 3:6). And the prophet Isaiah exclaimed, "I saw the Lord seated on a throne, high and exalted. My eyes have seen the King, the LORD Almighty" (Isa. 6:1,5). How can we reconcile these statements with those declaring God to be invisible?

Apparently, God sometimes chose to manifest Himself temporarily in visible form, although never in His full glory as Creator and Sovereign Lord of the universe. In the Old Testament we find instances when the angel of the Lord appeared; these are clearly references to the Lord Himself. As Sovereign God, He may elect to reveal Himself in various ways and on various occasions, but the general truth remains that God is without form and thus cannot be seen. Moreover, if He could be seen in His fully glory, the radiance of His presence would be more than a human could endure. As He stated to Moses, " 'You cannot see my face, for no one may see me and live' " (Ex. 33:20).

3. Spirituality means that God is alive. God is not inanimate. The Bible often refers to Him as the living God (see Josh. 3:10; Ps. 84:2; 1 Thess. 1:9). One of the most emphatic statements is the psalmist's contrast of God with idols in Psalm 115:3-7. Read those verses in the margin. Not only is God alive, but He is also the only living God!

> "Our God is in heaven
> and does whatever He pleases.
> Their idols are silver and gold,
> made by human hands.
> They have mouths, but cannot speak,
> eyes, but cannot see.
> They have ears, but cannot hear,
> noses, but cannot smell.
> They have hands, but cannot feel,
> feet, but cannot walk.
> They cannot make a sound with their throats" (Ps. 115:3-7).

4. Spirituality means that God is a person. God is not a thing, not an influence, but a person. According to the Bible, God has intellect, volition, and sensibility. These are the characteristics of a person—a person with whom we can have an intimate relationship.

Self-existence. God's self-existence means that His existence depends on no one other than Himself. All other beings—humans, angels, and animals—completely depend on God for their existence. Believers frequently ask themselves: *Where did God come from? Who made Him?* The biblical answer is found in the name of God, first given to Moses at the burning bush: "Moses asked God, 'If I go to the Israelites and say to them: The God of your fathers has sent me to you, and they ask me, "What is His name?" what should I tell them?' God replied to Moses, 'I AM WHO I AM. This is what you are to say to the Israelites: I AM has sent me to you' " (Ex. 3:13-14).

The name I AM (also expressed as Jehovah or Yahweh) essentially means *the One who was, who is, and who always will be—the eternally existing One.* God has always existed. This profound reality transcends our finite understanding, but it is nonetheless true.

Immensity. How big is God? Immensity refers to the fact that no matter how large this universe is, God is not contained in it. He is not limited or circumscribed by space. God transcends the universe. In fact, the universe depends on Him for its existence. It is not accurate to say that God is on the outside of the universe looking in, for He is also inside! Dedicating the temple in Jerusalem, Solomon said, "Will God indeed dwell on the earth? Behold, heaven and the heaven of heavens cannot contain You. How much less this temple which I have built!" (1 Kings 8:27, NKJV). Human language is inadequate to express God's immensity.

Eternity. The human understanding of time cannot be applied to God. For Him there are no past, present, and future. God is without beginning or end; He is the cause of time and is free from all succession of time. He knows the future as clearly as He knows the past or present. He simultaneously sees all dimensions of time. The prophet Isaiah quoted the Lord as saying,

> "I am God, and there is no other;
> I am God, and there is none like Me,
> Declaring the end from the beginning,
> And from ancient times things that are not yet done" (Isa. 46:9-10, NKJV).

The psalmist described God's eternal nature with these beautiful words:

> Your years continue through all generations.
> Long ago You established the earth,
> and the heavens are the work of Your hands.
> They will perish, but You will endure;
> all of them will wear out like clothing.
> You will change them like a garment,
> and they will pass away.
> But You are the same,
> and Your years will never end (Ps. 102:24-27).

Unity. God is one and cannot be divided. Although He has revealed Himself as Father, Son, and Holy Spirit, He is not ⅓ Father, ⅓ Son, and ⅓ Holy Spirit. He is one God. Furthermore, each person of the Godhead is fully God. The unity of God emphasizes His wholeness and means that He is indivisible. The Apostle Paul emphasized God's unity when he wrote of Christ, "In Him the entire fullness of God's nature dwells bodily" (Col. 2:9). Moses called the people to remember God's unity when he said, "Hear, O Israel: The LORD our God, the LORD is one" (Deut. 6:4).

Unity also refers to the fact that God is the only true and living God. He is unique—one of a kind. Humans recognize other so-called gods, but none of these are divine. They are either mythical inventions or human attempts to fashion a god in visible form. There is only one God, and He can easily be distinguished from all pagan attempts at deity.

These five qualities describe the fundamental nature of God. Of course, He is far more than the total of these feeble attempts to express who He is. When we try to characterize God, we must join Paul in his inspired expression of praise: "Now to the King eternal, immortal, invisible, the only God, be honor and glory forever and ever. Amen" (1 Tim. 1:17).

You probably know someone who does not believe in God. Use the following terms to briefly describe God's nature: *spirituality, self-existence, immensity, eternity,* and *unity.* Write as if you were speaking to your unbelieving friend.

_____

_____

_____

The Attributes of God

One of the oldest writings in the Bible is the Book of Job. Job desperately sought to understand why God allowed him to suffer many personal losses. One of his so-called friends asked Job these questions:

> "Can you search out the deep things of God?
> Can you find out the limits of the Almighty?" (Job 11:7, NKJV).

Was Job being presumptuous to expect God to make Himself and His ways known to him? And are we expecting too much by thinking we can even begin to know God—to comprehend His nature and character? Although it is unthinkable to suppose that mortals can know all about God, He has chosen to reveal certain attributes that help us understand His nature and know Him personally. Such knowledge is essential to our worship of Him, because the quality of our worship of God will be in direct proportion to our understanding of His greatness and goodness. We can know God better by learning the qualities ascribed to Him in His Word.

Omnipotence. The word *omnipotence* is formed by combining two words: *omni,* meaning *all,* and *potent,* meaning *power.* Therefore, God's omnipotence refers to the fact that He is all-powerful; there is no limit to His power. On at least two occasions Jesus spoke of the unlimited power of God when He said, " 'With God all things are possible' " (see Matt. 19:26; Mark 14:36). God can do whatever He pleases.

We are filled with awe as we contemplate God's omnipotence. He not only created everything from nothing but also governs His creation under His immediate and perfect control. He needs no help outside Himself and does not need to wait on processes and developments. At His will He accomplishes whatever He wants. Just as our finger moves at our will, the entire creation occurred in response to His word.

God exercises His omnipotence according to His nature. Thus, He does not use His omnipotence to act in an unrighteous manner. He is a person of the utmost integrity; He cannot be untrue to Himself or inconsistent with His promises. One of Job's complaints was that God was being unfair to him. Later he discovered how wrong he had been. God is love, and all His actions are consistent with that love.

God's Attributes
Omnipotence
Omnipresence
Omniscience
Holiness
Righteousness
Love

21

In the Scriptures we see evidence of God's omnipotence as He overcame what appeared to be insurmountable problems. One example is Sarah's conceiving and giving birth to Isaac in her old age. Another example is Jesus' virgin birth. Every miracle recorded in Scripture is a testimony of God's unlimited power to do His will. His sovereign control of the events of history clearly speaks of His supreme power. When Paul addressed the philosophers in Athens, he emphasized God's omnipotence: " 'The God who made the world and everything in it ... has made every nation of men to live all over the earth and has determined their appointed times and the boundaries of where they live. ... In Him we live and move and exist' " (Acts 17:24-28).

Later Paul wrote to the believers in Ephesus about the most wonderful expression of God's power. He said, "Now to Him who is able to do above and beyond all that we ask or think—according to the power that works in you—to Him be glory in the church and in Christ Jesus to all generations, forever and ever" (Eph. 3:20-21). God's power to produce spiritual transformation was very real and personal to Paul. He often recalled his own miraculous conversion—how his encounter with Jesus literally changed him from being the chief persecutor of Christians to their strongest advocate.

Omnipotence: God is all-powerful.
Omnipresence: God is present all the time in all places.
Omniscience: God is all-knowing.

Only God's omnipotence could achieve such a dramatic and permanent change. This aspect of God's supreme power encourages us to share with all people the good news that His power saves and transforms lives.

Omnipresence. *Omnipresence* means that all of God is present all the time in all places. He is present throughout His universe as the controlling, sustaining Sovereign who rules over all things and meets all needs. In fact, apart from His presence there could be no universe. However, the emphasis in the Bible is God's omnipresence in relationship to His people. As He promised Moses, " 'My Presence will go with you, and I will give you rest' " (Ex. 33:14). Although we sometimes think of coming into God's presence when we worship or pray, the truth is that we are never out of His presence. The psalmist affirmed this truth as he reflected on the inescapable presence of God:

> Where can I go to escape Your Spirit?
> Where can I flee from Your presence?
> If I go up to heaven, You are there;
> if I make my bed in Sheol, You are there.
> If I live at the eastern horizon
> or settle at the western limits,
> even there Your hand will lead me;
> Your right hand will hold on to me (Ps. 139:7-10).

This poet recognized the blessing and goodness of the omnipresent God. How comforting to know that we are never alone, never forsaken by Him. When Jesus gave His disciples their final commission, He promised, " 'I am with you always, to the end of the age' " (Matt. 28:20).

Is Omnipresence the Same as Pantheism?

Christians believe that God is present in all places all the time, but this is not the same as the Hindu and New Age teaching of pantheism. Pantheism claims that everything is either God or a part of God. God is viewed as an impersonal energy, power, or consciousness emanating throughout the universe. Therefore, all creation is considered divine.

In contrast, the Bible teaches that God is personal, not impersonal (see 1 Tim. 4:10). God relates to humans with personal qualities of love (see 1 John 4:7), mercy (see Ps. 143:1), grace (see Col. 1:6), righteousness (see Rom. 1:17), goodness (see Ps. 106:1), faithfulness (see 1 Thess. 5:23-24), wisdom (see Ps. 147:5), and justice (see Ps. 33:5). The Bible rejects the idea that God is the same as His creation:

"Claiming to be wise, they became fools and exchanged the glory of the immortal God for images resembling mortal man, birds, four-footed animals, and reptiles" (Rom. 1:22-23). Furthermore, neither the creation nor humanity can be equated with God. Although we are created in God's image, we are not and never will be God (see Gen. 1:26-27; Isa. 43:10).[13]

Scripture states that a Christian's body is actually God's dwelling place: "Do you not know that your body is a sanctuary of the Holy Spirit who is in you, whom you have from God?" (1 Cor. 6:19). Have you ever prayed, "God, please be with me"? Does that prayer reflect an understanding of God's omnipresence?

Knowing the fact of God's omnipresence is important, but appreciating why He is present is far more significant. Notice that each verse in the margin emphasizes the fact of God's presence in believers to do His work in them. How amazing that the God who is omnipresent throughout His universe is forever present in every Christian to work His will and purpose!

Omniscience. The root meaning of the word *science* is *to know* or *knowledge*. Therefore, *omniscience* means *all knowledge*. God knows everything that can be known—past, present, and future. The extent of His knowledge is unlimited. God does not acquire knowledge as we do, nor does He depend on memory to retain knowledge as we do. His knowledge is complete and perfect.

As we contemplate this attribute of God, we quickly exhaust our ability to comprehend such absolute and total knowledge. For example, how can God know the outcome of events before they occur? How can God know our choices before we make them and yet allow us the freedom to decide? Such questions refer to the foreknowledge of God and are valid, but ultimately, they are beyond our capacity to understand. I find help at this point in several statements from the Bible. First, read these words:

"I am sure of this, that He who started a good work in you will carry it on to completion until the day of Christ Jesus" (Phil. 1:6).

"It is God who is working among you both the willing and the working for His good purpose" (Phil. 2:13).

"Now may the God of peace … equip you with all that is good to do His will, working in us what is pleasing in His sight, through Jesus Christ, to whom be glory forever and ever" (Heb. 13:20-21).

"My thoughts are not your thoughts,
  Nor are your ways My ways," says the Lord.
"For as the heavens are higher than the earth,
  So are My ways higher than your ways,
  And My thoughts than your thoughts" (Isa. 55:8-9, NKJV).

We must remember that we are not God; we are not omniscient. Many things that are mysteries to us are perfectly clear to God.

As the psalmist faced the whys of life, he offered this prayer of humble confession:

LORD, my heart is not proud; my eyes are not haughty.
I do not get involved with things too great or too difficult for me.
(Ps. 131:1).

God welcomes all of our questions; He understands that we are often puzzled about His role in events that are beyond our comprehension. However, we must acknowledge our finite understanding and His infinite knowledge.

Notice the focus of Moses' counsel to his people: " 'The secret things belong to the LORD our God, but the things revealed belong to us and to our children forever, that we follow all the words of this law' " (Deut. 29:29). Moses pointed to the fact that our task is to do what God reveals and requires, not to speculate about mysteries beyond our ability to understand. A wise Christian teacher once said, "Always remember that God does not owe you an explanation for His ways, but you owe Him your trust and obedience to His commands."

God's omniscience also means that He sees all things in their proper perspective. While humans often evaluate happenings in light of our limited perspective, God knows the end as well as the beginning. Therefore, He knows the ultimate outcome of all events. His acts are always couched in the context of eternity. Because we cannot perceive consequences the way He can, we must trust Him when we cannot understand the reason we have certain experiences. As one wise leader declared, "When you cannot trace God's hand, you can always trust His heart." God never makes mistakes. He never allows situations that have no meaning or purpose for the believer who surrenders to His care.

Select one of the following attributes of God and describe a time when you became aware of this attribute through something that happened in your life: omnipotence, omnipresence, omniscience.

_____

_____

_____

Holiness. Isaiah's vision of God caused him to exclaim,

> "Holy, holy, holy is the LORD of hosts;
> The whole earth is full of his glory!" (Isa. 6:3, NKJV).

The basic meaning of the word *holy* is *separate, set apart*. Although God is present with us, He is also separate from us because of His nature as God. Holiness refers to the absolute moral perfection of God; He is the standard of truth, righteousness, and justice.

God's holiness evokes worship and adoration from us, as well as a conviction of our sinfulness. The Apostle Peter related God's holiness to Christian responsibility with the challenging words in the margin. A Christian's conduct is to be holy in the sense of being set apart from the conduct of the world—a different lifestyle. Such holiness is possible because believers have the Holy Spirit living inside us.

"As the One who called you is holy, you also are to be holy in all your conduct; for it is written, 'Be holy, because I am holy' " (1 Pet. 1:15-16).

Read 1 Peter 1:15-16. Based on the discussion above, how would you define *holy?*

_____

How should your being holy affect—

your work? _____

your home? _____

your social activities? _____

your entertainment? _____

your language? _____

Righteousness. One expression of God's holiness is His righteousness. *Righteousness* means that God is without sin; He never thinks or acts in ways less than perfect. God is also righteous in the sense that He actively opposes all sin and its consequences. God hates sin because of what sin has done and continues to do to His beautiful creation. He is determined to ultimately remove sin and all its influence.

Because He is righteous, God requires righteousness as the condition of being accepted by Him. His righteous justice demands perfection or else punishment. Knowing that humans' fallen nature makes right-

> *Holiness:* Moral perfection
> *Righteousness:* Being without sin
> *Love:* A decision to bless others and sacrifice for them

eousness impossible for them, God provides the righteousness He requires through the sacrifice of His Son on the cross for our sin. God offers His righteousness as a gift to all who will receive it through faith in Jesus Christ.

Moreover, we are comforted by the assurance of God's righteous dealings with us. He will never be unkind or unfair but always gracious and merciful. Read the psalmist's words in the margin.

Love. John declared that "God is love" (1 John 4:8). Love is the very essence of God. Divine love is unlike human love in that God's love is not an emotion but a decision to bless its object. Jesus is the perfect model of divine love. He chose to sacrifice Himself for the sake of others. A cross stands at the heart of God's love. As John stated, "This is how we have come to know love: He laid down His life for us" (1 John 3:16).

God expresses His love to us by grace and mercy. Grace is God's giving quality; it means that God gives us what we desperately need but do not deserve—forgiveness and salvation. Mercy is the kindness of God; it withholds what we deserve—condemnation and hell. We must never think of God's love as being less than righteous—God never overlooks sin. His love is a holy love that passionately cares for and provides the best for its object without compromising its just demands.

How awesome our God is! Each of His characteristics and attributes reveals His glory. What a mighty, wise, just, holy, loving, gracious God we worship and serve. I trust that you

> "The LORD is compassionate
>   and gracious,
> slow to anger and full of faithful
>   love. …
> He has not dealt with us
>   as our sins deserve
> or repaid us according
>   to our offenses.
> For as high as the heavens
>   are above the earth,
> so great is His faithful love toward
>   those who fear Him"
> (Ps. 103:8-11).

God's Love and Discipline

One expression of God's love that is sometimes misunderstood is His discipline of us as His children. The first readers of the Letter to the Hebrews were apparently discouraged because of various trials. The author of this practical letter reminded them of an important truth when he wrote, "You have forgotten the exhortation that addresses you as sons:

> 'My son, do not take the Lord's discipline lightly,
>   or faint when you are reproved by Him;
> for the Lord disciplines the one He loves,
>   and punishes every son whom He receives' " (Heb. 12:5-6).

God loves us the way we are—His love is unconditional—but He loves us too much to leave us the way we are. His love calls for the best we are capable of becoming by His grace. His is a tough love—one that offers discipline and correction as needed. For this we must be thankful, even though such love sometimes brings pain. A wise Christian once said, "Our trials come to prove and improve us."

find in these brief descriptions of His greatness and goodness a new appreciation of God—a desire to worship Him with more understanding and a motivation to offer yourself with complete abandon to His service.

Our first chapter of study has focused on two significant topics that are foundational to all that follows. What we believe about the Bible and God determines our beliefs about every other aspect of the Christian faith.

Review your 25-word description of God on page 7. Rewrite that description, using what you have learned in this chapter.

_____

_____

_____

_____

_____

_____

_____

[1] *The Baptist Faith and Message* (Nashville: LifeWay Christian Resources of the Southern Baptist Convention, 2000), 7.

[2] John Smyth, as quoted in James T. Draper Jr. and Kenneth Keathley, *Biblical Authority: The Critical Issue for the Body of Christ* (Nashville: Broadman & Holman, 2001), 54.

[3] The Second London Confession, as quoted in Draper and Keathley, *Biblical Authority,* 56.

[4] James P. Boyce, as quoted in Draper and Keathley, *Biblical Authority,* 60.

[5] B. H. Carroll, as quoted in Draper and Keathley, *Biblical Authority,* 63.

[6] *The Baptist Faith and Message,* 7.

[7] Josh McDowell, *Evidence That Demands a Verdict* (San Bernardino: Campus Crusade for Christ International, 1972), 150.

[8] David S. Dockery, *The Doctrine of the Bible* (Nashville: Convention Press, 1991), 98–99.

[9] Ibid., 100.

[10] Ken Hemphill, *LifeAnswers: Making Sense of Your World* (Nashville: LifeWay Press, 1993), 39.

[11] Dockery, *The Doctrine of the Bible,* 100.

[12] *The Baptist Faith and Message,* 8–9.

[13] Bill Gordon, "The New Age Movement: Part 1," in Tal Davis et al., *FAITH Discipleship: Faith Reaching Out to World Religions* (Nashville: LifeWay Press, 2001), 139–40.

CHAPTER 2

Who Are We, and How Can We Know God Personally?

One afternoon I was in my office at church when my secretary told me that a man wanted to talk with me. I greeted him and asked how I might help. He began by describing his search for meaning and purpose in life. When I asked him about his relationship with the Lord, he surprised me with his response. He said that he did not know what I meant by a relationship with God. After listening as I shared the gospel with him, he replied that he had never heard this news before. I was absolutely stunned. I could not believe that anyone could grow up in our nation and be totally unaware of Jesus, the Bible, and salvation.

Write the way you would explain how someone enters a personal relationship with God.

_____

_____

Sometime later, I read a news article that saddened me even more than the visitor to my office. This was the report of an interview with a prominent pastor, mayoral candidate, and Grammy-nominated singer (all the same person). When questioned about his Christian beliefs, he replied, "My posture is that all will be saved, with the exception of a few persons. I believe that most people on planet Earth will go to heaven because of God's unconditional love and the redemptive work of the cross." He went on to specify that this included sincere people who do not directly acknowledge Christ, such as Muslims, Hindus, and Buddhists. He believed the message we should deliver to the world is not that they need to receive Christ to be saved but that God loves them and has already reconciled them to Himself.

These two incidents emphasize the obvious need for a clear, Bible-based understanding of the nature of humanity, salvation, and God's grace. Because these truths are basic to all we believe as Christians, we must stand on solid ground in these areas. In this chapter we will discover the heart of the gospel message. Join me as we explore what the Scriptures reveal.

What Do We Believe About the Nature of Humanity?

Human beings are (check one)—
☐ created by God but are evolutionary in nature;   ☐ divine by nature;
☐ created in the image of God;   ☐ completely separated from God.

Explain why you chose your response. _____

_____

Philosophers have offered various answers to such questions as: Where did we come from? What is our nature? Why are we here? Where are we going? But only the Bible gives clear, reasonable answers to these important matters. Because we believe in the divine authority behind the Bible, we believe the following truths that are revealed in the Word.

Created by God, for God, and in God's Image

For years the debate has raged between those who believe in humanity's purposeful creation and our evolution by chance. This ongoing debate highlights the fact that the question of our origin is a critical one with important implications. If we are created in the image of God, human life is sacred and has special value. If we evolved, then human life has no greater significance than animal or plant life. Read some implications of these ideas in the box on this page.

Evolution Versus Creation

Evolution
• Humans evolved by time and chance.
• Humans are the product of the survival of the fittest.
• No absolutes: situation ethics, homosexuality, adultery, racism, abortion
• No moral obligation
• Human life has the same value as animal and plant life.
• Humans serve and satisfy self.

Creation
• Humans are created by God with purpose.
• Humans are made in God's image (see Gen 1:26).
• Humans are wonderfully made by design (see Ps. 139:13-14).
• God's Word is truth (see Ps. 119:160), including absolutes about all issues of life.
• Humans are obligated to the Creator (see Rom. 8:12-13).
• Human life has greater value than animal and plant life (see Gen. 1:28).
• Humans serve the Creator, not His creation (see Rom. 1:25).[1]

Christians believe that human origin can be traced to the opening statement of the Bible: "In the beginning God created" (Gen. 1:1). The term *created* is the Hebrew word *bara,* which means *to bring into being that which did not exist before.* The word is used in the Bible to refer only to God's activity, for only God creates something from nothing. After God created the universe and all plant and animal life, His crowning work of creation is expressed in these significant words: " 'Let Us make man in Our image, according to Our likeness.' ... God created man in His own image; He created him in the image of God" (Gen. 1:26-27). Every person is an original, unique creation of God.

This answers the question, Where did we come from? But what about human nature? Why are we wired the way we are? The Bible states that people are created in the image of God. What does that mean?

Spiritual beings. Being made in God's image means that although we are similar to animals in our physical makeup, we have an identity beyond our physical existence. Just as God is Spirit, humans were created to have spiritual life. We are made for fellowship with God—to know Him, love Him, worship Him, and share His life.

Higher intelligence. Created in God's image also means that people have a higher intelligence than animals, including the ability to reason, process information, recall what has been learned, and make decisions. In addition, we are endued with a sense of morality— a conscience that reminds us of right and wrong. We can understand our actions and judge between right and wrong. Our awareness of God as our Creator makes us accountable to Him. Because He has made us, we are the stewards of this life and all God has given to us.

Gender. Further insight into human nature comes from this biblical statement: "He created them male and female. God blessed them, and God said to them, 'Be fruitful, multiply, fill the earth, and subdue it. Rule ... every creature that crawls on the earth' " (Gen. 1:27-28). Gender is a special gift from God. Reproduction is one result of being male and female. But the differences between men and women are far more than physical. Being male or female describes intrinsic differences in personality, interests, and preferences—differences that contribute significantly to the quality of human life. This includes the gift of marriage.

Purpose. One expression of humanity's purpose is to populate the earth, subdue it, and rule over it (see Gen. 1:28). God planned for people to be the caretakers of His creation (see Gen. 2:15). The most noble expression of our purpose is found in these words by the Apostle Paul as he spoke of Christ: "the image of the invisible God, the firstborn over all creation; ... all things have been created through Him and for Him" (Col. 1:15-16). Created for Christ! This is our purpose—to belong to Christ and to fulfill His plan for our lives.

How would you present the biblical view of human origin to someone who believes in evolution?

_____

_____

Created with Free Will

Just as God exercised free will in choosing to create the universe and all its wonders, we who are made in His image have the capacity to make choices. Originally, before the entrance of sin, Adam and Eve enjoyed perfect free will. When faced with the opportunity to obey or disobey God's command to refrain from eating from the tree of the knowledge of good and evil, they chose to believe Satan's lie. Their disobedience was an act of rebellion against God, an act of choosing their way rather than God's way. This is the nature of sin.

> "You must not eat from the tree of the knowledge of good and evil, for when you eat of it you will surely die" (Gen. 2:17).

Read Genesis 2:17. What action did God specifically forbid?

_____

What were the stated consequences of violating God's instructions?

_____

God had clearly stated the consequences of disobedience before the first couple made that terrible choice—death. The Apostle Paul later declared, "The wages of sin is death" (Rom. 6:23). Death entered God's creation along with the first sin. Adam and Eve died spiritually by losing the intimate fellowship with God they had previously enjoyed, and the sentence of physical death on them was fulfilled later. A term often used to describe humanity's condition after this original sin is *total depravity*. This does not mean that people are as bad as they can be but that every part of human nature is affected by sin. All people inherit the sinful nature of Adam and Eve; all are prone to sin because of that original wrong choice. Thus, all humankind continues to be affected by the fall of God's first created man and woman; all people are born out of fellowship with God due to a natural proclivity to sin.

> *Total depravity:* The human condition of being so thoroughly tainted by sin that every part of human nature is affected

Check the path that Adam and Eve chose. Underline the path that you most often choose.

- ☐ God's instructions ⟶ human violation ⟶ negative consequences
- ☐ God's instructions ⟶ human obedience ⟶ positive consequences

In today's culture the idea of sin is widely rejected. Instead, people blame problems and mistakes on societal, educational, or socioeconomic factors. But the Bible teaches that sin is the fundamental human problem. Every imperfection in our human experience, whether due to evil behavior or natural catastrophes, is the direct result of humanity's choice to rebel against God. The history of the human race is a clear, consistent testimony to the consequences of sin.

Are Humans Divine?

Hinduism and its various branches, like the Unity School of Christianity and the New Age Movement, teach that all is God and that therefore human beings are divine. In this view humanity's greatest problem is ignorance of our divinity. The goal of life, then, is for people to realize their divinity through knowledge, self-improvement, and mystical experiences.

The Bible rejects this view of humanity. Although God created people in His image, they inherit a sinful nature and choose to sin against Him (see Rom. 3:23; 5:12). We are not part of God, and our basic problem is not ignorance of our divinity but rebellion against Holy God and His commandments (see Rom. 1:28-32; Gal. 3:22). We can be acceptable to Him only by accepting the atoning work of Jesus Christ for our sin (see Rom. 3:24-26).

Created with Sacred Value

In spite of the influence of sin on all humankind, God looks on humanity as His special creation, with the potential for restoration, and therefore worthy of His redeeming love. A term frequently used for the biblical view of humanity is *sanctity of human life*. The abortion of a human fetus is the issue most commonly associated with this term, but it also has implications for euthanasia, genetic engineering, cloning, fetal-tissue experimentation, and other similar practices. This is a vast field with many ethical and spiritual landmines.

We must affirm our base of authority for making judgments in this area. Problems arise when people look to human reason for their ultimate authority. Christians are committed to divine revelation—the Bible—as our ultimate authority. When we listen to philosophers, secular ethicists, educators, and scientists, we must evaluate their positions and determine our stance according to God's revelation through Scripture.

What is a situation you have faced in which you had to make a moral or ethical choice?

_____

How did you make your decision?
- ☐ I chose the action that seemed most comfortable.
- ☐ I chose what would be least embarrassing to me.
- ☐ I chose the action that was consistent with biblical instructions and God's character.
- ☐ I chose the action that would make me happy at the moment.

Because the abortion issue is the lightning rod of the sanctity-of-life debate, let's look at biblical teachings that must form our position. The Hebrew word *yeled,* routinely used in the Old Testament for *children,* also refers to the preborn child in Exodus 21:22. The same principle operates in the New Testament; in Acts 7:19 the Greek word *brephos* is used to refer to the killing of children at Pharaoh's command. In Luke 1:41 the same word describes John the Baptist while he was still in the womb. These are just two examples illustrating that God's Word gives the same identity and value to children before and after birth.

Psalm 139:13-16 is one of the most detailed and explicit passages in all of Scripture about God's creative work in the womb. Read those verses in the margin. When we read this beautiful and inspired account of God's work in fashioning a child in the womb, the thought of disrupting this divine work by the intrusion of instruments of death becomes revolting. The final verse points out the fact that God has recorded His plan for our lives before we were ever born. Intruding on God's intent is unthinkable.

Consider another biblical reference affirming the sacredness of all human life. The psalmist declares to the Lord, "Your hands made me and formed me" (Ps. 119:73). This is another clear statement of God's direct involvement in the creation of every person. From the moment of conception God determines every detail of each of us—regardless of race, gender, or ethnic status. Every human—born or unborn—is a person who is infinitely precious, unique, and handmade by God.

The Bible gives us a clear understanding of where we came from, who we are, and the great value God places on all human life. A healthy self-esteem is tremendously important because it is based on an understanding of who we are in God's eyes. His Word provides the only true revelation of the worth of every person to God.

"It was You who created
   my inward parts;
You knit me together in
   my mother's womb.
I will praise You
because I am unique
   in remarkable ways.
Your works are wonderful,
and I know this very well.
My bones were not hidden
   from You
when I was made in secret,
when I was formed in the
   depths of the earth.
Your eyes saw me when
   I was formless;
all my days were written in
   Your book and planned
before a single one of them
   began" (Ps. 139:13-16).

What Do We Believe About Salvation?

Our previous study about the nature of humanity established the fact that all people choose to rebel against God's commands—all people sin. One consequence of sin is separation from God, a condition described as spiritual death. According to the Bible, unless a person is rescued from this condition, he or she will ultimately suffer eternal punishment in hell. This truth underscores the importance of having a right understanding and belief about salvation.

Salvation means *spiritual rescue from the consequences of sin; redemption. Salvation* refers to all God does in reaching out to sinful humans to restore them to Himself. Because of sin we are estranged from God, alienated from Him. Sin separates a person from God, who is holy and cannot tolerate sin in His presence. *Salvation* refers to God's effort to bridge the gap between Him and sinners, provide the means of removing the guilt caused by sin, restore His original image in humans, and set sinful humanity free from all consequences of sin.

A Bible concordance lists four different Hebrew words and two Greek words that are all translated by the word *salvation*. The root meaning of these terms is *safety*. Sinners are in the process of perishing, but God's salvation offers safety. However, we must understand that salvation is far more than escaping hell. The Lord wants us to be with Him in heaven someday, but in the meantime His purpose in saving us is to restore our relationship with Him, give us His abundant life now, and allow us the pleasure of serving Him.

What is the primary purpose of salvation? Choose only one answer.
☐ I get to escape hell.
☐ I get to spend eternity in heaven.
☐ I can sin and be forgiven.
☐ I can have abundant life in this world and the next.

Circle the response that best characterizes the way you live your life.

The Bible presents a simple, clear revelation of God's plan of salvation.

The Person of Salvation

Although we often speak of the plan of salvation, a better description is the person of salvation. Salvation is God's work through one special Person—His Son, the Lord Jesus Christ. The Bible refers to Jesus as "His salvation," "the salvation of the Lord," "the Lord is my salvation," and "O God of our salvation." Salvation is a person.

The identity of this person first became clear through the prophecy of Zachariah, who said of his son, John the Baptist:

> "You, child, will be called a prophet of the Most High,
>   for you will go before the Lord to prepare His ways,
>   to give His people knowledge of salvation
>   through the forgiveness of their sins" (Luke 1:76-77).

Later Jesus was born to fulfill this prophetic word. The Apostle Peter boldly spoke of the person of salvation when he proclaimed, " 'There is salvation in no one else, for there is no other name under heaven given to people by which we must be saved' " (Acts 4:12). Jesus is the one and only way for any person to experience God's salvation from sin. As He said, " 'I am the way, the truth, and the life. No one comes to the Father except through Me' " (John 14:6).

Jesus is the person of salvation because no one else could provide the means by which guilty sinners could be saved. Jesus made two essential provisions.

1. Jesus made atonement for sin. The biblical concept of atonement is bringing reconciliation between God and humans by providing a covering (forgiveness) for the sin that caused the separation. Because Jesus had no sin, He was the perfect sacrifice for humanity's sin (see 2 Cor. 5:21; Gal. 3:13).

2. Jesus is our Redeemer. Sin brings bondage; sinners are enslaved by their sinful nature. The doctrine of redemption means that because of Jesus' death, believers have been purchased, delivered from the bondage of sin, and set free to serve God.

As a result of these two provisions, sinners can be reconciled to God and can be liberated from enslavement to sin.

Salvation is not found in a church, the ordinances of a church, or the good works of sincere people. Nor is it earned by making religious pilgrimages, sacrificing self for a religious cause, or completing any other act of religious devotion. God offers salvation as a free gift in the person of His Son. Let's be thankful that He took our sin on Himself and sacrificed His life for us. What a Savior!

Read the information in the box "Is Jesus the Only Way?" How would you respond to someone who claimed that Jesus is only one of many ways to salvation?

_____

_____

_____

Is Jesus the Only Way?

Three views of salvation are prevalent in today's culture.

1. *Universalism,* also known as pluralism, teaches that there are many ways—or even an unlimited number of ways—to God and that everyone will eventually be saved and reach heaven.

2. *Inclusivism* claims that Jesus is the only Savior; however, it is possible for Jesus to save people even though they may never have personally trusted Him for salvation. If they have never heard the gospel through no fault of their own, they will have the opportunity to respond to Jesus in the life to come.

3. *Exclusivism* is the biblical view that salvation is available only through faith in Jesus Christ as personal Savior and Lord. This belief affirms Jesus' statement in John 14:6: " 'I am the way, the truth, and the life. No one comes to the Father except through Me.' "[2]

Critics sometimes claim that the Christian view is much too narrow in excluding other ways to God. Billy Graham has responded to such criticism by saying that when he is a passenger on an airplane and it is time to land, he wants the pilot to be very narrow-minded—to follow one safe landing approach. That is no time for the pilot to try other possible ways to land. The same is true for the way of salvation from sin. There is one way, and that way is Jesus.

The Process of Salvation

Salvation is (check all that are correct)—

☐ a past event; ☐ an ongoing process;

☐ a religious theory; ☐ a future assurance.

What happens when a person turns to God from sin (repents) and by faith calls on the Lord for salvation? The simplest and perhaps best answer is that a miracle occurs! God brings about a miraculous change in the person, a change that begins with a new spiritual birth and continues until the believer safely arrives in heaven. In a sense, then, salvation is a process.

The process of salvation is sometimes expressed like this: "I have been saved; I am being saved; I will be saved." *The Baptist Faith and Message* states, "In its broadest sense salvation includes regeneration, justification, sanctification, and glorification."[3] These four theological terms help us understand the meaning and significance of salvation.

Regeneration. Regeneration refers to a spiritual rebirth—being born again. Prior to regeneration, sinners are spiritually dead. Stop and read the description of regeneration from Titus 3:5 in the margin.

Salvation begins when the Holy Spirit convicts a person of sin and of the need for Jesus. If that person turns to the Lord from sin, calling on Him for mercy, the Holy Spirit works the miracle of regeneration (new birth) in the person.

"He saved us—
not by works of righteousness
that we had done,
but according to His mercy,
through the washing of
regeneration
and renewal by the Holy Spirit"
(Titus 3:5).

The Bible recounts that a man named Nicodemus approached Jesus, seeking to know more about Him. Nicodemus was a religious leader, a teacher of God's law, and a man who was respected for his godly life. But Jesus knew this man's deepest need, so He responded by saying rather abruptly, " 'I assure you: Unless someone is born again, he cannot see the kingdom of God' " (John 3:3). It would be easy to understand why Jesus might have spoken these words to the woman who had been caught in adultery, but Nicodemus was a very religious man. We learn from this account that everyone needs regeneration, even someone who is considered a good person.

In this initial moment of salvation God takes us from the realm of sin and death and imparts His life to us—eternal life. The Spirit of God—the Spirit of Christ—lives in every believer from the moment of this new birth. Our new life is literally His life in us. And He promises that He will never leave us (see Heb. 13:5). Thus, regeneration is a one-time miracle that never needs repeating.

The Apostle Paul referred to this experience when he wrote, "If anyone is in Christ, there is a new creation; old things have passed away, and look, new things have come" (2 Cor. 5:17). Paul also described a new believer as being adopted into God's family: "You received the Spirit of adoption, by whom we cry out, 'Abba, Father!' The Spirit Himself testifies together with our spirit that we are God's children" (Rom. 8:15-16).

Recently, I met a businessman who shared his Christian testimony with me. He said, "I grew up in a religious family that regularly attended church, but I don't recall any emphasis on a personal relationship with God. Later, a business associate explained the gospel to me and led me to accept Christ by faith. I can't explain to you what happened; I just know I have never been the same." This is what occurs when we are born again—we are never the same.

So we begin our Christian pilgrimage by being reconciled to God. We are born and adopted into His eternal family. We who were dead because of sin are made alive spiritually. This is not our old life being made over but His life taking over—a true regeneration.

Justification. In *Fundamentals of Our Faith* Herschel Hobbs defines *justification* as "the judicial act of God whereby he declares the sinner righteous as though he had never sinned, removes the condemnation of sin, and restores him to divine favor (John 3:17-18; 5:24; Rom. 1:17; 8:1-2,30)." Hobbs explains that the Greek word for *justification* means not that a person is actually righteous but is declared righteous. Justification does not cause sinners to become perfect; however, God accepts believers as though they were perfect because Christ took all of the guilt and penalty for sin on Himself. Christians are thus blameless before God.[4]

> *Regeneration:* spiritual rebirth
> *Justification:* God's declaration of a believer as righteous through the blood of Christ
> *Sanctification:* the position and process of holiness by which a believer is set apart by and for God
> *Glorification:* the perfection of God's image and character in believers when they enter God's presence

The first half of Paul's letter to the Romans is basically a theological treatise. Most of the Bible's teaching on justification comes from this writing. Paul wrote, "All have sinned and fall short of the glory of God. They are justified freely by His grace through the redemption that is in Christ Jesus" (Rom. 3:23-24). The result of justification is that because believers are declared "not guilty" by the supreme Judge of the universe, they are not only restored to fellowship with God but are also able to enjoy peace with Him. As Paul declared, "Since we have been declared righteous by faith, we have peace with God through our Lord Jesus Christ" (Rom. 5:1). What a blessed relief to know that we will never be condemned for our sins. No longer are we under the oppression of guilt. We are free!

Notice another important truth from Romans 5:1: we become righteous (justified) "by faith." Justification cannot be earned by doing good works. We are justified because of God's grace; we receive justification by faith. Some Bible teachers interpret isolated Scripture passages to mean that human works are required to merit salvation. However, when the doctrine of salvation is considered from all the Bible material, the clear message of Scripture is accurately summarized in the words of Titus 3:5-7. Read those verses in the margin.

> "He saved us—
> not by works of righteousness
>   that we had done,
> but according to His mercy,
> through the washing
>   of regeneration
> and renewal by the Holy Spirit.
> This [Spirit] He poured out
>   on us abundantly
> through Jesus Christ our Savior,
> so that having been justified
>   by His grace,
> we may become heirs with
>   the hope of eternal life"
> (Titus 3:5-7).

Sanctification. Has anyone ever called you a saint? Probably not, but if you have been regenerated and justified by faith (which is true of every Christian), the Bible refers to you

Saved by Grace

Most world religions and cults teach that salvation can and must be earned through good works or self-enlightenment. Biblical Christianity alone teaches that salvation is a free gift of God for those who accept Jesus Christ as Savior. Therefore, it cannot be merited by our goodness or earned by our works (see Eph. 2:8-9).

Grace is God's disposition of favor toward us. Grace, working with God's love, is the quality in God that overrules the necessity that His holiness destroy us. If God were only holiness, we would all be deservedly dead. Grace works with holiness to bring us to acceptability with God. Notice the following qualities of grace.

1. *Grace is free.* We are "justified freely by His grace through the redemption that is in Christ Jesus" (Rom. 3:24).
2. *Grace is for all.* It is available to everyone who chooses to accept it, even those who have failed miserably (see Rom. 5:15,20).
3. *Grace abounds.* God's nature is to give and keep on giving (see Eph. 3:20; Jas. 1:5). In His kingdom the more grace you appropriate, the more you get.
4. *Grace is effective.* Grace covers any repented sin, and God eagerly awaits our confession (see 1 John 1:9). God's grace is so big that we will never reach the end of it.[5]

as a saint (see, for example, Acts 9:13,32,41; Rom. 1:7; 1 Cor. 1:2; Heb. 6:10; Rev. 5:8). A saint is a person who has been sanctified. Both words have the same root meaning, namely *to set apart, to consecrate to God's service. Holy* is another word for *sanctified.* All Christians, no matter how imperfect, are God's holy ones—His saints—because they have been set apart from all others and from the world's evil system to be God's special people and to serve His purpose.

Sanctification begins with regeneration. The new birth sets us apart from all who are not born again. As one leader says, "There are only two kinds of people in this world—the saints and the ain'ts!" We become God's holy ones when we accept Christ, and the Holy Spirit comes to dwell in our hearts. This is known as positional sanctification. In other words, new believers are immediately placed in the position of holiness—set apart by and for God.

Sanctification is not only a position but also a process—one that continues throughout a believer's lifetime. This process of Christian growth is known as progressive sanctification. Although God set us apart through regeneration, His plan is for us to grow in our faith— to advance from being babies in Christ to being mature believers. God calls every Christian to become progressively more and more like Jesus in terms of His character. This is the moral aspect of Christian growth. The Holy Spirit works in us to develop virtues called the fruit of the Spirit, which Paul listed in Galatians 5:22-23: "The fruit of the Spirit is love, joy, peace, patience, kindness, goodness, faith, gentleness, self-control." These nine qualities are not multiple fruits but one fruit that represents the character of Jesus in our lives. Only the Spirit of Christ can produce the evidence of Christ's character in us. It is not our fruit but His.

Sanctification, both positional and progressive, is God's work in a believer. Paul wrote, "It is God who is working in you, [enabling you] both to will and to act for His good purpose" (Phil. 2:13). Sanctification is not something we achieve; rather, we receive it by surrendering to God's control and purpose.

Some Bible teachers add another aspect to sanctification, called ultimate or final sanctification. This occurs when we are promoted from this life to be in heaven with Jesus forever. At that time every trace of sin and immaturity will be removed, and as John declared, "Dear friends, we are God's children now, and what we will be has not yet been revealed. We know that when He appears, we will be like Him, because we will see Him as He is" (1 John 3:2). We will reach an ultimate, final state of completion, a point at which we are fully sanctified. This brings us to the fourth aspect of salvation.

Glorification. God's process of salvation involves not only reconciling sinners to Himself but also fully restoring His original image and likeness in them. Our ultimate destiny, as far as character and morality are concerned, is to be as Adam was before his sin. *The Baptist Faith and Message* states, "Glorification is the culmination of salvation and is the final blessed and abiding state of the redeemed."[6] Glorification is the perfection of God's image and character in us when we enter His glorious presence in heaven.

> **Positional santification:** a believer's position of holiness after regeneration
> **Progressive sanctification:** the lifelong process of spiritual growth
> **Ultimate sanctification:** the final state of completion in God's presence

From Glory to Glory

When we are redeemed, God begins the process of bringing us into His personal glory to share it with us: "We all, with unveiled faces, are reflecting the glory of the Lord and are being transformed into the same image from glory to glory" (2 Cor. 3:18). This does not mean that we will become gods, for we do not share God's attributes of infinity and eternity. Rather, our glory derives from conforming to the image of His Son (see Rom. 8:29).

Being conformed to the image of Christ means that our moral character becomes increasingly like His through a process of sloughing off the old character and nurturing the character of Christ that is present in us. Because of His indwelling presence, we have attributes like holiness and righteousness. These come entirely from God, and we can receive them only as His gifts. Virtues like humility, faith, and self-control are also gifts from Him, but we have the ability to develop these qualities as we grow spiritually. "Glory to glory" is a process of experiencing more and more of Christ.

Jesus commanded us to be perfect (see Matt. 5:48). One primary meaning of both the Old and New Testament words for *perfect* is *finished*. We arrive at our final perfection through a process—we have to be finished. The word *perfect* can also mean *complete* and *without blemish*. We will be complete—without blemish—when we are finished, and that will be a glory beyond anything we have known![7]

The term *glorification* comes from the classic statement by Paul in Romans 8:28-30, which appears in the margin. Look at several other Bible references that help us understand the meaning of *glorification*. The Apostle Peter spoke of this several times in his first letter. He referred to himself when he wrote, "As a fellow elder and witness to the sufferings of the Messiah, and also a participant in the glory about to be revealed ..." (1 Pet. 5:1). He then said, "When the chief Shepherd appears, you will receive the unfading crown of glory" (v. 4). Finally, he reassured his readers by saying, "Now the God of all grace, who called you to His eternal glory in Christ Jesus, will personally restore, establish, strengthen, and support you after you have suffered a little" (v. 10). Peter repeatedly offered the promise of future glory to encourage believers who were enduring trials because of their faith. The writer of Hebrews also called his readers to anticipate their glorious future (see Heb. 2:10). In each of these references the glorification of saints is connected to the glory of Christ. We will reflect His glory.

> "We know that all things work together for the good of those who love God: those who are called according to His purpose. For those He foreknew He also predestined to be conformed to the image of His Son, so that He would be the firstborn among many brothers. And those He predestined, He also called; and those He called, He also justified; and those He justified, He also glorified" (Rom. 8:28-30).

> "It was fitting, in bringing many sons to glory, that He, for whom and through whom all things exist, should make the source of their salvation perfect through sufferings" (Heb. 2:10).

Included in this final state of believers is the promise of a new, glorified body. A person's original body is destroyed by death. However, we are assured that ultimately the body, as well as the spirit, will be redeemed. The major biblical treatment of this subject is found in 1 Corinthians 15, which states that the fact of Christ's resurrection is the guarantee and likeness of a Christian's resurrection. About that mystery Paul wrote, "Just as we have borne the image of the man made of dust, we will also bear the image of the heavenly man" (1 Cor. 15:49).

The entire process occurs because of God's unconditional love for His creation. He graciously pursues wayward humankind the way a good shepherd searches for lost sheep. All praise and gratitude for salvation belong to Him. He is the Author, Initiator, and Performer of His totally adequate design and work of completely restoring fallen humanity.

Match each term with its meaning.

____ 1. Regeneration   a. Restored to God's image

____ 2. Justification   b. Spiritual rebirth

____ 3. Sanctification   c. Set apart for God's service; growth in Christlikeness

____ 4. Glorification   d. Declared righteous

The Urgency of Salvation

Over the years I have had friends who were well informed about the biblical teachings on salvation, but they did not appropriate these truths for themselves. They had the head knowledge but not the heart experience of salvation. When E. F. "Preacher" Hallock was serving as the pastor of a Baptist church in Oklahoma, he invited an evangelist named T. T. Eaton to lead a revival meeting. During that week of services "Preacher" realized that he had never been saved. He was devoted to the Lord, had graduated from a seminary, believed the Bible, and preached its truths, but he had never personally trusted Jesus to save him. He was depending on his good works, not the gift of God in Christ. At the conclusion of the revival, he confessed his need, was saved, and was baptized by Brother Eaton. The church graciously urged him to remain its pastor.

"Preacher" was somewhat like Nicodemus—a religious man with high moral standards but lost. Could that be you? Has there been a time in your past when you realized your need for personal salvation? Have you repented of the sin of rejecting Jesus as your only hope of being forgiven and restored to God? When did you call on Jesus in faith, asking Him to save you and be your Lord? Does your life show evidence that you are a changed person?

I ask you these personal questions because of the urgency of salvation. No one is promised another breath or another heartbeat, but we have this moment. As the Bible declares, "Look, now is the acceptable time; look, now is the day of salvation" (2 Cor. 6:2). The title of this chapter asks, How can we know God personally? The purpose of salvation is to restore individuals to a personal relationship with God—one of intimacy with Him that brings abundant, eternal life. Please don't miss what God has provided for you.

How to Be Saved

The Roman Road tells how to go to heaven. The road begins at Romans 1:16: "I am not ashamed of the gospel, because it is God's power for salvation to everyone who believes." God gives power for salvation to all who believe.

We need God's power because we have a problem with sin: "All have sinned and fall short of the glory of God" (Rom. 3:23). *Sin* means *missing the mark* or *missing God's intended destination for us.* None of us can reach that destination on our own because everyone is a sinner.

When we work, we earn money. Sin earns wages as well—wages of death. Because God loves all sinners, He has provided another route: "The wages of sin is death, but the gift of God is eternal life in Christ Jesus our Lord" (Rom. 6:23).

The highway to heaven is found in Romans 10:9: "If you confess with your mouth, 'Jesus is Lord,' and believe in your heart that God raised Him from the dead, you will be saved." We need to confess our sin and ask God for forgiveness. To confess Jesus as Lord involves agreeing with God about our sin and our need for salvation. We must repent of our sin, turning away from the direction we are going in life. To "believe in your heart" is to place our faith in Jesus, trusting that He died on the cross to pay for our sins. "God proves His own love for us in that while we were still sinners Christ died for us" (Rom. 5:8).

To be saved, sincerely pray a prayer like this one: "Dear God, I confess to You my sin and need for salvation. I turn away from my sin and place my faith in Jesus as my Savior and Lord. Amen."

Share your decision with a Christian friend or pastor. Follow Christ in baptism and join a local church. Commit to lifelong spiritual growth and service to Christ.

Reflect on your answer to the activity on page 28, which asked how someone enters a personal relationship with God. How would you change your response after your study of salvation?

_____

Describe the time when you made that decision. _____

_____

_____

If you are saved, share your testimony with others. If you haven't accepted Jesus as Savior and Lord, read "How to Be Saved" on page 41 or speak with the leader of your study.

The Growth of a Christian

Being born again takes only a moment, while reaching spiritual maturity takes a lifetime. We cannot make any significant contribution to regeneration, but diligent, consistent personal discipline is necessary for Christian growth. We will look at essential biblical guidance for maturing in our walk with Christ.

Discipleship. Jesus' favorite word to describe His followers was *disciple.* The word *disciple* means *a learner, someone who follows a teacher with the intent of becoming like the teacher.* As Jesus once told His disciples, " 'A disciple is not above his teacher, but everyone who is fully trained will be like his teacher' " (Luke 6:40).

Disciple: A learner, someone who follows a teacher with the intent of becoming like the teacher

Agape: A self-sacrificing decision to put the welfare of others first

Jesus calls every believer to be His disciple, and He clearly outlines the requirements of discipleship. On one occasion He said to His disciples, " 'If anyone wants to come with Me, he must deny himself, take up his cross, and follow Me' " (Matt. 16:24). These are strong demands—a call to die to self and live only for Him. A similar challenge is found in these words: " 'If you continue in My word, you really are My disciples' " (John 8:31). Consistent obedience to Jesus' commands identifies His disciples.

Disciples are expected to keep one command above all others. Jesus put it like this: " 'I give you a new commandment: that you love one another. Just as I have loved you, you should also love one another. By this all people will know that you are My disciples, if you have love for one another' " (John 13:34-35). Several words for *love* can be used in the Greek language, but the word used four times in these verses is *agape.* This word, referring to the highest form of love, means *a self-sacrificing decision to put the welfare of others first.* As part of the fruit of the Spirit, this love is from God. Only He can produce this type of love in a person.

Jesus' first disciples learned from Him by following Him around, living with Him, observing His life and works, and listening to His teachings. How can we do this today?

1. *Learn from the Holy Spirit.* Jesus has sent the Holy Spirit to be our resident Teacher. As Jesus promised, " 'The Holy Spirit, whom the Father will send in My name, will teach you all things, and remind you of everything I have told you' " (John 14:26).

2. *Learn from God's Word.* Not only do we have the Teacher, but we also have the textbook. The Bible gives us an advantage the first disciples did not have. Peter gave wise counsel when he wrote, "Like newborn infants, desire the unadulterated spiritual milk, so that you may grow by it in your salvation" (1 Pet. 2:2). A serious learner gives prominence to the study of Scripture, asking the Teacher to give insight and understanding.

3. *Learn from prayer.* When Jesus' disciples asked Him to teach them to pray (see Luke 11:1), Jesus responded by giving them the Model Prayer. Prayer is one primary means for directly communicating with and relating to God moment by moment, day by day. We must learn to pray, not by listening to the prayers of our contemporaries but by following the Model Prayer as well as other prayers found in the Bible. Ask the Holy Spirit to teach you to pray.

4. *Learn from your church.* God has assigned the church the task of equipping believers and has bestowed spiritual gifts for accomplishing that task (see Eph. 4:11-13). Your church no doubt offers spiritual-growth opportunities through open Bible-study groups, closed discipleship studies, and specific ministry training. Taking advantage of these opportunities furthers your own spiritual growth and equips you to make disciples of others.

Complete the following sentence: I am growing in my knowledge of Jesus and His ways through—

_____

_____

Lordship. We also grow in Christ by surrendering to Him as Lord of our lives. An angel introduced Jesus as " 'Christ the Lord' " (Luke 2:11). Jesus is the same person known as Jehovah (Yahweh) in the Old Testament. He is Lord by virtue of being the Son of God, and He is Lord over the entire universe. Peter declared to Cornelius and his friends, " 'Jesus Christ—He is Lord of all' " (Acts 10:36). Paul affirmed the same truth when he wrote the beautiful verses printed in the margin.

> "God also highly exalted Him
>   and gave Him the name that
>   is above every name,
> so that at the name of Jesus
>   every knee should bow—
> of those who are in heaven
>   and on earth and under
>   the earth—
> and every tongue should confess
>   that Jesus Christ is Lord,
> to the glory of God the Father"
> (Phil. 2:9-11).

Submitting yourself to Jesus as Lord is inseparable from discipleship. As previously stated, a disciple chooses to deny self, take up his cross (die to self), and follow Jesus. Jesus becomes the Lord of that person. Christian growth is the process of increasing in your consistent surrender to Christ as Lord. Another expression for this is being filled with the Spirit. As we increase in our understanding of who Jesus is, we submit more and more to His authority. Being filled with the Spirit means to be guided by Jesus. The more He directs, the more of His fruit is displayed—the manifestation of Christ's character in our lives.

Filled with the Spirit

Ephesians 5:18 commands us to "be filled with the Spirit." Possessing the Spirit and being filled with the Spirit are different things. If you have received Christ, you have the Spirit living in you (see 2 Cor. 1:21-22). But the Holy Spirit wants to flow through you like a stream of living water (see John 7:38-39). You can't obey Christ's commands, witness, serve, or overcome a problem in your own strength. Christians today can be filled with the power of the Holy Spirit just as the early church was filled at Pentecost (see Acts 2:1-41).

The Holy Spirit will fill you completely if you acknowledge Christ's lordship and submit to His authority (see 1 Thess. 5:23). Confess your sin and your need for cleansing. Present your body as a righteous instrument for God's use. Then ask God to fill, control, and empower you (see Luke 11:13). Believe that God has answered your prayer. God wants you to be filled with His Spirit so that you will be found blameless, that is, Christlike (see 1 Thess. 5:23) and will be empowered to do His work (see Acts 1:8).[8]

When other people look at your life, would they determine—
- ☐ that your faith in God and your daily life are not connected?
- ☐ that a Christian lives like the world?
- ☐ that everything you do is based on biblical principles?
- ☐ that you've never understood what it means to have Jesus as your Lord?

What Do We Believe About Election?

The concept of election is a familiar one to those who live in a democracy. But what does election mean in the biblical sense? Both Old and New Testament passages can be cited to explain the concept of election. Let's do a brief word study. The Hebrew word for *elect* simply means *chosen*. Most Old Testament occurrences refer to God's choice of Abraham and his descendants to be a special people. For example, Moses said to them, " 'You are a holy people belonging to the LORD your God. The LORD your God has chosen you to be His own possession out of all the peoples on the face of the earth' " (Deut. 7:6). Election in the Old Testament refers primarily to God's choice of a nation to serve His purposes.

The New Testament word for *election* also means *chosen*. Peter wrote this about Christians:

> You are a chosen race, a royal priesthood,
> a holy nation, a people for His possession,
> so that you may proclaim the praises
> of the One who called you out of darkness
> into His marvelous light (1 Pet. 2:9).

The doctrine of election is the biblical teaching that God has chosen, called, and saved certain people to fulfill His purposes. *The Baptist Faith and Message* defines *election* this way: "Election is the gracious purpose of God, according to which He regenerates, justifies, sanctifies, and glorifies sinners."[9]

Election and God's Sovereignty

God is the supreme Ruler of this universe. He has the power, authority, and freedom to do whatever He pleases. Fortunately, God is not a harsh, unreasonable dictator. His sovereign control is always in perfect harmony with all of His other attributes. Therefore, God's sovereignty is always expressed in love. He always wants what is best for us.

Election is one aspect of God's sovereignty. He has a plan for humankind that He will bring to fulfillment. This plan includes the salvation of lost, condemned sinners. Apart from the loving choice of God, no one could be saved from sin and its consequences. Read the passage in the margin.

God takes the initiative in the salvation of humankind. Through the gospel He calls the unsaved to repent and believe in Jesus. No one would ever respond without being called. Those who answer God's call in faith are immediately justified and ultimately glorified. The Scripture clearly states that no one is excluded from God's plan of salvation. As Peter wrote, "The Lord ... is patient with you, not wanting any to perish, but all to come to repentance" (2 Pet. 3:9). Christ's death was an offering for the sin of all humankind, not a select few. Note the emphasis on *all* in these statements: "Christ's love compels us, since we have reached this conclusion: if One died for all, then all died. And He died for all so that those who live should no longer live for themselves, but for the One who died for them and was raised" (2 Cor. 5:14-15).

> "We know that all things work together for the good of those who love God: those who are called according to His purpose. For those He foreknew He also predestined to be conformed to the image of His Son, so that He would be the firstborn among many brothers. And those He predestined, He also called; and those He called, He also justified; and those He justified, He also glorified" (Rom. 8:28-30).

The concept of election means that—

☐ God has predetermined who will be saved;
☐ God's plan of salvation includes all people;
☐ salvation can be achieved only through good works;
☐ salvation is competitive; not everyone who pursues salvation will achieve it.

Election and Humanity's Free Will

The doctrine of election becomes a stumbling block for some students of Scripture. They struggle with this question: because God is sovereign and works all things according to His predetermined plan, how can humankind make free choices and be held responsible for those choices? We must admit the difficulty of this issue. However, we must also trust the revelation of Scripture. God is not only sovereign and wise but also gracious and merciful to all who call on Him. There is no conflict in the mind of God between His sovereignty and human beings' responsibility for their choices. If we hold to a belief in fatalism (the teaching that some are destined to be lost and therefore cannot be saved), we miss the clear teaching of the Bible that "everyone who calls on the name of the Lord will be saved" (Rom. 10:13). God chooses to offer salvation as a gift to all, but no one is forced to receive this gift. Therefore, everyone who hears the gospel is responsible for his or her response.

What about those who never hear the good news? Paul addressed that question: "How can they call on Him in whom they have not believed? And how can they believe without hearing about Him? And how can they hear without a preacher? And how can they preach unless they are sent?" (Rom. 10:14-15). Evangelism and missions find their place and motivation in the responsibility of the saved to reach the unsaved. Those who know Jesus have an obligation to share the good news of salvation with those who don't know. This is part of God's plan.

God is guiding history to a conclusion of His own choosing. The universe and all within it are under His control. He is bringing all creation to the perfection of His eternal kingdom. At the same time, people have free will to respond to God's plan and purposes. We can accept or reject God's plan and are therefore responsible for the choices we make.

Election and the Perseverance of Believers

Baptists are sometimes criticized for believing "Once saved, always saved." Critics sometimes point to a professing Christian whose life is a disgrace to Christ as evidence of the fallacy of this belief. But our response must not be based on what we think or what others have said but on what the Bible teaches about the perseverance of believers.

Perseverance, as used in this context, means, "All true believers endure to the end. Those whom God has accepted in Christ, and sanctified by His Spirit, will never fall away from the state of grace, but shall persevere to the end."[10] In other words, all who have been truly born again have eternal life and will never perish. Read in the margin our Savior's clear statement. If any true believer in Christ ever perished, Jesus would be a liar. He said that we are in His hand and in the hand of His Father and that no one can take us out of their hands.

"My sheep hear My voice, I know them, and they follow Me. I give them eternal life, and they will never perish—ever! No one will snatch them out of My hand. My Father, who has given them to Me, is greater than all. No one is able to snatch them out of the Father's hand" (John 10:27-29).

Our perseverance is secure because our salvation does not depend on us but on God. Because we did not save ourselves, we can do nothing to lose that salvation. Salvation is wholly initiated and accomplished by God, and those He saves, He secures. This does not mean that all professing Christians will be saved but that all true believers will. Peter, who at one time had denied knowing Christ, later said of the Lord, "He has given us … an inheritance that is imperishable, uncorrupted, and unfading, kept in heaven for you, who are being protected by God's power through faith for a salvation that is ready to be revealed in the last time" (1 Pet. 1:3-5).

Everlasting life is exactly what the term indicates—everlasting! Do not allow the Adversary to rob you of the peace and joy of knowing that the One you have trusted is "able to protect you from stumbling and to make you stand in the presence of His glory, blameless and with great joy" (Jude 24).

Can believers lose their salvation? ☐ Yes ☐ No Use Scripture to explain your response.

_____

_____

What Do We Believe About Sin in a Christian's Life?

Perhaps you have seen the bumper sticker that reads, "Christians aren't perfect, just forgiven." That's true. Sinless perfection should be every believer's goal, but as long as we live in this body and in this world, we will continue to fall short of perfection. The Apostle John gave this warning to some who may have claimed to be sinless: "If we say, 'We have no sin,' we are deceiving ourselves, and the truth is not in us" (1 John 1:8). Because sin continues to be a reality after a person is saved, it is important to learn how to deal with this problem.

The Christian Life Is Warfare

All Christians have the same three enemies: the flesh, the world, and the Devil (Satan). Let's be clear about who these enemies are.

The flesh. Although we have a new nature in Christ—a nature that is holy and righteous—the old sinful nature hangs on with its strong tendency to rebel against God. The Bible refers to this old nature as the flesh. Paul described the struggle with the flesh that believers continue to experience: "I know that nothing good lives in me, that is, in my flesh. For the desire to do what is good is with me, but there is no ability to do it. For I do not do the good that I want to do, but I practice the evil that I do not want to do" (Rom. 7:18-19).

The world. We also continue to live in a world that is contrary to God, which John described in 1 John 2:15-16 (in the margin). This is not God's beautiful creation but the kingdom of the world, under Satan's control.

The Devil. The Devil is a fallen angel who rules over a host of other fallen angels (demons). These form what Paul calls "the authorities … world powers of this darkness … the spiritual forces of evil in the heavens" (Eph. 6:12). Peter, who knew Satan's power from personal experience, wrote, "Be sober! Be on the alert! Your adversary the Devil is prowling around like a roaring lion, looking for anyone he can devour" (1 Pet. 5:8).

> "Do not love the world or the things that belong to the world. If anyone loves the world, love for the Father is not in him. Because everything that belongs to the world—the lust of the flesh, the lust of the eyes, and the pride in one's lifestyle—is not from the Father, but is from the world" (1 John 2:15-16).

The war rages every moment. The ultimate outcome is settled: Satan suffered eternal defeat through Christ's death, burial, and resurrection. However, until Christ's victorious return, His followers are subject to Satan's attacks in the form of temptations to sin. Satan is deceitful and persistent in his determination to destroy our Christian well-being and influence. He seeks to rob us of joy and subject us to a life of misery and uselessness. The Devil works through the flesh and the world to accomplish his evil purpose. But God's Word shows how we can have victory in the face of such overwhelming opposition.

"You must take up the full armor of God, so that you may be able to resist in the evil day, and having prepared everything, to take your stand. Stand, therefore, with truth like a belt
  around your waist,
righteousness like armor
  on your chest,
and your feet sandaled
  with readiness for the
  gospel of peace.
In every situation take the shield
  of faith,
and with it you will be able
  to extinguish
the flaming arrows of the
  evil one.
Take the helmet of salvation,
and the sword of the Spirit,
  which is God's word"
(Eph. 6:13-17).

The Christian Life Can Be Victorious

God provides everything we need to claim daily victory over the unholy trinity of evil. The Apostle Paul said, "We are more than victorious through Him who loved us" (Rom. 8:37). But we must learn how to defeat the enemy; we must become skilled in combat. Here are four helpful tactics.

Be alert. One of Satan's most effective strategies is to convince Christians that he is not a threat to them. Some doubt his existence; others fail to recognize his efforts to cause them to stumble. Recall Peter's words: "Be on the alert! Your adversary the Devil is prowling around like a roaring lion, looking for anyone he can devour" (1 Pet. 5:8). Keep up your spiritual guard. Believe the warning of God's Word. Live in a state of readiness to meet the enemy. Learn to recognize his tactics. Remind yourself every day that the enemy is real and dangerous.

Be armed. The Apostle Paul was a prisoner when he wrote his letter to the Ephesians. Perhaps while chained to an armed guard, Paul compared the soldier's equipment for battle to the spiritual armor needed by a Christian. In the margin read about the armor God provides to ensure victory over the Devil. God provides adequate armor, but we must put it on.

Be confident. At times we may feel that Satan is stronger than we are, but as we face this terrifying enemy, we must remember John's words of hope: "You are from God, little children, and you have conquered them, because the One who is in you is greater than the one who is in the world" (1 John 4:4). Jesus succeeded in overcoming every temptation from Satan;

How to Demolish Spiritual Strongholds

A spiritual stronghold is an idea, a thought process, a habit, or an addiction through which Satan has influence in your life. Use this biblical process to break free.

1. Identify the stronghold and the reason it violates God's Word and God's will.
2. Repent of the sin and ask for God's forgiveness.
3. Declare war on the stronghold by substituting biblical truth, claiming the mind of Christ, using spiritual weapons (see Eph. 6:13-17), praying for the Holy Spirit's power and guidance, requesting others' prayers and support, boldly making God's truth clear, and claiming the victory by faith.
4. Pray as you put on each piece of spiritual armor (see Eph. 6:13-17) and receive God's strength to fight the obstacle.
5. Win the victory in Christ by loving God, keeping His commandments, being sure that you are born of God, believing that Jesus is God's Son, and believing that God keeps you safe (see 1 John 4:4; 5:2-3,18-20).[11]

He is far superior to this adversary in every way. And we can also overcome because we can say with Paul, "Christ lives in me" (Gal. 2:20). Jesus Christ is the source of our confidence. We can also say with Paul, "I am able to do all things through Him who strengthens me" (Phil. 4:13).

Be clean. In spite of all God promises and provides, the enemy sometimes prevails. How do we deal with failure? The Bible shows us the way: "If we confess our sins, He is faithful and righteous to forgive us our sins and to cleanse us from all unrighteousness" (1 John 1:9). Confess your sins the moment you become aware of them. Acknowledge your disobedience and claim His promise to forgive and cleanse. Thank Him for the total removal of guilt and for the restoration of fellowship with Him. Then move on to greater experiences of worship of and service to the One who saved you and assures you of His faithful presence.

In the appropriate columns, list ways you are tempted to sin.

Your Old Nature	Social Temptations	Spiritual Indifference
_____	_____	_____
_____	_____	_____

Circle the temptation above that you deal with most often. Then use the following questions to develop a strategy for overcoming that temptation.

How can you be alert? _____

How can you be armed?_____

How can you be confident?_____

How can you be clean?_____

---
[1]Ken Hemphill, *LifeAnswers: Making Sense of Your World* (Nashville: LifeWay Press, 1993), 51.
[2]Daniel L. Akin, *Discovering the Biblical Jesus* (Nashville: LifeWay Press, 2003), 89–91.
[3]*The Baptist Faith and Message* (Nashville: LifeWay Christian Resources of the Southern Baptist Convention, 2000), 11.
[4]Herschel Hobbs, *Fundamentals of Our Faith* (Nashville: Broadman Press, 1960), 106.
[5]T. W. Hunt and Melana Hunt Monroe, *From Heaven's View* (Nashville: LifeWay Press, 2002), 131, 135–37.
[6]*The Baptist Faith and Message*, 11.
[7]Hunt and Monroe, *From Heaven's View*, 21–22, 53, 66, 147, 152.
[8]Avery T. Willis Jr., *MasterLife 2: The Disciple's Personality* (Nashville: LifeWay Press, 1996), 94–105.
[9]*The Baptist Faith and Message*, 12.
[10]Ibid.
[11]Avery T. Willis Jr., *MasterLife 3: The Disciple's Victory* (Nashville: LifeWay Press, 1996), 23–25.

CHAPTER 3

Why Did God Establish the Church, and What Is Our Role in It?

The story was beyond my imagination. A 21-year-old mother abandoned her baby, leaving her to die. Fortunately, the child was found and placed in a loving family. According to the law, this mother was guilty of a crime. Why? Because family relationships demand responsibility.

God created us for relationships not only in families but also in a fellowship of love, trust, and service with other believers. Our relationship with Jesus Christ is personal, but it is never intended to be lived in isolation. God's purpose is not just to save independent souls but also to build a family of redeemed individuals who worship and serve Him together. That family of faith is the church—a kingdom in which we are fellow citizens—a spiritual body in which Christ is the Head and we are His members. Only in this fellowship can we become all God intended for us to be as believers.

In 25 or fewer words, describe the purpose of the church as you understand it.

_____

_____

_____

_____

A certain microscopic form of life in the ocean is called plankton. This tiny organism serves as food for many of the smallest creatures in the sea. The term *plankton* comes from a Greek word meaning *to wander or drift*. Plankton seems to have no control of its destination; it simply drifts with the currents.

Many people of the 21st century are like plankton, having no sense of purpose and direction in life. This basic need can best be met by a relationship with God and His church.

In this chapter we will explore the nature of the church and a believer's role in this divinely designed fellowship. We will also learn about the purpose of the church, the way it functions, its leaders, its ordinances, and related issues like the Lord's Day and religious liberty. Through this study we will discover more about the responsibilities and blessings God gives us through His body, the church.

What Do We Believe About the Church?

A friend recently told me about a tornado that destroyed her church. Like many church members, she made the mistake of identifying the church with a building. Actually, the New Testament contains no mention of a church building. The church of Jesus Christ is not a building and not a denomination. What is the church?

The Nature of the Church

Let's begin with a definition. The word *church* is a translation of the Greek word *ekklesia*— a term that literally means *those who are called out—an assembly*. The Greek city-states, which followed a democratic form of government, held public meetings for the purpose of making decisions. Such an assembly was known as an *ekklesia*. Jesus chose this word to describe an assembly of His followers when He said, " 'I will build My church' " (Matt. 16:18).

The New Testament uses the word *ekklesia* 114 times.

- Three uses refer to a secular assembly (see, for example, Acts 19:39).
- Approximately 12 times the word indicates the complete assembly of all believers—the universal church (see, for example, Eph. 5:25,27).
- The remaining occurrences refer to an assembly of Christians at a specific place—a local congregation (see, for example, Rom.16:5).

> *Church:* Those who are called out—an assembly of believers

Which term best describes the New Testament word for *church*?

☐ A building or structure   ☐ A called-out assembly of believers
☐ Anyplace believers are gathered   ☐ A missions and educational organization

A church, in the biblical sense, is a fellowship of individuals who have been born again and have publicly acknowledged this new life by being baptized in water. A church is a living organism whose life is Christ, whose members submit to His authority, and whose mission is to do His will.

The church is God's plan for His people. Humans are created for relationships. All believers are redeemed to live in relationship with God and His eternal family. We need the church, and the church needs us. To refuse fellowship with other believers thwarts God's intention in two ways:

1. We withhold what God wants to contribute to other believers through us.
2. We miss what God wants to impart to us through others.

"As the body is one and has many parts, and all the parts of that body, though many, are one body—so also is Christ. For we were all baptized by one Spirit into one body. Now you are the body of Christ, and individual members of it" (1 Cor. 12:12-13,27).

Paul wanted believers in Corinth to understand the importance of their role in the church, so he compared the church to the human body. Read his explanation in the margin. Paul said that each part of our body is different from the other parts; yet each functions as part of the whole. No part can survive if cut off from the rest. In a similar way, the body of Christ is a living organism made up of unique members, each different yet each dependent on the others. And every Christian has an essential contribution to make to a local church. As a human body is handicapped by the loss of a finger or a toe, your church is less effective without a particular member's involvement.

The Mission of the Church

What is the purpose of the church? Why is Jesus building His church? Answers to those questions often point to a great deal of confusion today. Various nonbiblical traditions have developed that violate the original design given by Jesus and the New Testament writers.

What criteria do you use to evaluate the quality of your church experience?

☐ Choir's performance　　☐ Preacher's message　　☐ Ministry to the community
☐ Personal comfort　　　　☐ Worship style　　　　　☐ Availability of convenient parking
☐ Age-group ministries　　☐ Other: _____

"Go, therefore, and make disciples of all nations, baptizing them in the name of the Father and of the Son and of the Holy Spirit, teaching them to observe everything I have commanded you. And remember, I am with you always, to the end of the age" (Matt. 28:19-20).

Although a church can meet human needs in many ways, believers must maintain a clear focus on the original, fundamental mission of the church. Jesus' final words to His followers before His return to heaven, known as the Great Commission, are printed in the margin. Read those verses now.

From this classic statement, along with the first description of the church in Acts 2:42-47, in the margin on page 53, we can describe the church's basic mission in terms of the following five functions.

Evangelism. Jesus' first invitation to His disciples was " 'Follow Me, and I will make you fishers of men!' " (Matt. 4:19). In other words, "You make the choice to follow Me, and I will make the change from self-centered living to concern for the salvation of others." The words *evangelism* and *gospel* have the same root meaning: *glad tidings, good news.* The Book of Acts records that the first believers gave priority to reaching others with the good news. The first time Peter preached, the response was amazing: "Those who accepted his message were baptized, and that day about three thousand people were added to them" (Acts 2:41). A short time later this report was given: "Many of those who heard the message believed, and the number of the men came to about five thousand" (Acts 4:4).

In spite of the efforts of Jewish leaders to stop the spread of the gospel, the Scripture declares, "Every day in the temple complex, and in various homes, they continued teaching

The Church and the Kingdom

The central focus of Jesus' preaching was the kingdom of God, and many of His parables helped hearers understand the kingdom. The kingdom of God is the realm where God rules. Because He is sovereign over all creation, His kingdom extends over all nature, the holy angels, and all the redeemed of all time.

The kingdom of this world, under Satan's control, is in conflict with God's kingdom, but ultimately, God will prevail. The Apostle John's record of his vision includes this thrilling statement: "There were loud voices in heaven saying: 'The kingdom of the world has become the kingdom of our Lord and of His Messiah, and He will reign forever and ever!'" (Rev. 11:15).

The church is part of God's kingdom. He established the church as His primary means of overcoming the kingdom of Satan.

and proclaiming the good news that the Messiah is Jesus" (Acts 5:42). And God blessed the witness of His people: "The preaching about God flourished, the number of the disciples in Jerusalem multiplied greatly, and a large group of priests became obedient to the faith" (Acts 6:7). All of these indicators affirm the fact that the church is an assembly of believers whose primary mission is sharing with unbelievers the good news about salvation in Jesus Christ.

How important to your church is reaching unbelievers with God's love?

●————————————————————————————————————●

Very important   Not important

What can your church can do to express a greater commitment to evangelism?

_____

Discipleship. The Great Commission has one imperative: " 'Go, therefore, and make disciples of all nations' " (Matt. 28:19). A disciple is a learner— someone whose life is shaped by a chosen teacher. The New Testament mentions the disciples of John the Baptist, Moses, and the Pharisees, as well as the disciples of Jesus. For believers today, being a disciple of Jesus is a life-long process of becoming conformed to His likeness.

Evangelism is the first step in making disciples. Those who are won to Christ must be helped to grow in Christ and must be sent out to make new disciples for Him. The church is a school in which converts become disciples, who make disciples of others. Paul's relationship with Timothy is a classic example of disciple making. He wrote this challenge to his young disciple: "You, therefore, my child, be strong in the grace

"They devoted themselves to the apostles' teaching, to fellowship, to the breaking of bread, and to prayers. … All the believers were together and had everything in common. So they sold their possessions and property and distributed the proceeds to all, as anyone had a need. And every day they devoted themselves to meeting together in the temple complex, and broke bread from house to house. They ate their food with gladness and simplicity of heart, praising God and having favor with all the people. And every day the Lord added those being saved to them" (Acts 2:42-47).

that is in Christ Jesus. And what you have heard from me in the presence of many witnesses, commit to faithful men who will be able to teach others also" (2 Tim 2:2). Here are four generations of believers—Paul, Timothy, faithful men, and others. Each believer is called to reach and teach others to reach and teach others, and the process goes on and on.

How important is making disciples to your church?

Very important   Not important

Circle *T* for *true* or *F* for *false.*

I actively seek to learn more about Christ and the Christian life.	T	F
Every day I am more conformed to the image of Christ.	T	F
I help other believers grow in their faith.	T	F
My church has an intentional strategy for training disciples.	T	F

Functions of the Church
Evangelism
Discipleship
Fellowship
Ministry
Worship

Fellowship. The word *fellowship* is a translation of the Greek word *koinonia,* which means *that which is shared in common.* Every Christian is different from every other Christian in many ways, but all believers have one common experience that binds them together—the new birth, which brings new life in Christ. Unlike most organizations, the church is a family of God's redeemed people. Differences that divide, such as politics, race, ethnicity, social status, economic standing, gender, and many others, are all overcome when the children of the Heavenly Father assemble in His name. The only qualification for participation in a church fellowship is being an authentic disciple of Jesus—one who has been saved and baptized.

Fellowship has characterized the church from the beginning. Notice the role of fellowship in this first description of a church: "They devoted themselves to the apostles' teaching, to fellowship, to the breaking of bread, and to prayers. And every day they devoted themselves to meeting together in the temple complex, and broke bread from house to house" (Acts 2:42,46). These Christians' togetherness was not based on food and fun; they had a unity of heart because of their salvation in Christ.

How important to your church is encouraging fellowship among members?

Very important   Not important

Rank the following groups in the order of your preference for spending time with them. Write *1* beside the group you most want to spend time with, *2* beside the next group, and so forth. Circle the group you actually spend the most time with.

__ Coworkers   __ Social acquaintances   __ Neighbors
__ Sunday School class members   __ Other church friends   __ Strangers

If you adopt the characteristics of the people with whom you spend the most time, are you more likely to become like Christ or like the world?   ☐ Christ   ☐ The world

Ministry. The first church was characterized by mutual concern for one another's needs. Read this amazing description: "There was not a needy person among them, because all those who owned lands or houses sold them, brought the proceeds of the things that were sold, and laid them at the apostles' feet. This was then distributed to each person as anyone had a need" (Acts 4:34-35). We are reading about an unusual situation that arose in Jerusalem when many Jews traveled long distances from their homes to celebrate the religious festival called Pentecost. They brought enough food and money to last a few days but stayed much longer because of the outpouring of God's Spirit (see Acts 2).

The lesson for us is not that we must all sell our possessions and give away the proceeds; rather, we are to minister to one another when needs arise. And this ministry is certainly not limited to physical needs or to the immediate fellowship of believers. All persons need encouragement, comfort, affirmation, and other expressions of support. Every believer should occupy the role of a minister who serves others through the abilities and opportunities given by God. In this way we express Christ's love and create opportunities to share His good news.

How important to your church is ministering to others?

●————————————————————————————●

Very important   Not important

God Has No Orphans

Those who enter a relationship with God through Jesus Christ are automatically born into the family of God (see John 1:12-13). Unfortunately, many church members say, "My relationship with God is private" and have nothing to do with God's people. Our relationship with God is personal, but it was never meant to be private.

The Bible bears witness to the corporate life of God's children; this is by God's design and purpose. In a local church we are to be nourished, fed, protected, and guided toward spiritual maturity. Furthermore, the Spirit-filled life is obvious to all who see it. Christians are to be the salt of the earth who make a recognizable difference, a candle that gives light in a dark world, and a city set on a hill that all can see (see Matt. 5:13-16). Finally, the most convincing evidence that we have received the gift of salvation is that we demonstrate Christlike love to other believers (see 1 John 4:21).

No one who served God in the Bible had a relationship with God in private. Rather, each had a significant involvement with God's people, for that is where God's heart is found. Today God places His children in His family. The local church is crucial to every believer's unfolding relationship with God.[1]

Are people comfortable sharing their needs in your church? ☐ Yes ☐ No Why or why not?

_____

What can your church do to minister to needs in the community? _____

_____

Worship. This final function is actually the first in importance. True worship of God releases His love and power, which become our resources for performing the other functions of the church. Christians must learn to worship in spirit and truth; the church is the place for this essential practice. Jesus revealed a remarkable truth when He told the Samaritan woman, " 'An hour is coming, and is now here, when the true worshipers will worship the Father in spirit and truth. Yes, the Father wants such people to worship Him' " (John 4:23). How awesome that the Father wants our worship! Because our worship brings pleasure to Him, it is the most rewarding experience we can enjoy.

How important to you is worshiping with your church?

●————————————————————————————————————●

Very important   Not important

Select the phrase that best describes your understanding of worship.

☐ An event   ☐ An emotion   ☐ An attitude   ☐ A performance

We have taken a separate look at each of the five functions of the church, but none is independent of the others. Each contributes to the mutual edification and effectiveness of the church as a whole. Therefore, every Christian is expected to participate in every aspect of the church's mission. For example, we must not conclude that evangelism is not our responsibility because we may not feel comfortable sharing the gospel with others. Members of the body of Christ must beware of adhering to a spectator mentality. We are not the audience watching others perform. We are the performers! That leads us to our next teaching about the church.

The Ministers of the Church

One church has this motto: "Every member a minister." I like that because it affirms the teaching of the New Testament. Unfortunately, many people today think that only the pastor and other paid staff members qualify to be ministers. But the Bible clearly teaches that every Christian should consider himself or herself a minister of Christ. Paul wrote about the task of training believers "in the work of ministry" (Eph. 4:12). He concluded his letter to the Romans with a long list of men and women who had ministered to his needs. Each was a true minister of Christ (see Rom. 16:3-16). The Greek word most often translated *minister* means *one who serves.* All believers are called to serve Christ by serving one another.

How to Discover Your Gift(s)

1. Ask God to reveal to you your special serving ability. Claim His promises, such as "Call to Me, and I will answer you, and show you great and mighty things, which you do not know" (Jer. 33:3, NKJV).

2. Examine yourself. What do you enjoy doing to help others? Exercising your gift in the church will be something you enjoy.

3. Rather than assume a major responsibility at first, volunteer to be a helper in your church. Consider helping a Bible teacher of a particular age group, serving as an usher, singing in the choir, or volunteering for a committee or team.

How can you become a minister of Christ in your church? The Bible teaches that every believer possesses one or more spiritual gifts (see 1 Cor. 12:1-11; Eph. 4:11). A spiritual gift is a special skill or ability God bestows through His Holy Spirit that equips believers to serve God in the church. Peter wrote, "Based on the gift they have received, everyone should use it to serve others, as good managers of the varied grace of God" (1 Pet. 4:10). Peter was calling every Christian to use his or her spiritual gift(s) to serve others.

Insert your name in the blanks below.

Based on the gifts _____ has received, _____ should use it to serve others, as a good manager "of the varied grace of God" (1 Pet. 4:10).

Whatever your spiritual gift is, remember that every Christian is called to be a minister of reconciliation (see 2 Cor. 5:18), which means reaching others with the good news of Jesus.

Don't wait for someone to ask you to serve. Christ has already done that; obey Him by offering yourself as a minister in His body, the church. Remember, Christ saved you to serve!

The Polity of the Church

How does a church make decisions? Who makes the rules? Church polity encompasses these issues. The New Testament does not give detailed instructions about the way a local congregation should be governed. However, one fact is clear: the Head of the church is Jesus Christ. Every local congregation is an expression of His life and exists for His purpose in the world.

Because every believer has the Spirit of Christ, each is capable of participating in the process of discovering His will on any matter. Thus, a democratic approach to decision making is appropriate, and a church becomes a theocratic democracy. The term *theocracy* refers to God's rule over people. A pure democracy is the rule by the majority of the people involved. Local church government is a combination of these two. As *The Baptist Faith and Message* states, "Each congregation operates under the Lordship of Christ through democratic processes."[2]

Why is the structure of a Baptist church not a hierarchy?

☐ Because The Baptist Faith and Message teaches differently
☐ Because the pastor and staff serve only as long as the people allow
☐ Because it is a theocracy, with Jesus as the Head
☐ Because the hierarchical structure has proved ineffective

The pastor's authority comes from his call by God; however, the majority of the congregation must agree with his leadership. The same is true of deacons and other leaders. This principle affirms the ultimate authority of Christ and testifies to the faith of His people that He is always present to give them His divine guidance. Although church business meetings may often seem boring and unimportant, they are the best means of recognizing the priesthood of believers— the concept that every Christian has the same access to God and an equal opportunity to participate in determining His will for His church.

The Leaders of the Church

Two leaders were mentioned in the preceding paragraph—pastor and deacon. Most Baptist churches agree that these were the primary leaders in New Testament churches. The pastor is referred to by several names in Scripture. All three of the following terms refer to the same office and are used to point out the various roles a pastor must fulfill.

Pastor: Shepherd of a flock
Bishop: Overseer
Elder: Adviser and counselor

1. The word *pastor* (see Eph. 4:11) reflects a leader's role as the shepherd of a flock. This title conveys the ideas of personal care, protection, and guidance.
2. Scripture also calls the pastor a *bishop,* meaning *overseer* (see Phil. 1:1; 1 Tim. 3:1-2). This word emphasizes a pastor's administrative role.
3. A third function of the pastoral office is found in the word *elder* (see 1 Pet. 5:1), which refers to the pastor's wisdom and maturity as an adviser and counselor to the church.

In addition to these titles for *pastor,* the New Testament writers used the words *servant (underrower)* and *steward (manager)* to describe the office (see 1 Cor. 4:1). An underrower in the Roman navy was often a slave who was chained to the lowest level of a ship, where he joined others in pulling oars to propel the ship. Certainly, godly pastors earn their right to lead by first being servants of their flocks. A steward in Greek society was responsible for managing another person's estate. These two terms reveal that a pastor should serve others by being a good manager of all that is committed to his care.

Check all of the words that describe the biblical concept of pastor.

☐ Dictator	☐ Overseer	☐ Steward	☐ Bishop	☐ CEO
☐ Elder	☐ Servant	☐ Speaker	☐ Governor	

Deacons are also called to be servants of the church. A prototype of their role is found in Acts 6:1-7. This passage records that deacons were first chosen to bring harmony in the church fellowship; minister to the church's physical, emotional, and spiritual needs; and lead the church in spiritual growth and maturity. One of the deacons chosen to serve in this capacity, Stephen, is presented as a model for the ideal deacon (see Acts 6:3-15).

Paul gave clear instructions to Timothy about the qualifications of both pastors and deacons in 1 Timothy 3. This chapter emphasizes the importance of godly character for a church leader. A pastor must be "above reproach, the husband of one wife, self-controlled, sensible, respectable, hospitable, an able teacher, not addicted to wine, not a bully but gentle, not quarrelsome, not greedy" (vv. 2-3). Likewise, a deacon "should be worthy of respect, not hypocritical, not drinking a lot of wine, not greedy for money, holding the mystery of the faith with a clear conscience" (vv. 8-9). Although no pastor or deacon can be perfect, each one is required to be blameless in the sense of setting a high standard of both character and conduct.

> "Select from among you seven men of good reputation, full of the Spirit and wisdom, whom we can appoint to this duty" (Acts 6:3).

Can others be leaders in the church? Absolutely! Every church needs faithful leaders for Bible-study classes, discipleship groups, worship, missionary education, counseling, outreach, evangelism, and many other ministry areas. Such persons, chosen according to their spiritual gifts, are first required to lead by their Spirit-filled, godly lives.

Does the Bible Teach Ordination?

Baptist churches have traditionally practiced some form of ordination for pastors and deacons, although the New Testament does not give clear instructions about an ordination ceremony. However, the Greek word translated *ordain* or *appoint* occurs two times with reference to local church leaders. In Acts 6:3 seven men, the forerunners of deacons, were chosen and brought to stand before the apostles, "who prayed and laid their hands on them" (Acts 6:6). Later Paul wrote to Titus reminding him to "appoint elders in every town" (Titus 1:5). In other instances the laying on of hands was practiced as a form of commissioning (see Acts 13:3; 1 Tim. 4:14; 5:22; 2 Tim. 1:6).

These references give biblical support to the present practice of ordaining pastors and deacons. This solemn ceremony, usually performed publicly by other ordained persons, includes a challenge to the candidates, prayer, and laying on of hands. Although no special gift of authority or power is passed to the candidates by the laying on of hands, this ancient practice symbolizes the conferring of responsibility, trust, and God's blessing.

An unfortunate result of ordination is the nonbiblical custom of referring to ordained ministers as clergymen, as opposed to laypersons. These are not biblical terms, leading to a misunderstanding of church leadership. The term *laity*, which translates the Greek word *laos*, literally means *people*. All believers are the people of God; in this sense we are all laypersons. The only difference between those who have been ordained and other believers is one of leadership responsibility in light of God's call.

What about the role of women in ministry? The New Testament mentions several women leaders, such as Phoebe and Prisca, in Romans 16:1-16. Church history records the significant role women have played as leaders in various key capacities. Certain ministries of the church, such as women's and children's ministries, are often more effectively performed by women than men. Paul affirmed the teaching role of women in 2 Timothy 1:5; 3:15; and Titus 2:3-5.

The Baptist Faith and Message states, "While both men and women are gifted for service in the church, the office of pastor is limited to men as qualified by Scripture."[3] One reason for this position is that the list of qualifications given for pastors and deacons in 1 Timothy 3 requires that they be "husbands of one wife" (vv. 2,12). Most pastors and deacons are quick to acknowledge that their wives are a vital part of their ministries, providing encouragement and wise counsel. Paul instructed deacons' wives to be "worthy of respect, not slanderers, self-controlled, faithful in everything" (1 Tim. 3:11). Reverent and respectful women have an essential role in the work of the church.

The Ordinances of the Church

Jesus gave His church two commands about special events. Today these observances are often referred to as ordinances, although the New Testament does not identify them by this term. The words in the Bible that are translated *ordinance* generally mean *decree* or *command*. Traditionally, baptism and the Lord's Supper have been called ordinances because they were commanded by the Lord. One author defines a Christian ordinance as "a symbolic act commanded by Jesus to signify that which Christ did to effect salvation from sin."[4] Here is what Baptists believe about the ordinances of baptism and the Lord's Supper.

Baptism. A new believer said to me, "Pastor, I have accepted Jesus as my Savior. Why is it important for me to get dunked in front of a bunch of people?" The answer begins with the meaning of the word *baptism*. The Greek word *baptizo,* from which we get the word *baptize,* means *dip, plunge,* or *immerse*. The practice of the early church shows that the biblical form of baptism is the total immersion of a believer in water. For example, in Acts 8 the Lord sent the evangelist Philip to meet a man from Ethiopia who was traveling in a chariot from Jerusalem back to his home. Philip joined this man, shared the gospel with him, and led him to trust Jesus as his Savior. When they came to a pool of water, this new believer asked to be baptized. The text reads, "Both Philip and the eunuch went down into the water, and he baptized him. When they came up out of the water, the Spirit of the Lord carried Philip away, and the eunuch did not see him any longer" (Acts 8:38-39). Here is an obvious reference to the submersion of a believer. Because of this New Testament practice, Baptists have historically insisted on immersion rather than sprinkling or other modes of baptism.

The first record of baptism in the New Testament features the work of John the Baptist (literally, John the Baptizer), whom God sent to prepare the way for Jesus. He called for people to repent of their sins and be baptized as a symbol of being forgiven and cleansed from those sins. John's message addresses two kinds of baptism: " 'I baptize you with water for repentance.

> *Ordinance:* Decree or command
> *Baptize:* Dip, plunge, or immerse

Baptism: Symbol or Sacrament?

Roman Catholics and Eastern Orthodox teach that the seven sacraments of baptism, confirmation, Eucharist, penance, anointing of the sick, holy orders, and marriage confer grace on a person, changing the person inwardly through spiritual empowerment. In other words, they believe that salvation is available through the sacraments. The sacrament of baptism is practiced to remove sin and its punishment and to provide spiritual rebirth. Therefore, baptism is considered necessary for salvation.

In contrast, New Testament baptism is an outward ordinance that symbolizes a person's identification with Jesus' death, burial, and resurrection, as well as the person's new life in Christ. In 1 Corinthians 1:17 Paul contrasted baptism with preaching the gospel, indicating that only the gospel can lead someone to salvation. Evangelicals must insist that the only requirement for salvation is sincere, personal faith in Jesus Christ (see Acts 16:31).[5]

But the One who is coming after me is more powerful than I; I am not worthy to take off His sandals. He Himself will baptize you with the Holy Spirit and fire' " (Matt. 3:11).

John's baptism was in water as an indication of repentance. Jesus came to produce a spiritual baptism—an immersion in the Holy Spirit, bringing the power of new life (fire). This truth helps us understand why John was reluctant to baptize Jesus. As the Gospel account states, "Jesus came from Galilee to John at the Jordan, to be baptized by him. But John tried to stop Him, saying 'I need to be baptized by You, and yet You come to me?' " (Matt. 3:13-14). John knew that Jesus had no need of repentance and thus did not need to be baptized by him. However, Jesus insisted on being baptized: " 'Allow it for now, because this is the way for us to fulfill all righteousness' " (v. 15). Jesus requested baptism because He wanted to be an example for others to follow. The phrase *fulfill all righteousness* means *to do all that is required for a life of obedience to God.* Jesus knew that He would soon call for those who believed in Him to be baptized, so He set the example by His own baptism. The strongest reason believers should be baptized comes from this example of Jesus and His command " 'Go, therefore, and make disciples of all nations, baptizing them in the name of the Father and of the Son and of the Holy Spirit' " (Matt. 28:19). One reason the Trinity is named in a person's baptism is that all three members of the Godhead are involved in bringing an unsaved person to salvation.

Check the purposes of baptism, as taught by the New Testament. Check your answers as you read.

☐ It signifies church membership.
☐ It is a denominational mandate for all members.
☐ It is a way of counting annual conversions.
☐ It signifies a new believer's new life in Christ by picturing His death, burial, and resurrection.
☐ It represents the spiritual baptism of new birth.

A New Testament church recognizes the following three significant functions of baptism.

1. Baptism allows the believer to publicly declare faith in the death, burial, and resurrection of Jesus as the means of deliverance from sin. Therefore, Baptists offer baptism for believers only, rejecting infant baptism. Baptism by immersion symbolically presents the simple truths of the gospel, namely, "that Christ died for our sins," "was buried," and was raised from the dead (1 Cor. 15:3-4). When believers obey Christ's command to be baptized, they give a visual statement not only of Christ's death, burial, and resurrection but also of their own death to sin and spiritual resurrection to new life in Christ. Paul affirmed this truth when he wrote, "We were buried with Him by baptism into death" (Rom. 6:4). Dead bodies are buried by being placed underground. The submersion of a believer is a picture of his death to an old life of sin. Raising a believer out of the water symbolizes that person's spiritual resurrection to a new life in Christ. Baptism should always be a public action because it is a Christian's testimony to others of having received Jesus as Savior and of obeying Him as Lord.

> "We were all baptized by one Spirit into one body" (1 Cor. 12:13).

2. Water baptism pictures the spiritual baptism a believer receives at the moment of new birth, when the Holy Spirit comes to abide in the person's heart.

3. Baptism unites the believer with a local church (see 1 Cor. 12:13).

Having considered these truths, can we agree that "getting dunked in front of a bunch of people" is important? Jesus willingly endured the shame and agony of public crucifixion for us. Shouldn't we gladly identify with Him in the meaningful ordinance of baptism?

If you have been baptized, briefly explain the significance of your baptism. If you have not been baptized even though you have accepted Christ as your Savior, state why you need to follow Him in baptism. Then make sure you are baptized as soon as possible!

_____

_____

The Lord's Supper. Through the years many communities in America have erected statues of war heroes. These monuments are reminders of those who gave their lives to gain and preserve our freedom. Jesus left a monument to Himself, a most unusual reminder of His sacrifice for the sins of the entire human race. On the night before His death, Jesus gathered with His disciples to observe the Passover feast, a celebration of God's deliverance of His people from bondage in Egypt. During this memorial supper Jesus introduced two symbols of His imminent death. The four New Testament accounts of this supper (see Matt. 26:26-30; Mark 14:22-26; Luke 22:14-20; 1 Cor. 11:23-26) record that Jesus used unleavened bread to symbolize His body and the cup of "the fruit of the vine" (Mark 14:25) to symbolize His blood.

What makes this monument unlike any other is the fact that observers are commanded to eat it and drink it. When we observe the Lord's Supper, why don't we simply look at the bread and the cup, hold them, and pass them around? The answer is found in Jesus' words in the margin, recorded only by the Apostle John.

As believers partake of the elements of the Lord's Supper, they are reminded that Jesus sacrificed His body and blood to provide eternal life for all who receive Him by faith. Just as we physically eat and drink the symbols of His body and blood, we must spiritually partake of Jesus in order to share in His eternal life. That is the reason Jesus insisted that the disciples eat and drink the elements.

Two terms are used for this important ordinance, and both occur only in 1 Corinthians. Paul first referred to this event as a communion: "The cup of blessing which we bless, is it not the communion of the blood of Christ? The bread which we break, is it not the communion of the body of Christ? For we being many are one bread, and one body: for we are all partakers of that one bread" (1 Cor. 10:16-17, KJV). Paul was emphasizing the fact that believers have communion, or fellowship, with Christ as well as communion with one another ("we … are … one body"). Because of this reference some churches use the term *communion service*. One insight suggested by this term is the fact that this ordinance loses some of its meaning if not conducted by the church family. The New Testament records no instances of the communion service being observed alone. Fellowship with other believers results from our fellowship with Christ.

> "I am the living bread that came down from heaven. If anyone eats of this bread he will live forever. The bread that I will give for the life of the world is My flesh. I assure you: Unless you eat the flesh of the Son of Man and drink His blood, you do not have life in yourselves. Anyone who eats My flesh and drinks My blood has eternal life, and I will raise him up on the last day, because My flesh is true food and My blood is true drink. The one who eats My flesh and drinks My blood lives in Me, and I in him" (John 6:51,53-56).

Receiving Christ's Body and Blood

Religious groups hold different views about the meaning of Jesus' words "This is My body … My blood" (1 Cor. 11:24-25).

1. The Roman Catholic and Eastern Orthodox teaching is called transubstantiation. According to this view, the elements of bread and juice become Jesus' literal flesh and blood when the priest prays over them in the Mass.
2. Lutherans hold a view known as consubstantiation, claiming that Jesus is present with the elements of the supper.
3. Others maintain a mystical view, believing that a person receives special grace from partaking of the Lord's Supper.
4. Baptists and other evangelicals interpret the elements to be symbolic. The bread and juice could not have been Jesus' literal body and blood, because His physical body was present when He spoke those words. Furthermore, His words " 'Do this in remembrance of Me' " (Luke 22:19) convey the idea of a figurative memorial. For these reasons we know that the bread and juice are only symbols or pictures of Jesus' body and blood.

Read "Receiving Christ's Body and Blood," page 63. Then match these terms with their meanings.

_____ 1. Transubstantiation

_____ 2. Consubstantiation

_____ 3. Mystical view

_____ 4. Symbolic view

a. The belief that Christ's presence is in the elements

b. The belief that the elements of the Lord's Supper symbolize Jesus' body and blood

c. The belief that the bread and juice literally become Jesus' flesh and blood

d. The belief that a person receives special grace from partaking of the Lord's Supper

The second and most commonly used term for this memorial to our Savior is *Lord's Supper* (see 1 Cor. 11:20). Paul chose this descriptive term because the original event was a supper hosted by Jesus. In this same passage Paul recorded Jesus' commands for eating the bread and drinking the cup: " 'Do this in remembrance of Me' " (v. 24). Let me suggest three truths to remember about Jesus as we observe the Lord's Supper.

First, remember the past. Christ's death for our sins, symbolized in the breaking of bread (His body) and the pouring of juice (His blood), is the central message of this ordinance. As Peter wrote,

> "He Himself bore our sins
> in His body on the tree,
> so that, having died to sins,
> we might live for righteousness" (1 Pet. 2:24).

Second, remember the present. When believers partake of the elements, we are reminded that we must receive Jesus in order to obtain eternal life. He wants us to remember Him in the present as our indwelling Lord and life. An old communion hymn has these thought-provoking lines: "Bread of heaven, on Thee we feed."[6] He is not present in the elements or in some mystical way around the elements, but He is present in our hearts and wants us to remember Him in this way.

"I will give you a new heart and put a new spirit within you. … I will put My Spirit within you and cause you to walk in My statutes. … You shall be My people, and I will be your God" (Ezek. 36:26-28, NKJV).

Another present remembrance is that because of Jesus' death, believers live in a new covenant relationship with God. At that first Lord's Supper Jesus said, " 'This cup is the new covenant in My blood' " (Luke 22:20). Through His prophets Jeremiah and Ezekiel, the Lord promised a new covenant relationship, based on His gifts rather than human works. Read His words in the margin. The Lord's Supper commemorates this new relationship of grace.

Third, remember the future. Paul added this comment about the Lord's Supper: "As often as you eat this bread and drink the cup, you proclaim the Lord's death until He comes" (1 Cor. 11:26). Christ's return is a future event that the church not only anticipates but also proclaims each time the Lord's Supper is observed. Jesus' last words at the first Lord's Supper pointed to the future: " 'I tell you, from this moment I will not drink of this fruit of the vine until that day when I drink it new in My Father's kingdom with you' " (Matt. 26:29). While the Lord's Supper we observe is temporary, each observance brings us one step closer to the final Lord's Supper. When Jesus returns for His church, there will be no more need for a memorial event; we will all be with Him face-to-face!

How frequently should the meaningful ordinance of the Lord's Supper be observed? Some churches include communion as a part of worship every Sunday; others prefer monthly, quarterly, or less frequently. My belief is that we should observe the supper often enough to prevent us from losing a sense of gratitude for our Lord's sacrifice but not so often that it becomes a ritual without meaning.

More important than frequency is proper preparation. The church at Corinth had divisions in the fellowship and allowed drunkenness at the supper. Paul chastised the church at Corinth for failing to observe the Lord's Supper with a proper attitude of reverence and consideration for others: "Whoever eats the bread or drinks the cup of the Lord in an unworthy way will be guilty of sin against the body and blood of the Lord. So a man should examine himself; in this way he should eat of the bread and drink of the cup" (1 Cor. 11:27-28). Careful self-examination should always precede our participation in this sacred ordinance. We must make certain that our attitude is one of reverence toward Christ, gratitude for His sacrifice, and willingness to build unity in His church.

What Do We Believe About the Lord's Day?

Sunday has been a very special day for me for as long as I can remember. Our family always regarded this first day of the week not only as the day for church services but also as a day of rest. As a child I never questioned the reasons for this practice. As an adult I discovered biblical reasons for our observance of the Lord's Day.

The term *Lord's Day* occurs only once in the Bible. The Apostle John, exiled to the island of Patmos, received a series of revelations from God. He reported, "I was in the Spirit on the Lord's day, and I heard behind me a loud voice like a trumpet" (Rev. 1:10). Most interpreters understand the Lord's Day to be a reference to Sunday. John was accustomed to joining other believers for worship on the first day of the week. We do not know whether other Christians were with him on this island, but John was apparently worshiping when the visions began.

"By the seventh day God had finished the work he had been doing; so on the seventh day he rested from all his work. And God blessed the seventh day and made it holy" (Gen. 2:2-3).

Let's go from Revelation back to the first chapters of Genesis to discover the roots of a special day of worship. Following six days of creation, God rested from His work (see Gen. 2:2-3). The first occurrence of the word *sabbath,* from the Hebrew word *shabath,* meaning *to cease or rest,* is found in Exodus with reference to gathering manna. Moses said to the people, " 'This is what the LORD commanded: "Tomorrow is to be a day of rest, a holy Sabbath to the LORD" ' " (Ex. 16:23). Later the principle of a Sabbath rest became part of the Ten Commandments (see Ex. 20:8-10). The penalty for violating this law was death (see Ex. 31:14-15). The Old Testament and the Gospels make many other references to the Sabbath Day. As Jews, Jesus and His disciples observed the Sabbath.

This history brings us to a logical question: Who changed God's law? Today some groups, including Seventh-Day Baptists and Seventh-Day Adventists, still observe the seventh day as the proper time for rest and worship. Why do the vast majority of believers ignore the seventh day and meet on Sunday?

The change occurred when Jesus was raised from the dead on the first day of the week—the most significant event in history. Jesus' first appearances to His followers after His resurrection were on Sunday. The Gospels record five appearances that first day (see Matt. 28:9-10; Mark 16:9; Luke 24:13-32,33-35; John 20:19-25). Jesus was next seen on the following Sunday (see John 20:26-31). After these events there is no New Testament account of Jesus' followers worshiping on the seventh day. Instead, clear references are made to the gathering of believers on the first day of the week (see Acts 20:7; 1 Cor. 16:2). The early church obviously chose Sunday as the proper day to celebrate its relationship with the risen Lord. His resurrection ushered in a new era for God's people.

> "Remember the Sabbath day by keeping it holy. Six days you shall labor and do all your work, but the seventh day is a Sabbath to the LORD your God. On it you shall not do any work" (Ex. 20:8-10).

Another pivotal event that greatly influenced the change of the day of Christian worship was the day of Pentecost. *Pentecost* means *50*. According to Leviticus 23:15-16, Pentecost occurred on the first day of the week 50 days after Passover. Jesus promised that when He returned to heaven, He would send the Holy Spirit on all of His followers. That promise was fulfilled on the day of Pentecost. This spiritual baptism marked the birth of the church (see Acts 2:1-4), and the Christian community continued to gather on the first day of the week to commemorate the fulfillment of Jesus' promise. Thus, the change from Saturday to Sunday was not made by Jesus' followers but by the Lord Himself. His resurrection, His ascension (see Luke 24:50-51), and the gift of the Holy Spirit all contributed to the change from the end of the week to the beginning, as Christians celebrated the beginning of the covenant of grace.

The observance of the Sabbath shifted from Saturday to Sunday because—
☐ many businesses were already closed or had reduced hours;
☐ Jesus' resurrection, His ascension, and the gift of the Holy Spirit occurred on Sunday;
☐ not a lot is on television on Sunday;
☐ Christians wanted to meet at the synagogues, so they had to wait until they were available.

The practice of gathering on Sunday to worship the Lord has continued from New Testament times to the present. Although most churches provide opportunities for assembling and worshiping on days other than Sunday, priority should be given to this first-day observance because it celebrates and focuses on our Savior and Lord, Jesus Christ. *The Baptist Faith and Message* states that the Lord's Day, as a commemoration of Christ's resurrection, is properly observed by "exercises of worship and spiritual devotion, both public and private. Activities on the Lord's Day should be commensurate with the Christian's conscience under the Lordship of Jesus Christ."[7] Appropriate observances of this special day, in addition to church activities, may include rest, prayer, devotional study, personal worship, deeds of mercy, and witnessing.

If Christians cannot be in church on Sunday because their jobs require them to work, are they disobeying the Lord? The answer to this question depends on our understanding of the basis of our relationship with God. The old covenant was based on obedience to God's laws— a covenant of works. The new covenant offers a relationship of grace with God. Ever since Christ's death, burial, and resurrection, a person comes into a right relationship with God by His grace through faith. Therefore, we must not be legalistic about Sunday worship. The Pharisees, some of Jesus' strongest critics, were very rigid about religious rules and condemned His disciples for what they considered to be work on the Sabbath. Jesus replied, " 'The Sabbath was made for man, and not man for the Sabbath. Therefore the Son of Man is Lord even of the Sabbath' " (Mark 2:27-28).

Paul wrote about Sabbath observance, "Don't let anyone judge you in regard to food and drink or in the matter of a festival or a new moon or a sabbath day. These are a shadow of what was to come; the substance is the Messiah" (Col. 2:16). What is most important is not what day we worship or where we worship but the sincerity of worship from a heart that loves God. Again, Paul wrote, "One person considers one day to be above another day. Someone else considers every day to be the same. Each one must be fully convinced in his own mind. Whoever observes the day, observes it to the Lord" (Rom. 14:5-6).

The truth is, every day belongs to the Lord. Every day should be a day of worship and service to Him. We are free in Christ to choose the best time to meet with other believers to celebrate our life in Him. However, we have significant biblical reasons to give preference to a Sunday gathering to honor the Lord. We must beware of an attitude that says, "I can worship the Lord just as well at the lake as at church." We cannot improve on the biblical model of meeting together on the first day of the week, not just for what we can receive but, more importantly, for what we can contribute to others (see Heb. 10:24-25).

"Let us be concerned about one another in order to promote love and good works, not staying away from our meetings, as some habitually do, but encouraging each other, and all the more as you see the day drawing near" (Heb. 10:24-25).

True or false? The gift of the Holy Spirit enables Christians to worship just as well at the lake as at church. ☐ True ☐ False **Explain your response.**

_____

_____

Believers do well to avoid the two extremes of legalism and failure to observe the Lord's Day, seeking instead to celebrate and honor Christ on Sunday and every day.

What Do We Believe About Religious Liberty?

Baptists have long been outstanding advocates of religious liberty. We must give attention to this subject not only to understand its implications today but also to appreciate the rich heritage bequeathed by our Baptist forefathers. One of the earliest references to religious liberty appeared in 1612, when John Smyth published an extensive confession of faith insisting that civil authorities must not "meddle with religion, or matters of conscience."[8] Other Baptist leaders, such as Thomas Helwys, John Bunyan, and John Milton in England, then John Clarke, Roger Williams, Isaac Backus, and John Leland during colonial times in America, continued the call for the free expression of religious beliefs. Many such leaders were severely persecuted for their views. Belief in religious liberty is founded on the biblical doctrine of soul competency—that individuals are capable of forming religious beliefs and are responsible solely to God for them.

The Biblical Foundation of Religious Liberty

Our Lord clearly spoke about true liberty when He promised, " 'If you continue in My word, you really are My disciples. You will know the truth, and the truth will set you free. ... If the Son sets you free, you really will be free' " (John 8:31-32,36). In these verses Jesus was referring to freedom from sin, a freedom that comes by knowing and acting on the truth. When Jesus stood before Pilate to be sentenced to the cross, He spoke of His mission in these words: " 'I was born for this, and I have come into the world for this: to testify to the truth. Everyone

Early Champions of Religious Liberty

In colonial America religious liberty was not guaranteed. State churches were the norm, and Baptists were expected to pay taxes to support them. Those who resisted lost their property, which was sold for tax costs. The following men are examples of Baptist leaders who fought for guarantees of religious freedom in this country.

- John Clarke—Immigrating from England, Clarke was a Baptist or became one soon after arriving in America. He established First Baptist Church of Newport, Rhode Island, in 1638.
- Roger Williams—Banished from the colony of Massachusetts for his view on the separation of church and state, Williams founded Rhode Island Colony in 1636, where religious liberty was guaranteed. He became a Baptist in 1639 and helped establish First Baptist Church of Providence.
- Isaac Backus—After helping form a Baptist church in Middleborough, Massachusetts, in 1756, Backus actively opposed the taxation of Baptists for state churches. In 1774 he argued for religious freedom before the Continental Congress.
- John Leland—A Baptist preacher in Orange, Virginia, Leland articulated principles of religious freedom and became its leading advocate. He was instrumental in ensuring the provisions for religious freedom in the federal Constitution and the Bill of Rights.

who is of the truth listens to My voice' " (John 18:37). Ultimate truth about God's plan for humankind is found in Jesus' words, and these words will lead every believer to true liberty.

Jesus also addressed the individual's obligation to civil government. On one occasion the Pharisees asked His opinion on paying taxes to the Roman government. Jesus replied by asking them to show Him a Roman coin. Pointing to Caesar's image on the coin, He said, " 'Give back to Caesar the things that are Caesar's, and to God the things that are God's' " (Matt. 22:21). Jesus thus affirmed the rightful claim of government on its citizens.

The most extensive discussion of the relationship between God and government is found in Paul's words in Romans 13:1-7. Three times in these verses Paul stated that civil government is God's servant (see vv. 4,6). He further stated that civil authority comes from God and should be accepted by Christians (see vv. 1-2). Paul concluded with this command: "Pay your obligations to everyone: taxes to those you owe taxes, tolls to those you owe tolls, respect to those you owe respect, and honor to those you owe honor" (v. 7). *The Baptist Faith and Message* affirms these biblical teachings: "Civil government being ordained of God, it is the duty of Christians to render loyal obedience thereto in all things not contrary to the revealed will of God."[9]

"Submit to every human institution because of the Lord, whether to the Emperor as the supreme authority, or to governors as those sent out by him to punish those who do evil and to praise those who do good" (1 Pet. 2:13-14).

Are Christians ever justified in refusing to conform to civil laws? Consider the example of Peter, whose words in the margin instruct believers to submit to civil authority. However, prior to this letter, Peter and the other apostles had been arrested in Jerusalem for preaching about Jesus. Their response to the authorities was " 'We must obey God rather than men' " (Acts 5:29). Christians are obligated to give first allegiance to Jesus Christ. If government regulations are contrary to God's commands—and this has been the case many times throughout history—Christians should obey God rather than human authorities. *The Baptist Faith and Message* summarizes, "God alone is Lord of the conscience, and He has left it free from the doctrines and commandments of men which are contrary to His Word or not contained in it."[10]

The Separation of Church and State

The Scriptures we just examined form the basis for the strong Baptist stance that insists on the separation of church and state. Civil government and the church of Jesus Christ should recognize God's hand in establishing both, but both should also insist that the two entities remain free from each other's control. *The Baptist Faith and Message* asserts, "Church and state should be separate. ... A free church in a free state is the Christian ideal."[11]

From the beginning of church history, as we read in the Book of Acts, civil authorities have attempted to interfere with religious freedom. History records the staunch determination of Christians, especially Baptists, to resist external control. On the other hand, as the church grew in power and influence, church leaders occasionally sought to control the state. Again, Baptists disagreed with this position and denounced the corruption that went with it. An insistence on the complete separation of religious and civil authority is our Baptist heritage.

The separation of church and state has important implications. As *The Baptist Faith and Message* explains, "The state owes to every church protection and full freedom in the pursuit of its spiritual ends. In providing for such freedom no ecclesiastical group or denomination should be favored by the state more than others. ... The church should not resort to the civil power to carry on its work. ... The state has no right to impose taxes for the support of any form of religion."[12] The concept of separation of church and state guarantees that neither one shall attempt to exercise control over the other. Nor can the state favor one religious group over another, taxing citizens for its support. According to Romans 13:1-7, God established government to provide safety and protection from evildoers for all persons, religious and nonreligious. Civil authorities must relate to people of every religious persuasion by upholding their right to assemble and worship according to their own conscience and beliefs.

Separation of church and state does not mean that believers cannot share their faith in the public arena. The government must ensure "the right of free and unhindered access to God on the part of all men, and the right to form and propagate opinions in the sphere of religion without interference by the civil power."[13]

Furthermore, separation should not be interpreted so to prevent Christians from influencing law and government. Jesus called believers to be salt and light (see Matt. 5:13-16)—to be a strong, positive influence on the culture. Many Christians have found a place of ministry by becoming involved in the political arena, feeling that God has called them to improve social and moral conditions through better laws and law enforcement. Although Christians know that the only sure way to change personal morality is through spiritual regeneration, a Christian influence benefits government and society as a whole.

Many times Christians have affected the safety and well-being of all citizens by advocating biblical principles in social, economic, and government policies. One significant example occurred when Southern Baptists introduced True Love Waits, a Bible-based emphasis on sexual abstinence prior to marriage, in Uganda in the early 1990s. Since then "the number of AIDS cases has decreased more than 30 percent."[14]

"First of all, then, I urge that petitions, prayers, intercessions, and thanksgivings be made for everyone, for kings and all those who are in authority, so that we may lead a tranquil and quiet life in all godliness and dignity" (1 Tim. 2:1-2).

In America evangelical Christians encouraged Congress to pass the Equal Access Act in 1984. This legislation recognizes the rights of high-school-student groups to use public-school buildings as meeting places for student-led organizations, including Bible-study clubs. Christians can and must make a difference as moral, productive, involved citizens.

The Apostle Paul advocated the most effective way for believers to influence civil government. Read his words in the margin. Every Christian can participate through prayer in the spiritual warfare between the kingdom of God and the spiritual forces of evil. This intercession will make a positive impact for all humankind.

Although we live in a world that is increasingly hostile to God, the church is here to be His witness. We must devote ourselves to make a positive impact for the kingdom of God.

Religious Freedom Under Attack

The First Amendment of the Constitution, the guarantor of religious liberty in this country, is now being misinterpreted to deny religious persons their rights and to exclude religion and values from public expression. Organizations like the American Civil Liberties Union are insisting on a strict interpretation of the First Amendment, which undermines religious liberty in the following ways.

1. *Excluding religiously grounded moral positions from the formation of law.* Prohibiting moral positions from influencing our nation's laws allows secular philosophies free reign over our legal system. As a result, we are witnessing the rejection of a societal moral code in favor of an individual's determination of right and wrong. This path has already led to devastating court decisions in the areas of abortion and homosexual rights.

2. *Denying religious persons the equal right of expression.* This position upholds the erroneous assumption that the public arena, especially public education, must be secular. Consequently, students and adults have routinely been prohibited from the free expression of their Christian faith in the classroom and on the job.

Our nation's founders intended the First Amendment to protect the free expression of religious faith, not to discriminate against people of faith or to shield public life from religion.[15]

In light of your study, rewrite your description of the church's purpose on page 50.

_____

_____

---

[1] Henry T. Blackaby and Melvin D. Blackaby, *Your Church Experiencing God Together* (Nashville: LifeWay Press, 2003), 17–19.

[2] *The Baptist Faith and Message* (Nashville: LifeWay Christian Resources of the Southern Baptist Convention, 2000), 13.

[3] Ibid.

[4] Herschel H. Hobbs, *Fundamentals of Our Faith* (Nashville: Broadman Press, 1960), 114.

[5] Bill Gordon, "The Roman Catholic Church," in Tal Davis et al., *FAITH Discipleship: Faith Reaching Out to World Religions* (Nashville: LifeWay Press, 2001), 213–14.

[6] Josiah Conder, "Bread of Heav'n, on Thee We Feed," in *The Modern Hymnal,* ed. Robert H. Coleman (Nashville: Broadman Press, 1926), 45.

[7] *The Baptist Faith and Message,* 14.

[8] Robert G. Torbet, *A History of the Baptists,* 3rd edition (Valley Forge: Judson Press, 1963), 519.

[9] *The Baptist Faith and Message,* 20.

[10] Ibid.

[11] Ibid.

[12] Ibid.

[13] Ibid., 20–21.

[14] James T. Draper Jr., "A Century of Business and Ministry," *The Tennessean,* 15 June 2003, sec. E, 2.

[15] Perry L. Glanzer, "Religious Liberty," *CitizenLink* [online], 23 April 1998 [cited 30 June 2003]. Available from the Internet: *www.family.org.*

CHAPTER 4

What Is Our Purpose in Life?

What is your purpose in life?

☐ Make all the money I can and live comfortably.

☐ Grow in my service to God and help others grow in their faith.

☐ Impress everyone with my possessions and position.

☐ Raise children who don't get into trouble.

☐ Survive.

One of the truly remarkable truths of God's Word is that God has a special plan for every person. The psalmist described this phenomenal fact in these words:

> Your eyes saw me when I was formless;
> all my days were written in Your book and planned
> before a single one of them began (Ps. 139:16).

What an amazing revelation! Before we were born, God recorded all the days of our lives as if they had already happened. The Apostle Paul wrote, "We know that all things work together for the good of those who love God: those who are called according to His purpose" (Rom. 8:28). God created us and redeemed each of us for a unique purpose. Discovering this truth gives significance to our lives; discovering this purpose makes life an exciting adventure!

Read Romans 8:28. How does this verse relate to your purpose in life? _____

_____

_____

I was 12 years old when I first learned that God had a special purpose for me. I sensed that He was calling me to His service. Although I knew that God wanted me to be a minister, I did not know whether I should serve Him as a missionary, an evangelist, a pastor, a musician, or a teacher. Yet I urgently wanted to know what God had in mind for me.

Gradually, I realized that knowing all of the details of God's plan for my life was not necessary. His will was for me to learn to obey Him one step at a time. My part was to surrender to God's purpose for my life. His part was to reveal His will and purpose for me as He chose. He was always faithful to reveal His purpose as my life unfolded.

When I publicly surrendered to ministry at the age of 14 in a small east-Texas town, I had no idea where God would lead. Later I discovered that God had gifted me to preach His Word. As a high-school senior, I began preaching in revivals in and around Houston. I would never have dreamed the future God planned for me. My first pastorate was a small country church. Next He moved me to a town of approximately 350 people, then to a city of 50,000, and finally to a metropolitan area. After many years of serving God as a pastor, He called me to serve Him and the churches of our denomination as the president of LifeWay Christian Resources. What has happened in these many years of service can be traced to the time when I acknowledged Christ's lordship over my life and surrendered myself to obey Him step by step.

God has a purpose for each of us—a mission for us to fulfill in life. Whether a person serves the Lord in church leadership or through another occupation, the greatest sense of joy and fulfillment comes by surrendering to and living that purpose.

God's Word provides clear guidelines for understanding and discovering God's purpose.

What Do We Believe About God's Purpose for Our Lives?

God's purpose for our lives is His gift to us through a personal relationship with Jesus Christ. The abundant life Jesus brings to us satisfies all of our needs. Only He provides us a worthwhile purpose for living—something that calls for our best effort, a worthy and challenging reason for getting out of bed each morning, a conviction that says, "I was made for this purpose."

The Great Commission clearly states the life purpose Jesus intends for each of His followers (see Matt. 28:19-20). Of the four verbs in this passage—*go, make disciples, baptize,* and *teach*—only *make disciples* is in the imperative mood. The other three are participles. Therefore, making

Frameworks of God's Plan

You can gain perspective by viewing your purpose in life against the backdrop of God's grand purposes for all humankind. Before God made the universe, His plan was to create a people who would enjoy His glorious presence throughout eternity. He is accomplishing this through three broad works:
1. Creation (see Gen. 1)
2. Redemption (see Rom. 3–8)
3. Bringing His children to glory (see Heb. 2:10)
All of God's other actions in the Bible and in our lives today fit into His greater plan as defined by these three frameworks.[1]

disciples is the primary goal that Jesus established. All disciples are called to be disciple makers. As individual Christians and as churches, this is our priority task. Let's seek to understand the full nature of the call to make disciples. What does disciple making include? As we examine each component of God's purpose, ask yourself, *Am I giving priority to the things Jesus said should come first in my life?*

"Go, therefore, and make disciples of all nations, baptizing them in the name of the Father and of the Son and of the Holy Spirit, teaching them to observe everything I have commanded you. And remember, I am with you always, to the end of the age" (Matt. 28:19-20).

Rank the following priorities in your life by numbering them 1–6.
___ Earning a living
___ Rearing children
___ Making disciples
___ Accumulating possessions
___ Achieving social recognition
___ Maintaining a healthy lifestyle

Read Matthew 28:19-20 and check your responses against Jesus' instructions.

"If anyone is in Christ, there is a new creation; old things have passed away, and look, new things have come. Now everything is from God, who reconciled us to Himself through Christ and gave us the ministry of reconciliation: that is, in Christ, God was reconciling the world to Himself, not counting their trespasses against them, and He has committed the message of reconciliation to us. Therefore, we are ambassadors for Christ; certain that God is appealing through us, we plead on Christ's behalf, 'Be reconciled to God' " (2 Cor. 5:17-20).

Our Purpose Includes Personal Evangelism

The process of making a person into a disciple of Jesus begins when an unsaved person repents of unbelief and, by faith, receives Jesus Christ as Savior and Lord. This new birth marks the person's initiation into a life of discipleship. Apart from such a conversion experience a person remains spiritually dead because of sin. A person must decide to turn to Jesus, the life giver, before discipleship can begin.

No one can make this life-changing decision apart from hearing the gospel. The term *gospel* means *good news,* the good news that " 'God loved the world in this way: He gave His One and Only Son, so that everyone who believes in Him will not perish but have eternal life' " (John 3:16). The word *evangelism,* which comes from the same root as *gospel,* means *sharing the message of good news.*

Every person who hears and believes the good news is responsible to pass it on to those who haven't heard it. God calls all Christians to be evangelists in the sense of sharing with others the message of life in Christ. Read in the margin this call to evangelism as expressed by Paul. This passage teaches that every follower of Jesus is His ambassador—His personal representative. Christ sends us with the message of reconciliation. In the Bible we find more than 30 references to the will of God, and all involve the salvation of the lost or the witness of the believer. God's will is for the lost to be saved and for every believer to play a role in evangelism. The most joyful, radiant Christians are those who consistently seek to pass on to others the new life that has been passed on to them.

How can you carry out your purpose of sharing God's good news?

1. *Share your testimony of how you became a believer in Christ.* Write a brief account of this experience and practice telling your salvation story to others. Perhaps your family members and other Christians would listen as you practice.

2. *Learn a simple method of presenting Bible verses that show someone how to become a Christian.* Perhaps your church offers training in how to share the plan of salvation. Several resources are also available that can help. [2]

3. *Pray for the ministry of evangelism.* Begin by asking God to lead you to those who need to hear your testimony and the gospel presentation. Ask Him to make you sensitive to the opportunities He brings your way. Compile a prayer list of unsaved persons you know. Pray for evangelistic events. Join a team of prayer warriors who claim the salvation of the lost. And don't forget to thank God as He brings the unsaved to Himself.

4. *Look for opportunities to spread the gospel.* For example, I know an elderly woman who is not articulate in sharing the gospel, but she continually invites friends, neighbors, and strangers to her church, where they hear the gospel from her pastor. She prays for these prospects, and many of them have become Christians. Others participate in evangelism by going on short-term mission trips, handing out gospel tracts, providing funds for evangelistic endeavors, praying daily for unsaved persons and missionaries, and encouraging their church to reach the unsaved. Most Christians will admit that maintaining a priority on evangelism is one of the most difficult aspects of discipleship. Satan works diligently to distract us from being consistent in our concern for the lost. One Christian has a small note taped to his bathroom mirror that says, "Do something today to help another person know Jesus."

Our Purpose in Life
Personal
  evangelism
Church
  involvement
Spiritual
  growth
Global
  missions

List the four ways you can carry out your purpose of sharing God's good news.
1. Share my _____.
2. Learn a simple way to present _____ _____ that tell how to be saved.
3. Pray for the ministry of _____.
4. Look for opportunities to spread the _____.

Circle the way that is most difficult for you. Spend time praying that God will help you overcome any obstacles so that you can be a more effective witness for Him.

After finding Zacchaeus and leading him to salvation, Jesus described His own mission in these noteworthy words: " 'The Son of Man has come to seek and to save the lost' " (Luke 19:10). When we follow Jesus, we must be involved with Him in the most important mission in life—searching for and rescuing the lost.

Our Purpose Includes Church Involvement

God's plan is for babies to be born into families. Newborns need parental care as they begin to grow toward maturity. Likewise, spiritual infants need relationships that encourage their

"They devoted themselves to the apostles' teaching, to fellowship, to the breaking of bread, and to prayers. ... All the believers were together and had everything in common. So they sold their possessions and property and distributed the proceeds to all, as anyone had a need. And every day they devoted themselves to meeting together in the temple complex, and broke bread from house to house. They ate their food with gladness and simplicity of heart, praising God and having favor with all the people. And every day the Lord added those being saved to them" (Acts 2:42-47).

development. Jesus spoke of this need in the Great Commission with the phrase " 'baptizing them in the name of the Father and of the Son and of the Holy Spirit' " (Matt. 28:19). In the New Testament, as people believed in Christ and were baptized, they became members of a local fellowship called a church. Following this pattern, new Christians today are baptized and enter a fellowship of love, where they find support for growing in and learning about their new life in Christ, especially during the initial weeks and months. Read in the margin a biblical picture of a church that nurtured members of the body.

Established by Jesus Christ, the church is essential to God's plan for all humankind. Authentic Christianity is Christ-centered and church-centered. Paul spoke of the church as "the body of Christ" (1 Cor. 12:27). Fellowship with other believers meets a vital need for the proper development of disciples. God never intended for believers to live in isolation from other believers. All of His children need a family of faith.

You learned in chapter 3 that the church exists for evangelism, discipleship, fellowship, ministry, and worship. To fulfill its mission, the church needs your support and involvement. All believers are called to actively participate in church life to strengthen its ministry to the community, its worship of the one true God, and its witness to the world.

What about your relationship to a local church? Do you regularly participate with other believers in a fellowship of mutual support and service to Christ?　☐ Yes　☐ No　Name a first step you can take to improve your church involvement.

Our Purpose Includes Spiritual Growth

One aspect of the Great Commission focuses on the instruction of believers, which is expressed in Jesus' phrase " 'teaching them to observe everything I have commanded you' " (Matt. 28:20). The Greek word translated *teaching* means *instructing*. The new birth is the beginning of an entirely new and different life. Jesus commissioned His disciples to give complete instruction about everything He had first commanded them. Notice His emphasis on teaching believers to observe all of His commands. *To observe* means *to obey, to put into practice.* Believers must be taught to obey Jesus' commands, not merely to know them. Consistent obedience is the proof of effective teaching.

In the New Testament Jesus was often called a teacher. For example, Nicodemus, who was himself a teacher, referred to Jesus as a teacher who had come from God (see John 3:2). Jesus publicly and privately taught those who were with Him. His final commission before leaving His disciples, according to Matthew, included the command to teach all nations. Thus, one

Making Disciples

Part of your growth as a disciple is helping others grow spiritually. Think of your discipleship in terms of the following stages of development.

1. *Spiritual child.* When you turn from your sin and ask Christ into your life, you are born again as God's spiritual child. You must be established in your faith and in relationship to God and other believers.

2. *Spiritual disciple.* At this stage you grow in Christ by spending time with Him, living in His Word, praying in faith, fellowshipping with believers, witnessing to the world, and ministering to others.

3. *Disciple maker.* Jesus expects His disciples to bear fruit (see John 15:1-4). A disciple maker bears the fruit of other disciples. You do this by equipping them to understand, adopt, and obey biblical teachings, just as you learned to do.

4. *Co-laborer in ministry.* At this stage you are ready to go out and make disciples through intentional ministry. You are a colaborer with Christ in multiplying disciples.[3]

of our purposes in life is to teach believers a curriculum that includes everything Jesus taught. The outcome of such an education goes beyond the acquirement of information. The intended goal is spiritual transformation—a transformation that begins with a new birth and results in a new creation in Christ (see 2 Cor. 5:17).

The measure of spiritual transformation is the degree to which a person becomes like Jesus. The ultimate teacher in this process is the Holy Spirit. Jesus promised His disciples, " 'The Counselor, the Holy Spirit, whom the Father will send in My name, will teach you all things and remind you of everything I have told you' " (John 14:26). This Teacher uses all of life's experiences, as well as the intentional instruction of the church, to produce the spiritual transformation of Christlikeness in each Christian.

The measure of spiritual transformation is—

☐ how good you feel after worship;

☐ the degree to which you are becoming like Jesus;

☐ how you compare to other Christians;

☐ the number of leadership positions you hold in the church.

Do you think of yourself as a student of Christ who seeks to grow in Christlikeness? If so, you must give prominence to the textbook, the Bible, and you must constantly remain available for the Holy Spirit's instruction. Do you regularly participate in Bible study, on your own and in a group at church? Do you take advantage of the discipleship training provided by your church? Do you seize opportunities to pass on to others what you have learned? Paul admonished young Timothy, "Be diligent to present yourself approved to God, a worker who doesn't need to be ashamed, correctly teaching the word of truth" (2 Tim. 2:15).

Our Purpose Includes Global Missions

A disciple of Jesus Christ is a person on mission—someone He sends to minister to others. The terms *send* and *sent* are found more than 60 times in the Gospel of John. Most of these refer to Jesus being sent by His Father or Jesus sending His disciples to perform various tasks. For example, on the first Easter evening Jesus appeared to His followers and said, " 'Just as the Father has sent Me, I also send you' " (John 20:21). What was true for those first believers has been just as true for every believer since then. Jesus sends all who are saved to reach those who are not saved. Every person in this world is either a missionary for Christ or needs a missionary from Christ.

The Baptist Faith and Message states: "It is the duty and privilege of every follower of Christ and of every church of the Lord Jesus Christ to endeavor to make disciples of all nations. The new birth of man's spirit by God's Holy Spirit means the birth of love for others. Missionary effort on the part of all rests thus upon a spiritual necessity of the regenerate life, and is expressly and repeatedly commanded in the teachings of Christ. The Lord Jesus Christ has commanded the preaching of the gospel to all nations."[4] The extensive nature of the Great Commission is found in Jesus' words: " 'Go, therefore, and make disciples of all nations' " (Matt. 28:19). "All nations" literally includes everyone everywhere in every generation.

Although Southern Baptists support organizations that perform a significant missionary service (see box below), the responsibility for missionary advance rests on every believer and every church. Outreach to the unsaved should begin locally and extend globally. Each

On Mission with God

Southern Baptists have a long and distinguished history of missions effort. When the Southern Baptist Convention was organized in 1845, two missions agencies were formed to appoint and support missionaries worldwide. Their names today are the International Mission Board, responsible for overseas outreach, and the North American Mission Board, which has responsibility for the United States, its territories, and Canada.

The first overseas mission field was China, followed by Africa, Italy, Mexico, Brazil, and Japan.[5] Today more than 5,000 missionaries serve 153 countries. More than 15,000 overseas missionaries have been appointed since 1845, with ⅓ of these serving today. The International Mission Board's mission statement explains, "The mission of the International Mission Board, SBC, is to lead Southern Baptists in international missions efforts to evangelize the lost, disciple believers, develop churches and minister to people in need."[6]

The North American Mission Board "exists to proclaim the gospel of Jesus Christ, start New Testament congregations, minister to persons in the name of Christ, and assist churches in the United States and Canada in effectively performing these functions." This agency also communicates the gospel through radio and television, coordinates ministry to disaster victims, and serves the spiritual needs of military personnel through about 2,500 chaplains.[7]

of us should think of ourselves as missionaries whom Jesus sends to share His gospel with others. Missionary involvement is not optional but mandatory for a follower of Jesus. Believers cannot be true to their faith if they do not share it. Likewise, an authentic church evangelizes and participates in missions. Any concept of Christianity is inadequate if it allows believers to be comfortable with what has been received and not have a passion for sharing with others.

You are responsible for helping spread the gospel to all nations. Identify ways you are obeying God's expectation.

_____

The challenge of evangelizing the world is compelling. America has about 9 percent of the world's population but about 90 percent of the world's preaching. Only 3 percent of the giving of our churches is for overseas missionary work. The remainder is consumed by the churches. I can imagine our Lord looking over hundreds of cities that have populations of over one million but no gospel witness. He loves these people and longs for someone to tell them the good news. Jesus sends us to be missionaries first to our families, neighborhoods, schools, social relationships, and workplaces. Wherever we interact with others, Jesus sends us to be His ambassadors. But He also expects us to have significant involvement through our churches in extending the kingdom worldwide. When this becomes our way of thinking, each day can be an exciting adventure of being on mission with Christ.

Do you feel inadequate when you think about being on mission? The truth is, we are all inadequate! Jesus addressed our weakness in John 15:4-5.

Read John 15:4-5. Rewrite these verses as if Jesus is speaking directly to you about your attitude toward evangelism.

_____

_____

_____

_____

"Remain in Me, and I in you. Just as a branch is unable to produce fruit by itself unless it remains on the vine, so neither can you unless you remain in Me. I am the vine; you are the branches. The one who remains in Me and I in him produces much fruit, because you can do nothing without Me" (John 15:4-5).

A feeling of inadequacy is actually an essential qualification for being on mission with Christ. Success in missionary service results from a constant sense of depending on Christ—abiding in Him as a branch abides in the vine. Jesus' final words before His ascension, according to Acts 1:8, identify the resource of power He supplies for fulfilling the Great Commission: " 'You will receive power when the Holy Spirit has come upon you, and you will be My witnesses in Jerusalem, in all Judea and Samaria, and to the ends of the earth.'" The remainder of Acts records the amazing account of how the Holy Spirit mightily used these first believers, who seemed so incompetent, to extend the kingdom of God throughout the world of that era. That same resource of spiritual power is available to us today. We can all say with Paul, "I am able to do all things through Him who strengthens me" (Phil. 4:13).

Spreading Christianity is illegal in many countries. Should Christian missionaries be sent into those countries? ☐ Yes ☐ No **Why or why not?**

_____

_____

The Bible clearly states God's general purpose for all believers—to make disciples of all nations through personal evangelism, church involvement, spiritual growth, and global missions. Have you ever wondered why God doesn't take us to heaven as soon as we are saved? The answer is clear: God wants us to be witnesses of His salvation to others. Just as He used someone to show us the way to eternal life, He calls us to pass on the good news to others, to multiply disciples, and to extend God's kingdom everywhere.

Rate your effectiveness in carrying out each purpose. Let 1 = poor and 3 = excellent.

Personal evangelism	1 2 3
Church involvement	1 2 3
Spiritual growth	1 2 3
Global missions	1 2 3

What Do We Believe About God's Calling?

We have discussed how God calls all Christians to fulfill the Great Commission. God also calls every believer to serve Him through a vocation. The word _vocation_ comes from the Latin root _vocare,_ meaning _to call._ How can we discover God's calling to a particular vocation?

Following the Good Shepherd

"The LORD is my shepherd; there is nothing I lack. ... He leads me along the right paths for His name's sake" (Ps. 23:1-3).

God's Word promises that God is faithful to answer our prayers and to guide us to know and do His will. God wants to help all who call on Him. When we wonder what God wants us to do, we can remember that our Lord speaks of Himself as "the good shepherd" (John 10:11). A shepherd's primary responsibility is providing for the needs of his sheep; a good shepherd gives all the guidance the sheep need (see Ps. 23:1-3).

Hearing God's Voice

"You and I cannot understand the truth of God unless the Holy Spirit of God reveals it. He is the Teacher. When He teaches you the Word of God, sit before Him and respond to Him. As you pray, watch to see how He uses the Word of God to confirm in your heart a word from God. Watch what He is doing around you in circumstances. The God who is speaking to you as you pray and the God who is speaking to you in the Scriptures is the God who is working around you. ...

"God speaks by the Holy Spirit through the Bible, prayer, circumstances, and the church to reveal Himself, His purposes, and His ways. ... The key to knowing God's voice is not a formula. It is not a method you can follow. Knowing God's voice comes from an intimate love relationship with God. ... The *relationship* is the key to knowing God's voice, to hearing when God speaks."[8]

How does the Good Shepherd guide us? The prophet Isaiah declared of the Lord,

> He will be very gracious to you at the sound of your cry;
> When He hears it, He will answer you. ...
> Your ears shall hear a word behind you, saying,
> "This is the way, walk in it" (Isa. 30:19-21, NKJV).

One of my favorite passages in Proverbs reassures us of God's guidance:

> Trust in the Lord with all your heart,
> and do not rely on your own understanding;
> think about Him in all your ways,
> and He will guide you on the right paths (Prov. 3:5-6).

To what extent is your vocation integrated with God's purpose for your life?
☐ My vocation and my purpose in life are somewhat connected.
☐ My vocation is how I discovered my purpose in life.
☐ My purpose in life determines my vocation.
☐ My spiritual life is what happens on Sunday; it has no bearing on my vocation.

The Lord knows the vocation He created you to follow; He promises to guide you in knowing His will. But you must ask Him, believing His promise to hear and answer. As soon as you ask God to guide you in knowing His will, thank Him for hearing and answering. Giving thanks before you receive an answer affirms your faith. And before the answer is made clear, commit yourself to follow God's leading—no matter what or where that may be.

Discovering Your Gifts

Your spiritual gifts often indicate God's will for your calling in life. As you learned in chapter 3, a spiritual gift is a God-given ability to serve Christ through His church. Paul wrote about spiritual gifts and their purpose in his letter to the Romans. Using the human body as an example of the way a church functions through its many members, Paul wrote, "As we have many parts in one body, and all the parts do not have the same function, in the same way we who are many are one body in Christ and individually members of one another. According to the grace given to us, we have different gifts" (Rom. 12:4-6).

Paul then identified seven types of essential ministry, each the result of a special spiritual gift. These are prophecy, service, teaching, exhorting, giving, leading, and showing mercy (see Rom. 12:6-8). Although Paul mentioned other gifts in 1 Corinthians, many Bible interpreters consider these seven gifts to be a comprehensive expression of all gifts for ministry. Here is a brief description of each gift.

- Prophecy is the ability to proclaim God's truth. Before the completion of the Bible, this gift enabled a speaker to give direct revelation of God's message for a specific situation. Today this gift is expressed through inspired preaching based on scriptural truths.
- Service is the ability to render practical service to others in the body of Christ. This is also referred to as the gift of helping (see 1 Cor. 12:28) and is probably the gift most often exercised by believers.
- Teaching is the ability to accurately interpret, apply, and communicate biblical truth.
- Exhortation is the ability to give wise counsel to others, including rebuke, encouragement, and affirmation.
- Giving is the ability to earn and give money for the advancement of the kingdom.
- Leading is the ability to guide others in accomplishing the mission of the church.
- Showing mercy is the ability to express compassion toward persons who are suffering for any reason.

Check the gift you believe to be your primary spiritual gift.

☐ Prophecy   ☐ Service   ☐ Teaching   ☐ Exhortation
☐ Giving   ☐ Leading   ☐ Showing mercy

Describe how you express your gift in your daily life. _____

All Christians should express certain gifts, such as showing mercy and giving. However, God has gifted some in His church with a special sense of burden and joy in exercising these particular abilities. Therefore, these persons are more highly motivated than others, and they are usually more effective in serving in these ways.

No matter what your gift is, these New Testament principles should govern its expression:
1. *Every Christian has been given at least one spiritual gift.* Although you may not know what your gift is, you can be certain that God has gifted you.

Equipped to Serve

The acrostic SERVE represents five ways God has prepared you for His service.
Spiritual gifts that God has given you for His service
Experiences that God has brought into your life
Relational style—behavioral traits that you possess
Vocational skills that you have gained through training and experience
Enthusiasm—the passion God has given you for a particular ministry[9]

2. *God determines by His own sovereign will what each Christian's gift is.* No one can choose a preferred gift; God makes this decision.
3. *God bestows all spiritual gifts to be used in building up the body of Christ.* Your gift is not intended to bring you honor or recognition but to make the church more effective.
4. *Each Christian is responsible for discovering and using his or her gift, guided by the Holy Spirit.*
5. *Love must be the controlling motive in using spiritual gifts.* First Corinthians 13, the love chapter, should be interpreted in the context of Paul's discussion of spiritual gifts. Believers are to use their gifts because of love for God and others.[10]

If you seek the Holy Spirit's guidance in discovering and using your gifts, you will be well on your way to becoming involved in the work to which God has called you.

What Do We Believe About Serving God?

You cannot discover your gift or gifts without actually getting involved in ministry. Just as a person cannot learn to swim by reading books on swimming, a Christian must take the plunge and allow God to clarify His call. If you need help finding a suitable avenue for ministry, ask your pastor or a Christian friend to suggest possible opportunities. Discovering and using your spiritual gift will open a new adventure with many gratifying rewards, and you will enable your church to better fulfill its mission.

John had been a Christian for many years but had never been personally involved in ministry. His church began a ministry to homeless men called Room in the Inn. On Monday nights during the winter the church van brought 12 men from downtown to the church building. They were given a warm meal, clean clothes, and a place to sleep, followed by breakfast and the gift of a sack lunch before being returned to the rescue mission.

When John was asked to help with this weekly outreach, he was somewhat reluctant because he had never done anything like it before. However, he soon found himself becoming more and more enthusiastic about this means of serving persons in need. Today John not only leads this ministry of compassion but also trains volunteers from other churches. Best of all, several men have been saved and are being discipled. John discovered that God had given him the spiritual gift of mercy. Now he is an effective, enthusiastic minister of Christ. John knows that God has a purpose for his life, and he is finding true joy as he seeks to fulfill that purpose.

The same discovery and reward can be yours. Christian ministry is not just for a few chosen people or the paid church staff. Rather, it is expected of every believer. Claim God's guidance in finding your place in ministry and make yourself available to Him. The Holy Spirit not only imparts spiritual gifts to you but also dwells in you to supply all the wisdom and power you need to fulfill God's wonderful purpose for your life. As the Apostle Paul declared, "My God will supply all your needs according to His riches in glory in Christ Jesus" (Phil. 4:19).

Two significant ways you can serve God are through education and stewardship.

Fulfilling God's Purpose Through Education

Education is the process of developing a person's knowledge, skill, mind, and character through teaching and training. This process begins at birth and continues throughout life. Education is vitally important because God created us with the need and capacity for learning.

Unfortunately, this ability to learn has been severely corrupted by sin. Many educators today base their efforts on the false premise that better education is the ultimate remedy for most human problems. However, well-educated persons are sometimes the most evil, greedy, lustful, dissatisfied, and unhappy. Therefore, the primary human need is not for education but for spiritual transformation. Education holds the greatest value for those who have been spiritually reborn, because only then is a person's capacity for learning restored.

The primary human need is for—

☐ education;   ☐ popularity;   ☐ spiritual transformation;
☐ self-esteem;   ☐ security.

Spiritual transformation. Spiritual transformation is not the result of learning the error of our ways and turning over a new leaf. Spiritual transformation begins with the miracle of a new birth—a miracle that only God can perform. Until this occurs, a person is separated from God, spiritually dead, and incapable of reaching full potential in any field of endeavor. The Bible identifies Jesus Christ as the ultimate source of wisdom and knowledge: "In Him [Christ] all the treasures of wisdom and knowledge are hidden. For in Him the entire fullness of God's nature dwells bodily" (Col. 2:3,9). *The Baptist Faith and Message* affirms this truth: "Christianity is the faith of enlightenment and intelligence. In Jesus Christ abide all the treasures of wisdom and knowledge. All sound learning is, therefore, a part of our Christian heritage. The new birth opens all human faculties and creates a thirst for knowledge."[11]

All educators agree that the primary center for learning is the mind. Read in the margin on page 85 the statements about the condition of an unsaved person's mind. These Scriptures testify to humankind's mental depravity in the sense that sin affects our ability to think clearly, reason logically, and understand truth.

The good news of the gospel of Christ is that a person's mind can be renewed—made completely new, resulting in a new way of thinking. Paul described this miracle: "You took off your former way of life, the old man that is corrupted by deceitful desires; you are being renewed in the spirit of your minds; you put on the new man, the one created according to God's likeness in righteousness and purity of the truth" (Eph. 4:22-24). The writer of Hebrews explained how this change occurs as he recounted the promise of God's new covenant, first revealed to Jeremiah:

> This is the covenant that I will make with them
> after those days, says the Lord:
> I will put My laws on their hearts,
> and I will write them on their minds (Heb. 10:16).

"The god of this age has blinded the minds of the unbelievers so they cannot see the light of the gospel of the glory of Christ" (2 Cor. 4:4).

"… men whose minds are depraved and deprived of the truth"(1 Tim. 6:5).

"… men who are corrupt in mind, worthless in regard to the faith" (2 Tim. 3:8).

Paul showed the relationship between the key words *transformed* and *renewing* in this statement: "Do not be conformed to this age, but be transformed by the renewing of your mind, so that you may discern what is the good, pleasing, and perfect will of God" (Rom. 12:2). A believer in Christ has the potential of being totally transformed spiritually, and this transformation happens by the renewing of the mind. Renewing occurs as God writes His laws on the hearts and minds of all who turn from unbelief and receive Jesus by faith. Spiritual transformation is the process, beginning with a new birth, by which a believer progressively becomes like Jesus Christ.

"To the pure, everything is pure, but to those who are defiled and unbelieving nothing is pure; in fact, both their mind and conscience are defiled" (Titus 1:15).

The role of teaching. The Bible affirms the importance of teaching in the process of spiritual transformation. The first biblical reference to the essential role of teaching is found in Exodus, when God said to Moses, " 'Now go! I will help you speak and I will teach you what to say … and will teach you both what to do' " (Ex. 4:12-15). The ultimate and original teacher is God Himself. Jesus affirmed His divine role as a teacher: " 'Take My yoke upon you and learn from Me' " (Matt. 11:29). Nicodemus, a teacher of God's law, testified to Jesus' reputation as a teacher when he said, " 'Rabbi, we know that You have come from God as a teacher' " (John 3:2). Jesus promised, " 'The Counselor, the Holy Spirit, whom the Father will send in My name, will teach you all things and remind you of everything I have told you' " (John 14:26). Education was a very significant part of Jesus' ministry.

Jesus and the apostles instructed their followers to teach others. A key element in the Great Commission is the command to teach all nations to observe everything Jesus commanded (see Matt. 28:19). Paul spoke of the teaching role of Christian leaders: "He [Christ] personally gave some to be apostles, some prophets, some evangelists, some pastors and teachers, for the training of the saints in the work of ministry, to build up the body of Christ" (Eph. 4:11-12). The goal of this education is to equip believers to serve the Lord—"to build up the body of Christ." A church's educational ministry is vitally important to the work God calls us to do.

The Church's Educational Ministries

Southern Baptist churches offer several programs that educate members in various aspects of the Christian life.

- Sunday School Ministry is the church's strategy for engaging believers in evangelistic Bible study, foundational discipleship, fellowship, ministry, and worship.
- Discipleship Ministry equips believers through spiritual growth for a vital relationship with God and for ministry to others.
- Music Ministry provides musical training for church members and leads the church to worship through music.
- Baptist Men on Mission and Women on Mission teach missions and guide men and women to become personally involved in missions through ministry, prayer, and giving.

Baptists have a long history of providing organized instruction in biblical truth. The first church in America to provide a Sunday School for religious instruction was Second Baptist Church of Baltimore, Maryland, in 1804. Subsequently, many others followed this pattern. The Southern Baptist Convention formed the Sunday School Board, now LifeWay Christian Resources, in 1891, which began publishing materials to be used as teaching curriculum. Today most churches have organizations for Bible teaching as well as training in discipleship and Christian service. Many churches also use education to bring life change through support groups and family and marriage enrichment.

Evaluate the importance of each of the following to your personal spiritual growth.
Let 1 = not important and 5 = absolutely crucial.

Your Sunday School class	1	2	3	4	5
Discipleship studies	1	2	3	4	5
Music ministry	1	2	3	4	5
Missions organizations	1	2	3	4	5

Circle a category in which you need more involvement.

A biblical worldview. Human life, as seen from God's perspective, is not divided into religious and secular compartments. Christian education relates to life as a whole. The Bible teaches the truth about God, humanity, the world, life and death, the future, marriage and family life, the church, the kingdom of God, sin and evil, salvation, and every subject essential to a full and meaningful life.

From a serious study of Scripture comes a growing awareness of life and the world as seen from God's perspective—the perspective of truth. Some Christian leaders refer to this perspective as a biblical worldview. One writer defines *biblical worldview* as "the sum total of assumptions and beliefs based on the absolute truth of God's Word that shape the thoughts, attitudes, and actions of an individual or culture."[12] All worldviews seek to provide answers to the following five sets of questions.

1. Who or what is God? What is God like?
2. Who am I? Where did I come from?
3. What is truth? How do I know and experience truth?
4. What is right and wrong?
5. What is the purpose of life? Where am I going?[13]

One goal of a believer's education is to discover clear, biblical answers to all of these questions.

> **Worldview:** the set of assumptions and beliefs that guide your thoughts, attitudes, and actions

The believer's textbook. The knowledge of truth is the beginning point of education. However, we need further help to understand truth and the wisdom to apply truth to life situations. God meets our need in each of these areas. The writer of Proverbs expressed the value of wisdom and understanding:

> Happy is a man who finds wisdom
> and who acquires understanding,
> for she is more profitable than silver,
> and her revenue is better than gold.
> She is more precious than jewels;
> nothing you desire compares with her.
> Long life is in her right hand;
> in her left, riches and honor (Prov. 3:13-16).

Job is a biblical character who wrestled with the issues of wisdom and understanding. He concluded,

> "Behold, the fear of the Lord, that is wisdom,
>   And to depart from evil is understanding" (Job 28:28, NKJV).

One special sourcebook teaches us to have an authentic "fear of the Lord" (respect for Him), and that is the Bible. Psalm 119, the longest chapter in the Bible, celebrates the immeasurable value of God's Word. The Holy Spirit uses Scripture to impart both wisdom and understanding about the truth God wants His people to know. Read in the margin the value the psalmist attributed to the Word of God.

The Bible must be the basic text for the education of every believer. Parents should begin this biblical instruction, and Christian schools are well equipped to continue the process. Whether or not the children attend Christian schools, parents are responsible for providing biblical instruction in the home. The church augments this instruction through Bible teaching.

"How I love Your teaching!
It is my meditation all day long.
Your command makes me wiser
   than my enemies,
for it is always with me.
I have more insight
   than all my teachers
because Your decrees
   are my meditation.
I understand more
   than the elders
because I obey Your precepts.
The revelation of Your words
   brings light
and gives understanding
   to the inexperienced"
(Ps. 119:97-100,130).

A Commitment to Educational Excellence

For many years Southern Baptists have provided Christian education at every level. For example, an increasing number of churches provide day care for the preschool children of working parents, nurturing these children from a strong Christian perspective. Christian schools for elementary and secondary instruction are also increasing in number. More than 50 Southern Baptist colleges and universities are in the United States. In addition, the Southern Baptist Convention endorses and supports six theological seminaries. Seminary training through extension is available to students who cannot attend classes on a seminary campus. This advanced training is available at almost 500 centers in the United States and overseas. Individual learning plans are offered through independent study by correspondence, with various courses available on CD-ROM and the Internet.

Our principal teachers. Parents have the primary responsibility for imparting biblical truth to their children. One of the most revered passages in the Old Testament is the Shema (the Hebrew word for *hear*): " 'Listen, Israel: The LORD our God, the LORD is One. Love the LORD your God with all your heart, with all your soul, and with all your strength. These words that I am giving you today are to be in your heart. Repeat them to your children. Talk about them when you sit in your house and when you walk along the road, when you lie down and when you get up' " (Deut. 6:4-7).

The Apostle Paul passed on to Christian fathers this same teaching responsibility: "Fathers, don't stir up anger in your children, but bring them up in the training and instruction of the Lord" (Eph. 6:4). Both fathers and mothers have the God-given role of being their children's most influential teachers, and the home is the children's first school.

The primary responsibility for the spiritual education of children belongs to—

☐ the public or private school system;   ☐ the parents;
☐ the church;   ☐ the government.

Does a time come in a believer's mental and spiritual development when we have learned enough? Is there an end to our need for education? As long as our minds are capable of learning, we need to "grow in the grace and knowledge of our Lord and Savior Jesus Christ" (2 Pet. 3:18). We are healthier and happier when we seek to learn and grow in Christ. Greater learning can also enable us to be increasingly useful as servants of the Lord. Learning is a lifelong privilege for every Christian.

Fulfilling God's Purpose Through Stewardship

Another important way you can serve God is through stewardship. Stewardship relates to everything a Christian is, has, says, and does.

The New Testament uses two Greek words to describe a steward. The first term (see, for example, Gal. 4:2) views the steward as a guardian. This member of the household staff has responsibility for the care, instruction, and guardianship of the children. The second word (see, for example, Luke 16:1), used more frequently, stresses the fact that a steward is a manager who deals primarily with property; the word literally means *to arrange a house*. This person is a responsible trustee of another's possessions. Although the words are sometimes used interchangeably, the first word emphasizes a relationship with people, while the second focuses on responsibility for managing another's estate.

From these two words we can define *steward* as *a servant who is entrusted with the care of persons and possessions belonging to another and is accountable to the owner for this position of trust.* Jesus told several parables about stewardship, each emphasizing the steward's accountability (see Matt. 18:23-35; 25:14-30; Luke 19:11-26). These parables illustrate that a steward is a trusted servant who is responsible to use or manage what belongs to another.

> **Steward:** a servant who is entrusted with the care of persons and possessions belonging to another and is accountable to the owner for this position of trust

Stewardship principles. The Bible reveals the following basic principles of stewardship.

- *God is the owner of all things because He created them.* The psalmist declared,

> The earth and everything in it,
> the world and its inhabitants, belong to the Lord (Ps. 24:1).

We commonly speak as if we were owners: my life, my family, my money, my house, my time. The truth is that we possess, but we do not own. Everything ultimately belongs to God; all we possess comes as a gift from Him. As the Apostle Paul asked, "What do you have that you didn't receive?" (1 Cor. 4:7).

- *God has given us all we possess as an expression of His grace and love.* Every heartbeat, every breath, every moment of life is a love-gift from our Father. God's amazing love causes Him to pour out innumerable gifts on us. Not one of these comes to us because we deserve it. Every gift is an unmerited blessing from a gracious God. As James said, "Don't be deceived, my dearly loved brothers. Every generous act and every perfect gift is from above, coming down from the Father of lights; with Him there is no variation or shadow cast by turning" (Jas. 1:16-17).

- *Stewards are responsible to God for the way we use all that is entrusted to us.* Personal accountability is a fundamental principle of stewardship: "We will all stand before the judgment seat of God. Each of us will give an account of himself to God" (Rom. 14:10,12). The standard by which God judges stewards is faithfulness. Stewards are to faithfully use for His glory what He has committed to us. Again Paul explained, "A person should consider us in this way: as servants of Christ and managers of God's mysteries. In this regard, it is expected of managers that each one be found faithful" (1 Cor. 4:1-2). A steward's rewards in heaven are bestowed on the basis of the faithful use of resources on earth.

• *Stewardship responsibility includes all of a person's life.* Unfortunately, the term *stewardship* is often applied primarily to the use of financial resources. Scriptural stewardship embraces everything God gives us—time, abilities, talents, gifts, influence, the gospel, testimony, opportunities, and physical health, as well as material possessions.

The ideal steward sees all of life as an opportunity to serve God. A servant desires that nothing be wasted, withheld from God's use, misused, or used selfishly. Instead, a faithful steward joyfully sacrifices all resources to the Lord's service.

Who owns it? Beside each item below write who owns it—you or God.

_____ My house   _____ My car   _____ My checking account   _____ My savings account

_____ My Christian service   _____ My family   _____ My present life   _____ My future life

Based on your responses, are you a steward or an owner? _____

Stewardship and tithing. Tithing is returning to the Lord the first tenth of a person's material gain. Abram was the first to engage in this practice when he brought tithes to Melchizedek, a priest of the Most High God some five hundred years before God gave the law to Moses (see Gen. 14:18-20). The Scripture clearly teaches that the first tenth of a person's increase, whether crops, herds, or other resources, belongs to the Lord (see Lev. 27:30; Mal. 3:10). By tithing, a person acknowledges that God is the owner of all things. Moreover, returning the first tenth shows your gratitude to God for allowing you to use the remaining nine-tenths.

"Every tenth of the land's produce, grain from the soil or fruit from the trees, belongs to the LORD; it is holy to the LORD" (Lev. 27:30).

Jesus, who must have practiced tithing as an orthodox Jew, affirmed tithing when He said to the Pharisees, " 'Woe to you, scribes and Pharisees, hypocrites! You pay a tenth of mint, dill, and cumin, yet you have neglected the more important matters of the law—justice, mercy, and faith. These things should have been done without neglecting the others' " (Matt. 23:23).

" 'Bring all the tithes into
   the storehouse,
That there may be food
   in My house,
And prove Me now in this,'
Says the LORD of hosts,
'If I will not open for you
   the windows of heaven
And pour out for you
   such blessing
That there will not be room
   enough to receive it' "
(Mal. 3:10, NKJV).

God places great importance on our obedience in tithing. In Malachi 3:8 God charged His people with robbing Him by not bringing tithes and offerings to Him. This statement reveals the serious nature of withholding what the Lord requires.

Tithing is the beginning of a believer's financial response to God. The first tenth belongs to God and is holy (set apart) to Him, but we make offerings to Him as we give beyond the tithe. Many Christians begin by giving 10 percent, then increase by 1 percent each year until they reach 20 percent or more.

Tithing is God's imperative. His law requires it, and His love demands it. Because our tithes are used to spread the gospel and minister to others, the mission of the church and the need of the world call for our faithfulness in tithing.

Tithing is—

☐ a nice thing to do; ☐ optional;

☐ required by God; ☐ only for the wealthy.

The Cooperative Program. The 11 men who first heard the Great Commission understood the necessity of working together to accomplish the challenging goal of making disciples of all nations. Throughout church history various plans have been formulated to enable churches to work together in missionary and benevolent outreach.

Since 1925 Southern Baptists have partnered together to reach the world for Christ through a plan called the Cooperative Program. Through this method of missionary outreach, all cooperating churches pool their financial resources to fulfill the Great Commission. Each church determines the amount of money to be sent to its state convention. Annually, the state convention decides how much money to allocate for Cooperative Program funds and how much to reserve for ministry within the state (the original goal was a 50-50 division).

Messengers from the churches who attend the annual meeting of the Southern Baptist Convention determine how Cooperative Program gifts to the Southern Baptist Convention are distributed. The majority of support is allocated to the International Mission Board, the North American Mission Board, and six Southern Baptist seminaries. Southern Baptists' contributions also fund the convention's Executive Committee, the Ethics and Religious Liberty Commission, the Annuity Board, and the Woman's Missionary Union.

We must always remember that our love for Christ is the supreme motive for steward-ship. Our faithful use of all His gifts to us is not the result of ought or must; rather, "Christ's love compels us" (2 Cor. 5:14). Our love for Him and others is a response to His greater love for us. When we love Him, we want to commit our lives and possessions to His purpose.

Making a Difference

Cooperative Program missions, simply defined, is caring people partnering together to touch the world. More than 16 million Southern Baptists in more than 42,000 churches—all working together under the lordship of Jesus Christ—can make an eternal difference in the world. The effectiveness of the Cooperative Program plan of financial cooperation is reflected in these statistics:

- Cooperative Program missions supports the work of more than 5,000 international missionaries who are engaging different people groups in 153 countries. Church-planting efforts saw 5,700 new churches started in one year.
- The North American Mission Board supported more than 5,000 missionaries and helped start more than 1,600 new churches in the year 2000.
- Six seminaries annually educate more than 13,400 future pastors, missionaries, and church leaders.[14]

Considering God's purpose for our lives fills us with a deep sense of gratitude. How amazing it is that God has a special plan for each of us and reveals His plan through His Word and His Holy Spirit. May we respond as His faithful servants, committing all we are and all we have to carry out His will for our lives.

Based on your study of this chapter, write a description of your purpose in life. Then spend time in prayer asking God whether your written statement reflects His plan and priorities.

_____

_____

_____

_____

_____

_____

_____

[1]T. W. Hunt and Melana Hunt Monroe, *From Heaven's View: God Bringing His Children to Glory* (Nashville: LifeWay Press, 2002), 16.

[2]Suggested resources are *Share Jesus Without Fear* and *Learning to Share My Faith*. To order, write to LifeWay Church Resources Customer Service; One LifeWay Plaza, Nashville, TN 37234-0013; fax (615) 251-5933; phone toll free (800) 458-2772; e-mail *customerservice@lifeway.com;* order online at *www.lifeway.com;* or visit a LifeWay Christian Store.

[3]Avery T. Willis Jr., *MasterLife 4: The Disciple's Mission* (Nashville: LifeWay Press, 1997), 123–25.

[4]*The Baptist Faith and Message* (Nashville: LifeWay Christian Resources of the Southern Baptist Convention, 2000), 16.

[5]H. Leon McBeth, *The Baptist Heritage* (Nashville: Broadman Press, 1987), 413–23.

[6]"God at work from 1845–2002" and "Our Mission" [online], [cited 30 July 2003]. Available from the Internet: *www.imb.org.*

[7]"About NAMB" [online], [cited 30 July 2003]. Available from the Internet: *www.namb.net/about.*

[8]Henry T. Blackaby and Claude V. King, *Experiencing God: Knowing and Doing the Will of God* (Nashville: LifeWay Press, 1990), 36–37.

[9]C. Gene Wilkes, *Jesus on Leadership: Becoming a Servant Leader* (Nashville: LifeWay Press, 1996), 33.

[10]James E. Harvey, "Helping Christians Discover Their Gifts for Ministry" (D.Min. dissertation, Golden Gate Baptist Theological Seminary, 1979), 20–25, 110.

[11]*The Baptist Faith and Message,* 16.

[12]"Toward Spiritual Transformation Through Developing a Biblical Worldview" (internal document) (Nashville: LifeWay Christian Resources of the Southern Baptist Convention), 5.

[13]Ibid.

[14]"Cooperative Program" [online], [cited 30 July 2003]. Available from the Internet: *www.sbc.net/cp.*

CHAPTER 5

Should Christians Try to Shape Society?

Growing up as a preacher's kid had advantages and disadvantages. One advantage was the godly influence of my parents. They not only taught me biblical principles for righteous living but also lived as good examples for me. One disadvantage was the high expectations others had of me. Although I was a good kid, I loved to have fun and would sometimes find myself in trouble!

As a teenager I tried very hard to live a model Christian life but continually fell short. I soon developed a predictable pattern. During church revival meetings and summer camps I would rededicate my life to Christ, promising to do better. But before long I would yield to peer pressure and drift back into a compromised lifestyle. Finally, God got my attention when He called me to preach His Word. Just before my sophomore year in high school, I made a public decision to follow God's call. After that I learned to stop depending on my best efforts, instead trusting Christ to live His life in me. That marked a turning point in my behavior and influence.

One incident made me realize how much others respected my changed lifestyle. One day at football practice a lineman twisted his ankle and let out a string of curse words. The other players became very quiet and looked at me. The coach turned to me and asked, "That wasn't nice, was it, Draper?" I replied, "No, it wasn't." My very presence on that team and in our school was making a difference. Today I realize that such a reaction is the natural effect of faith that is expressed in everyday life.

The Bible tells us that Christians are new creations in Christ (see 2 Cor. 5:17). Personal transformation not only changes a person but also changes those who are influenced by that person. Believers stand for honesty, kindness, diligence, persistence, integrity, and purity. We display the virtues of love, forgiveness, and faithfulness. These qualities have the potential to strengthen and transform family, society, and culture. Tragically, the converse is also true. If Christians do not shape society, society will shape them. The Apostle Paul warned, "Do not be conformed to this age, but be transformed by the renewing of your mind, so that you may discern what is the good, pleasing, and perfect will of God" (Rom. 12:2).

What is Paul's command in Romans 12:2? _____

_____

What is the outcome of obeying that command? _____

_____

Paul was saying not to let the world squeeze you into its mold. Either we will be a mold that transforms society, or we will be molded by society. Christianity is not just a way of doing certain religious things like praying and worshiping God. Authentic Christianity is a new lifestyle, a transformed way of living. And that can make a powerful, positive impact on society.

This chapter deals with your Christian influence—the change you, as a believer, can bring in society, in the world, and in the family.

What Do We Believe About Influencing the Social Order?

I once read about a man who had died. After the funeral a friend of his asked the man's employer if he had someone in mind to fill this man's vacancy. "No, it isn't necessary," his boss replied. "Fred didn't leave a vacancy." Fred's work was of such poor quality that the business was actually better off without him. Many people make no lasting impact for good on others. How sad to live without making a positive difference—what a waste of life! God has something far better for each of us.

Changed People Changing the World

In 1947 Southern Baptists established an agency to encourage and equip believers to make a moral impact on their culture. Now known as the Ethics and Religious Liberty Commission, this agency works "to awaken, inform, energize, equip, and mobilize Christians to be the catalysts for the biblically based transformation of their families, churches, communities, and the nation." Publishing resources on a wide range of critical social issues, the commission educates individual believers and churches about the ethical demands of God's Word. It also maintains a full-time office in Washington, D.C., that shares biblical perspectives on moral issues with national organizations and government agencies. Issues the agency addresses include citizenship and religious liberty, racial reconciliation, sanctity of human life, pornography, world peace, the environment, gambling, substance abuse, world hunger, Christian persecution, community service, entertainment and pop culture, family issues, and sexual purity.[1]

Which of the following are appropriate ways for Christians to influence society?
- ☐ March in a peaceful protest
- ☐ Destroy abortion facilities
- ☐ Write letters to the editor of the local newspaper
- ☐ Refuse to pay taxes
- ☐ Christians shouldn't try to influence society.

A Biblical Mandate for Social Involvement

Jesus came into this world to make a difference. In the margin read Luke's description of the occasion when Jesus declared His reason for coming.

What did Jesus say was His reason for coming to the world? _____

_____

What does this say about the purpose of the Christian life? _____

_____

"He came to Nazareth, where He had been brought up. As usual, He entered the synagogue on the Sabbath day and stood up to read. The scroll of the prophet Isaiah was given to Him, and unrolling the scroll, He found the place where it was written, 'The Spirit of the Lord is upon Me, because He has anointed Me to preach good news to the poor, He has sent Me to proclaim freedom to the captives and recovery of sight to the blind, to set free the oppressed, to proclaim the year of the Lord's favor' " (Luke 4:16-19).

In verse 18 the phrase *preach good news* translates a single Greek word that can also be translated *evangelize*. The priority of Jesus' mission was to bring about spiritual change in people. In this passage the terms *the poor, the captives, the blind,* and *the oppressed* all refer to the spiritual needs of those who heard Jesus. He came to deliver them from the consequences of their sin, making them new persons. Jesus knew that every person's greatest needs are spiritual—the need for a right relationship with God, resulting in a transformed life. He devoted His entire three-year ministry to bringing abundant, eternal life.

However, Jesus also cared about physical and social needs. After Jesus stated His mission, He delivered a demon-possessed man (see Luke 4:31-35) and healed a woman who suffered from a high fever and other sick people (see Luke 4:38-40). He "healed many people of diseases, plagues, and evil sprits, and He granted sight to many blind people" (Luke 7:21). Another Gospel account tells us that He fed hungry multitudes (see Mark 6:30-44; 8:1-10). His first miracle was to save a wedding host from the embarrassment of not having enough wine for the guests (see John 2:1-11). All of these references show Jesus' compassion for hurting people. He cared not only for their eternal, spiritual conditions but also for their immediate, physical needs. He is truly the Great Physician.

Jesus continues His work of changing people and changing society as He works in and through His followers today. He promised, " 'The one who believes in Me will also do the works that I do. And he will do even greater works than these, because I am going to the Father' " (John 14:12). Toward the end of His earthly ministry, Jesus articulated His challenging vision for our involvement in social change. When you read His words in the margin (Matt. 25:31-40), you realize that He expects us to serve Him by relieving human suffering.

Scripture makes clear that salvation and service belong together; they are the two sides of the Christian coin. Ephesians 2:8-9 assures us, "By grace you are saved through faith, and this is not from yourselves; it is God's gift—not from works, so that no one can boast." But we must also grasp the importance of the next sentence: "For we are His making, created in Christ Jesus for good works, which God prepared ahead of time so that we should walk in them" (v. 10). The Book of James confronts those who claim to believe in Christ but fail to prove their faith by their actions: "What good is it, my brothers, if someone says he has faith, but does not have works? Can his faith save him? If a brother or sister is without clothes and lacks daily food, and one of you says to them, 'Go in peace, keep warm, and eat well,' but you don't give them what the body needs, what good is it? In the same way faith, if it doesn't have works, is dead by itself" (Jas. 2:14-17). Authentic faith expresses itself in obedience to the Lord Jesus' command to love others as we love ourselves (see Mark 12:31).

Jesus used two simple, familiar words to illustrate a Christian's influence on society: *salt* and *light*. Read in the margin His words to His disciples (Matt. 5:13-14,16).

Salt was used in biblical times to preserve meat. Just as salt must permeate meat in order to prevent spoilage, Christians are to have a saving, purifying influence as they permeate society. Sin always brings decay and corruption. All social relationships need Christians' preserving influence in order to maintain their health.

When Jesus compared believers to light, He further defined our influence. Just as light penetrates the darkness, enabling us to see our surroundings clearly, Jesus' followers manifest the light of His life in a world of spiritual and moral darkness.

A Changed World Begins with a Changed Heart

When we think about influencing society for Christ, we are not talking about the popular concept of social work. Many local, state, and federal government agencies involve both saved and unsaved people in assisting needy persons. Believers can support and participate in these efforts as long as we do not compromise our loyalty to Jesus Christ and His Word.

The difference between secular social work and Christian social involvement is a recognition of and an attention to every person's fundamental spiritual need. Christian ministry is always offered in Jesus' name

"When the Son of Man comes in His glory ... all the nations will be gathered before Him, and ... the King will say to those on His right, 'Come, you who are blessed by My Father ... For I was hungry and you
   gave Me something to eat;
I was thirsty and you gave
   Me something to drink;
I was a stranger and you
   took Me in;
I was naked and you clothed Me;
I was sick and you took care
   of Me;
I was in prison and you
   visited Me.' ...
Whatever you did for one of the least of these brothers of Mine, you did for Me" (Matt. 25:31-40).

"You are the salt of the earth. But if the salt should lose its taste, how can it be made salty? It's no longer good for anything but to be thrown out and trampled on by men. You are the light of the world. A city situated on a hill cannot be hidden. ... Let your light shine before men, so that they may see your good works and give glory to your Father in heaven" (Matt. 5:13-14,16).

Christlike Character Traits You Can Show the World

The Beatitudes (see Matt. 5:3–12)	Christlike Love (see 1 Cor. 13)		Faith
Poor in spirit	Patient	Rejoices in the truth	Gentleness
Mourn	Kind	Bears all things	Self-control
Gentle	Does not envy	Believes all things	
Hunger and thirst for righteousness	Is not boastful	Hopes all things	Christlike Virtues (see Jas. 3:17)
	Is not conceited	Endures all things	
Merciful	Does not act improperly		Pure
Pure in heart	Is not selfish	The Fruit of the Spirit (see Gal. 5:22–23)	Peace-loving
Peacemakers	Is not provoked		Gentle
Persecuted for righteousness	Does not keep a record of wrongs	Love	Compliant
		Joy	Merciful
	Finds no joy in unrighteousness	Peace	Fruitful
		Patience	Without favoritism
		Kindness	Without hypocrisy
		Goodness	

for the purpose of demonstrating God's love and salvation through Jesus Christ. As you learned in chapter 2, all humans are born with a serious heart problem. The Lord told Jeremiah, " 'The heart is deceitful above all things, and desperately wicked; who can know it?' " (Jer. 17:9). Read in the margin Jesus' description of the depraved human heart. Is it surprising that so much evil is in the world when every person is born with this sinful nature?

Wickedness and ungodliness also result from Satan's work in the world. Peter said that the unsaved live "under the tyranny of the Devil" (Acts 10:38). This adversary has the power to cause spiritual blindness, as well as to bring persons into bondage to sinful practices. Scripture states that he "has blinded the minds of the unbelievers so they cannot see the light of the gospel of the glory of Christ" (2 Cor. 4:4). Jesus compared Satan to a thief who " 'comes only to steal and to kill and to destroy' " (John 10:10).

Only a biblical worldview enables us to understand the true reason for society's ills. Until someone's heart is changed, the person can experience no permanent change in character and conduct. Because of God's love for humanity, He made this promise: " 'I will give you a new heart and put a new spirit within you. ... I will put My Spirit within you and cause you to walk in My statutes, and you will keep My judgments and do them. ... You shall be My people, and I will be your God. I will deliver you from all your uncleannesses' " (Jer. 36:26-29, NKJV). His Son, Jesus, offered a new birth that results in new life that is abundant and eternal (see John 3:5,16; 10:10). He is the only hope for changing individuals. As

"Out of people's hearts, come evil thoughts, sexual immoralities, thefts, murders, adulteries, greed, evil actions, deceit, lewdness, stinginess, blasphemy, pride, and foolishness. All these evil things come from within and defile a man" (Mark 7:21-23).

Meeting Needs, Sharing Christ

Many churches use ministry evangelism to meet persons' physical and spiritual needs. Ministry evangelism is "caring for persons in the name of Jesus Christ. It is meeting persons at the point of their need and ministering to them physically and spiritually. The intent of ministry evangelism is to present the good news of God's love in order to introduce persons to Jesus. Ministry evangelism is not manipulative. Ministry is given lovingly and unconditionally. But the reason for it all, God's love for lost persons, is always shared."[2]

"The gospel is a message of Jesus' incarnation in human flesh. The only way it can be biblically shared is to focus on whole persons, with all of their hurts and needs, and to involve the church in ministering to those persons and in leading them to Christ. ... Evangelism that does not minister to the needs of the whole person falls short of the New Testament standard. Evangelism is incarnational when it recognizes that Christ, who came in human flesh, is concerned about persons—body, mind, and spirit." Ministry evangelism is a way God's people can witness and minister in an incarnational way.[3]

people accept Jesus Christ as Savior and Lord and are discipled to grow in their relationships with Him, they are equipped and empowered to reach out and change their world as well.

Reread the previous paragraph and complete the sentence:
Until someone's _____ is changed, the person can experience no permanent change in _____ and _____.

Describe how Jesus has changed your heart. _____

_____

How well do your character and conduct reflect a changed heart?

Not at all   All the time

Understanding the source of all evil and every person's deep need for salvation helps us love sinners while despising their sin. In the Scriptures we see many examples of this love: when Jesus offered His salvation to sinners like the woman at the well (see John 4:1-26), the woman caught in adultery (see John 8:1-11), and the Apostle Paul (see 1 Tim. 1:12-16). Although Jesus hated evil, He loved evildoers enough to die for them. We are challenged to maintain Christlike love for others in the midst of an evil, perverted society.

You read in chapter 4 that evangelism is the process of sharing the good news of God's offer of a new heart and a new life in Christ. Countless examples could be given of the transforming power of the gospel. Consider one example of someone who experienced spiritual change and then went on to help change society.

Chuck Colson was known as a White House hatchet man during the four years he served on President Nixon's staff. His reputation for being coldhearted and ruthless led one observer to state that Colson was "incapable of humanitarian thoughts." Because of his involvement in the Watergate scandal, he spent six months in a federal prison. During that time Colson turned to Christ and was born again. In 1976 he wrote his first book, *Born Again*. A news reporter commented, "If Mr. Colson can repent of his sins, there has to be hope for everybody."

Following his months in prison, Colson began a ministry to prisoners called Prison Fellowship, which has grown to involve more than 50,000 volunteers. These believers minister to prisoners, their families, and the victims of their crimes. This ministry operates a prison in Texas, where the number of inmates who have become repeat offenders has greatly declined. Sociologists at the University of Pennsylvania did a five-year study to analyze this very successful Christian approach to rehabilitating convicts. Chuck Colson commented on the results of the study by saying, "When your friends tell you that your faith is merely private and you ought to keep it to yourself, tell them about this report. Faith isn't just a private experience. Faith, when it is lived out, changes not only people—it also changes cultures, countries. It reduces recidivism. It eventually will reduce crime."[4]

What is the explanation for the transformation of people whose lawless, violent behavior made them a threat to society? The same power that changed Chuck Colson from a man who was "incapable of humanitarian thoughts" to a man whose passion is to help others find permanent hope and change—the gospel. The Apostle Paul also had firsthand knowledge of this power. As a result, he wrote, "I am not ashamed of the gospel, because it is God's power for salvation to everyone who believes" (Rom. 1:16). Like Paul and like Chuck Colson, we must recognize that any lasting change in society must begin with a change of heart. The most important social change Christians can bring to their culture is to take the good news of Jesus Christ to everyone.

Describe a situation in which you have been involved in helping a needy person.

_____

_____

Describe how you shared the gospel through your ministry to that person.

_____

_____

Making a Difference

The biblical mandate to make a difference in society can be applied to many areas of concern. *The Baptist Faith and Message* reads, "In the spirit of Christ, Christians should oppose racism, every form of greed, selfishness, and vice, all forms of sexual immorality, including adultery, homosexuality, and pornography. We should work to provide for the orphaned, the needy, the abused, the aged, the helpless, and the sick. We should speak on behalf of the unborn and contend for the sanctity of all human life from conception to natural death. Every Christian should seek to bring industry, government, and society as a whole under the sway of the principles of righteousness, truth, and brotherly love. In order to promote these ends Christians should be ready to work with all men of good will in any good cause, always being careful to act in the spirit of love without compromising their loyalty to Christ and His truth."[5]

What a challenge! We can't examine each of these issues in our brief study, but let's look at some of the most critical ones and consider a biblical view of each. Is the Lord calling you to get involved and make a difference in one or more of these areas?

Race relations. Though all races are subject to discrimination, minority groups have historically been susceptible to mistreatment by the majority. In America, Blacks were once enslaved, then segregated. Southern Baptists were slow to acknowledge the worth and dignity of Blacks, even when they were brothers and sisters in Christ. Fortunately, our denomination has acknowledged this sin and has embraced the biblical teaching that all believers are one in Christ (see 1 Cor. 12:13-14). The Book of Revelation teaches that in heaven "every nation, tribe, people, and language" (7:9) will stand before the throne and worship the Lamb. Southern Baptists are now attempting to desegregate churches and to express love and acceptance toward all minorities.

> "We were all baptized by one Spirit into one body—whether Jews or Greeks, whether slaves or free—and we were all made to drink of one Spirit" (1 Cor. 12:13-14).

Read 1 Corinthians 12:13-14. Write what you think God would say to a racially prejudiced person.

_____

_____

Pornography. The lucrative pornography industry directly harms society by fostering a false and damaging view of sex, undermining chastity and marital fidelity, encouraging promiscuity, and perverting the minds of children. Individuals can easily develop an addiction to pornography by becoming dependent on the emotional and physical stimulation it offers.

Paul taught believers to deny the lusts of the flesh (see Titus 2:12) and instead to "walk with decency, as in the daylight: … not in sexual impurity and promiscuity" (Rom. 13:13). John warned Christians that "the lust of the flesh, the lust of the eyes, and the pride in one's lifestyle—is not from the Father, but is from the world. And the world with its lust is passing away" (1 John 2:16-17).

Homosexuality. A homosexual is someone who has consciously chosen to engage in sexual relationships with persons of the same gender. The homosexual lifestyle is detrimental to society in its promotion of self-indulgence, hedonism, and sexual promiscuity and in its influence on young people. In addition, well-organized homosexual-rights groups actively seek a protected status for homosexuals, attempt to change the definition of marriage, advocate for the normalization of homosexuality in public-school education, and work for the decriminalization of prostitution and other sexual contacts.

Several passages in the Bible clearly forbid homosexual behavior.

Match the Scripture references with their teachings.

____ 1. Leviticus 18:22   a. Sexual immorality, murder, idolatry, and lying are sins.

____ 2. Romans 1:26-32   b. Homosexuality is unnatural.

____ 3. Revelation 22:15   c. To God, homosexuality is detestable.

Although some denominations have accepted homosexual behavior, Southern Baptists are committed to the authority of the Bible in this matter. Although we condemn homosexuality as a perversion of God's gift of sexuality, we affirm that God loves the homosexual person and can deliver him or her from this lifestyle.

World hunger. Hunger is one of the most desperate needs of millions of people around the world. As a result of war, drought, flooding, famine, economics, political corruption, and overpopulation, more than 700 million people suffer from malnutrition. One agency estimates that as many as 280,000 malnourished children die every week.

We have already seen that Jesus fed the hungry on several occasions (see Mark 6:30-44; 8:1-10) and that He calls believers to do the same (see Matt. 25:31-40). The early church willingly shared with those who had physical needs (see Acts 2:41-47; 4:34-35). In Acts 6:1-7 the church selected deacons to ensure that widows were fed. The church today has a similar responsibility to meet the physical needs of people.

Since 1974 Southern Baptists have tried to make a difference in the world-hunger crisis. More than 5,600 projects exceeding $6.3 million annually have been devoted to this effort. Every year churches are asked to observe World Hunger Day by bringing a special offering. Feeding the hungry is one way we fulfill the mission Jesus left for us in this world.[6]

Bioethics. The broad field of bioethics includes ethical issues related to the beginning of life, death, and many medical experiences in between. For Christians the question is how biblical principles and Christian values apply to ethical issues in medicine. The goals of bioethics should be the glory of God and the benefit of people, who are created in God's image.

Bioethics includes such issues as organ transplantation, human-reproductive technologies, stem-cell research, cloning, euthanasia, genetic screening, in vitro fertilization, artificial insemination, and surrogate motherhood. Believers must approach each of these issues from a commitment to the sanctity of all human life—born and unborn (see Eccl. 11:5; Isa. 49:1,5; Gal. 1:15). The Bible teaches that all human life is a gift from God (see Gen. 1:26-27; 2:21-23;

1 Cor. 11:7; 2 Cor. 3:18; Eph. 4:24; Col. 3:10; Jas. 3:9). Let's apply this biblical principle to several bioethical issues.

- *Organ donation and transplantation.* Most Christians believe that these actions are morally acceptable as long as the donor volunteered the organ. Although no specific biblical reference supports these practices, they fit the general Christian principles of helping others and preserving human life.

- *Infertility.* The use of fertility drugs presents few ethical difficulties as long as the couple is willing to risk the possibility of multiple births. Using a husband's sperm for artificial insemination is likewise acceptable to most Christians. However, ethical problems may arise from other technologies for treating infertility, such as artificial insemination using a donor's sperm, in vitro fertilization, and the use of a surrogate mother. Adoption may be the most ethical option for Christian couples who are unable to conceive children.

- *Genetic screening.* When tests reveal that an unborn child has physical defects that will affect its quality of life, some parents choose to abort the infant. This decision violates the biblical principle of the sanctity of human life. The Bible also teaches that persons with disabilities should not be discriminated against, either before or after birth (see Ex. 4:11; Isa. 43:7-8; Acts 10:34).

- *Cloning.* When it was announced in March 1997 that a sheep had been cloned, the scientific world immediately faced the possibility of human cloning. Manufacturing a human would violate biblical principles, for human life is the express creation of God and is made in His image and likeness (see Gen. 1:26-27).

- *Stem-cell research.* A stem cell is a human cell that has the ability to develop into any of the nearly 220 types of cells in the human body. These stem cells show great promise for curing illnesses. The ethical problem arises when scientists abort and destroy human embryos in order to obtain their tissues. This practice is contrary to the biblical principle of the sanctity of every human life from conception (see Gen. 1:27; Ps. 139:13-16) and the prohibition against taking human life (see Gen. 9:6; Ex. 20:13).

- *Abortion.* Because human life begins with conception (see Ps. 139:13-16), all abortion is the destruction of a person. The Bible does not distinguish between the nature and value of a person before birth and after birth. Both are people created by God in His image and likeness (Gen. 1:26-27; Ps. 119:73). The Bible never teaches or condones the killing of an unborn child. In fact, if an unborn child was hurt or killed through another person's actions, God required a penalty (see Ex. 21:22-25).

- *Euthanasia.* Active euthanasia is an action that causes the death of another person who is suffering from a terminal and imminently fatal condition. An example is when a doctor gives a dying patient a lethal injection to relieve pain and suffering. Southern Baptists oppose active euthanasia and doctor-assisted suicide because they are direct, intentional acts of killing. The only biblical justification for taking human life is society's punishment for violating certain laws that God has established. A Christian's duty is to care for the dying with compassion, believing that God creates human life and determines its duration:

Ten Commandments for Christian Citizens

1. *Honor your citizenship.* We do not deserve to be Americans; we are privileged to be Americans. We have the right to see our faults and challenge elected officials but not to dishonor our country. "To love America is to honor all that is good about her, while seeking to protect her from all that would destroy her goodness."

2. *Know your heritage.* We must make sure that revisionists with a secular-humanist agenda do not undermine the Christian foundation of our country.

3. *Live your values.* It is not enough to extol high moral values; we must live them to God's glory (see 1 Pet. 2:12). Vote, pay your taxes, and volunteer for community service.

4. *Maintain your prayer life.* Pray for government officials (see 1 Tim. 2:1-2), for those with whom you disagree (see Matt. 5:44), for issues facing our country, and for our nation's preservation and protection.

5. *Voice your convictions.* Be proactive. Send letters and e-mails to elected officials expressing your views. Become involved with others who share your cause. Share information with fellow believers.

6. *Discipline your criticism.* Not everything in government is wrong. Commend officials who sponsor moral legislation and are positive influences.

7. *Analyze your zeal.* We can't give equal time to every social issue, but we should be balanced in our concern for legitimate needs and not be motivated by personal prejudice.

8. *Protect your family.* Satan is targeting home and family life in America. We must stand on God's definition of family and family values.

9. *Extend your compassion.* Your desire to change society should ideally move beyond public condemnation to hands-on involvement with those who are victimized by sin.

10. *Declare your hope.* Our hope ultimately lies not in our human efforts but in the hands of our sovereign God. He will win in the end. Focus on Him and be ready to share the hope offered by His Son, Jesus Christ.[7]

"There is a time for every purpose under heaven; a time to be born, and a time to die" (Eccl. 3:1-2; also see 1 Cor. 15:22-23). God alone determines these times. We have examined only a few ethical and moral issues in our nation and our world. How can believers make a difference in the face of such overwhelming need? Jesus said, " 'Whatever you ask in My name I will do it, so that the Father may be glorified in the Son' " (John 14:13). If we confess our inadequacy and yield to His purposes, He will equip us for His work of transforming society. Indeed, we can confidently say with Paul, "I am able to do all things through Him who strengthens me" (Phil. 4:13). Jesus lives in us (see Gal. 2:20). He will give us wisdom and power to speak and act in ways that influence our society for the kingdom of God.

Identify one way you can be a positive social influence while sharing your Christian witness.

What Do We Believe About Peace and War?

Any discussion of a Christian's involvement in social issues must include the subject of peace and war. One research study discovered that in 3,530 years of recorded human history, only 286 years have been without war.[8] Numerous wars are being waged throughout the world at the time of this writing, and American troops are directly involved in several hostile military engagements. Many of these men and women are devout Christians. Other believers refuse to go to war, basing their position on biblical teachings. What does the Bible say about waging war?

The Prince of Peace

About seven hundred years before Jesus was born, the prophet Isaiah described His ministry:

> Unto us a Child is born, …
> And His name will be called …
>   Prince of Peace.
> Of the increase of His government and peace
> There will be no end (Isa. 9:6-7).

"Peace I leave with you. My peace I give to you. I do not give to you as the world gives. Your heart must not be troubled or fearful" (John 14:27).

Later Jesus identified with this promise.

Read Jesus' words in the margin. What do these verses say about Jesus' attitude toward war?

☐ Jesus said He was totally against war.
☐ Jesus was talking about inner peace, not international peace.
☐ Jesus never wants Christians to be involved in war.

"I have told you these things so that in Me you may have peace. In the world you have suffering. Be courageous! I have conquered the world" (John 16:33).

When we consider what happened to Jesus and His first disciples after He made those statements, it is clear that the peace He possessed and promised was not external in nature. Jesus had many enemies; they declared war on Him and ultimately arrested Him, severely punished Him, and put Him to death. Some historians believe that all 11 of His disciples were put to death by their enemies. What kind of peace was Jesus promising?

The peace Jesus gives to those who trust Him as Savior and Lord is an inner peace—the kind of peace described in these words: "Since we have been declared righteous by faith, we have peace with God through our Lord Jesus Christ" (Rom. 5:1). Peace with God means we are no longer at war with Him—no longer living in rebellion against Him. God has declared us not guilty as the result of our turning to Christ from sin. We have the assurance of His mercy and His gift of eternal life. God's peace reigning in our hearts is the beginning of all peace. This is true peace, a spiritual peace the world cannot conceive and only God can give through His Son, Jesus Christ (see Phil. 4:7).

Blessed Are the Peacemakers

Because Christians have the peace of Jesus Christ, He sends us to be peacemakers in the world (see Matt. 5:9). We bear witness of the availability of peace with God for everyone. Furthermore, we are to live at peace with others. Paul wrote,

> If possible, on your part, live at peace with everyone. Friends, do not avenge yourselves; instead, leave room for His wrath. For it is written: "Vengeance belongs to Me; I will repay," says the Lord. But
>> If your enemy is hungry, feed him.
>> If he is thirsty, give him something to drink (Rom. 12:18-20).

We are instructed to cultivate peaceful relationships with all people, even our enemies. We should never wage war against another individual except to protect someone's life.

The Bible indicates that wars will continue as long as sin rules the hearts of humankind. James wrote: "What is the source of the wars and the fights among you? Don't they come from the cravings that are at war within you?" (Jas. 4:1). The disciples once asked Jesus, " 'What is the sign of Your coming and of the end of the age?' " (Matt. 24:3). Included in His answer were these words: " 'You are going to hear of wars and rumors of wars. See that you are not alarmed, because these things must take place, but the end is not yet. For nation will rise up against nation, and kingdom against kingdom' " (Matt. 24:6-7).

"Blessed are the peacemakers, because they will be called sons of God" (Matt. 5:9).

War will continue until Jesus' ultimate reign. At that time

> They shall beat their swords into plowshares,
> And their spears into pruning hooks;
> Nation shall not lift up sword against nation,
> Neither shall they learn war anymore (Isa. 2:4, NKJV).

Until then believers should do all they can to prevent war. We are thankful for Christians who serve as diplomats, seeking peaceful solutions to potential conflicts. Others help prevent wars by building a strong military force to defend our nation. And many have given their lives to bring about the surrender of hostile forces that have attacked our nation and others.

Although Christians have peace, seek to be peacemakers, and despise violence, at times we must take up arms to defend our nation and those who cannot defend themselves. Christians have advocated this just-war position since the time of Augustine in the fourth century A.D. A just war is entered only as a last resort to secure justice and ensure peace. Martin Luther said, "Without armaments peace cannot be kept; wars are waged not only to repel injustice but also to establish a firm peace."[9] Having been the victim of terrorist attacks and having witnessed cruel aggression in other parts of the world, our nation must maintain a strong military force to protect ourselves and to aid our allies.

John Stuart Mill said, "War is an ugly thing but not the ugliest of things; the decayed and degraded state of moral and patriotic feelings that thinks that nothing is worth war is much worse."[10] Explain what you think this statement means and why you agree or disagree.

_____

_____

War is ultimately a spiritual matter. As Paul stated, "Our battle is not against flesh and blood, but against the rulers, against the authorities, against the world powers of this darkness, against the spiritual forces of evil in the heavens" (Eph. 6:12). Because spiritual warfare must be waged with spiritual weapons, Paul admonished us to "put on the full armor of God so that you can stand against the tactics of the Devil. Pray at all times in the Spirit, and stay alert in this, with all perseverance and intercession for all the saints" (Eph. 6:11,18). Prayer is the most effective antiwar weapon we have. We must be diligent as soldiers of the cross to wage spiritual warfare daily, always remaining aware that, as _The Baptist Faith and Message_ states, "the true remedy for the war spirit is the gospel of our Lord. The supreme need of the world is the acceptance of His teachings in all the affairs of men and nations, and the practical application of His law of love. Christian people throughout the world should pray for the reign of the Prince of Peace."[11]

What Do We Believe About the Family?

What is a family? Check the definition you affirm.
☐ A community of individuals who share goals and an authority and responsibility structure
☐ A God-ordained institution composed of persons related by marriage, blood, or adoption

What is the difference between these two definitions? _____

_____

God has established three social institutions for the welfare of humankind: family, government, and church. After the creation of Adam and Eve, every person has been born into a family, the descendant of a mother and a father. _The Baptist Faith and Message_ states that "God has ordained the family as the foundational institution of human society."[12] The family is also the most influential force in our lives. While growing up in a home, we develop our foundational values and skills for life.

God's Word establishes clear guidelines for marriage and family life. Let's look at some of the fundamental truths we believe about the family.

The Biblical Concept of Marriage

We live in a time when a strong attempt is being made to change the definition of marriage. The homosexual agenda is persistently lobbying for the legalization of same-sex marriages. Scripture is clear, however, that from the beginning God intended marriage to be a covenant relationship between a man and a woman. Jesus' words in the margin reflect this fact. *The Baptist Faith and Message* affirms the biblical definition of marriage: "Marriage is the uniting of one man and one woman in covenant commitment for a lifetime."[13]

From a legal standpoint, marriage is a contractual relationship that can easily be dissolved. As a result, more than half of all marriages end in divorce. But the biblical view focuses on a covenant relationship characterized by a mutual promise to be faithful to each other for life. The Hebrew word for *covenant* literally means *to fetter together*. The implication is that a husband and a wife are united for the remainder of their lives. Unlike a contract, a covenant is not intended to be broken. It represents a spiritual bond, not a legal one. Such a marriage covenant also includes God, who joins the couple together, and any children who are born to that union. A covenant marriage is possible only when the partners understand their mutual responsibilities as given in God's Word. And they must recognize their dependence on God for the motivation and power to live up to their responsibilities.

"He who created them in the beginning 'made them male and female.' …
For this reason a man will
leave his father and mother
and be joined to his wife,
and the two will become
one flesh.
So they are no longer two, but one flesh. Therefore what God has joined together, man must not separate" (Matt. 19:4-6).

Read the covenant-marriage vow in the box below. Underline characteristics of a Christian marriage.

Biblical Principles for Spouses

The Apostle Paul wrote his letters to readers in a culture that considered women inferior to men in many ways. In Hebrew families a woman was viewed more as a thing than a person. For example, women had no rights of divorce, but a Jewish man could put away his wife for the most trivial reason. Among the Greeks many women were used as prostitutes; respectable women were secluded and often did not even appear at meals. Companionship in marriage was not important; men found pleasure and friendship outside marriage. A wife managed her home and cared for the legitimate children, but she had little contact with her husband.

Covenant Marriage

The Southern Baptist Convention has endorsed the concept of covenant marriage. Couples who commit to a covenant marriage make this vow: "Believing that marriage is a covenant intended by God to be a lifelong fruitful relationship between a man and a woman, we vow to God, each other, our families, and our community to remain steadfast in unconditional love, reconciliation, and sexual purity, while purposefully growing in our covenant marriage relationship."[14]

Among the Romans the situation was even worse. Although there was not a single case of divorce in the first five hundred years of the Roman Empire, by New Testament times family life had broken down. Seneca wrote, "Women were married to be divorced and divorced to be married." The climate was adulterous. Chastity became the victim of the luxurious lifestyle of the rich. Marital fidelity was practically unknown. Against this pagan, immoral background, Paul's instructions about the roles of spouses in marriage greatly improved the perception of women and called for faithfulness, purity, companionship, and fellowship in married life.

The letter from Paul to the believers in Ephesus begins by devoting three chapters to doctrinal matters—the foundation of the faith. The final three chapters then apply theology to life situations. Chapter 4 begins with this challenge: "I, therefore, the prisoner in the Lord, urge you to walk worthy of the calling you have received" (Eph. 4:1). All that follows relates to a Christian's walk, or behavior.

The theme of Ephesians 5 is: "Be imitators of God, as dearly loved children. And walk in love, as the Messiah also loved us and gave Himself for us" (vv. 1-2). In this context the apostle called for believers to "be filled with the Spirit" (v. 18). One expression of the Spirit's control is "submitting to one another in the fear of Christ" (v. 21). Paul then applied this principle to the marriage relationship.

Instructions for wives. We know from the preceding teachings that Paul's guidelines are for Christian marriages in which both the husband and the wife are believers. Wives are admonished to "submit to your own husbands as to the Lord" (Eph. 6:22). The grammatical form of *submit* suggests that this submission is not from fear of the husband but as an expression of reverence for Christ. A wife is to submit to Christ because He is worthy of her faith; she submits to her husband because he is worthy of her trust. Such submission does not imply that a woman is inferior to a man but recognizes God's established roles in marriage. Someone must be the leader in the marriage; God places the husband in that role. The wife is to be supportive, helping the husband be an effective leader. Even within the Godhead, Christ is portrayed as being submissive to the will of His Father, not because of inferiority but because of His role in God's redemptive purpose.

The Baptist Faith and Message reinforces this biblical understanding of the wife's role in marriage: "The husband and wife are of equal worth before God, since both are created in God's image. ... A wife is to submit herself graciously to the servant leadership of her husband even as the church willingly submits to the headship of Christ. She, being in the image of God as is her husband and thus equal to him, has the God-given responsibility to respect her husband and to serve as his helper in managing the household and nurturing the next generation."[15]

In Paul's letter to Titus he added the following to a wife's duties: "Encourage the young women to love their husbands and children, to be sensible, pure, good homemakers, and submissive to their husbands, so that God's message will not be slandered" (Titus 2:4-5). The Greek word for *love* here is *agape,* a self-sacrificing love that puts others' needs above self.

Instructions for husbands. The Bible sets a very high standard for husbands when it declares, "Husbands, love your wives, just as also Christ loved the church and gave Himself for her" (Eph. 5:25). The Greek word *agape* is again used for *love* throughout this passage. Jesus demonstrated this kind of love when He chose to die on the cross to make possible the offer of God's forgiveness for the sins of all humankind. Paul referred to this act when he said, "Christ loved the church and gave Himself for her" (Eph. 5:25). A husband who sacrificially loves his wife literally submits himself to her, just as Paul stated all believers are required to do (see Eph. 5:21). Christian love never seeks to exercise tyranny or control over another. Rather, the husband is to "provide for, to protect, and to lead his family."[16]

Thus, the ideal for marriage is that two persons give themselves to each other, each putting the other first and giving himself or herself to meet the other's needs. Such a spirit of complete unselfishness builds the strongest union possible between two persons. In contrast, separation and divorce usually result from selfishness on the part of one or both marriage partners. The Bible gives couples a clear statement of what is essential to a successful marriage relationship.

Paul continued, "Husbands should love their wives as their own bodies. He who loves his wife loves himself" (Eph. 5:28). The teaching here is not that the husband loves his wife in the same way he loves his own body but that he loves her as actually *being* his own body. To understand this, we must read verse 31:

> For this reason a man will leave his father and mother
> and be joined to his wife,
> and the two will become one flesh.

The one-flesh concept does not refer just to a sexual union. The sexual union of two bodies is an outward, physical extension of the inner union of two lives. Thus, the husband who "provides and cares" (v. 29) for his wife is doing himself a great favor. Conversely, a husband who neglects and mistreats his wife harms not only his marriage but also himself, for his wife's welfare is indissolubly bound up with his own.

Love finds practical ways of expressing itself. Peter, who was married, gave wise counsel to husbands with the words in the margin. To show honor to the wife means to cherish her as a person of great value. The statement about her weaker nature refers to the fact that most women have less physical strength than men. Peter reminded husbands that apart from the proper treatment of their wives, they cannot be in the kind of relationship with God in which He will answer their prayers.

"Husbands ... live with your wives with understanding of their weaker nature yet showing them honor as co-heirs of the grace of life, so that your prayers will not be hindered" (1 Pet. 3:7).

Summarize the biblical instructions for wives and husbands.

Instructions for Wives	Instructions for Husbands
_____	_____
_____	_____
_____	_____
_____	_____

Review the box "Meeting Your Spouse's Needs" on this page and underline the needs that you feel you adequately meet in your spouse's life. Circle the areas to which you need to pay more attention. Write a note of thanks to your spouse for meeting your needs in specific areas.

Biblical Principles for Parents

God's plan is for children to be reared by a mother and a father. Both are needed for the healthy development of children. Unfortunately, a growing number of single parents today must attempt to fill the role of both father and mother. In some American cities as many as 90 percent of children are born out of wedlock, so most of these children grow up without the influence of a father.[17]

"The one who will not use the rod hates his son, but the one who loves him disciplines him diligently" (Prov. 13:24).

"Discipline your son while there is hope" (Prov. 19:18).

"Foolishness is tangled up in the heart of a youth; the rod of discipline will drive it away from him" (Prov. 22:15).

Paul also addressed the role of parents in Ephesians 6: "Fathers, don't stir up anger in your children, but bring them up in the training and instruction of the Lord" (v. 4). A father has the primary responsibility to provide discipline and spiritual teaching for his children. Of course, mothers play a vital role in child rearing, but God's desire is for the father to provide leadership in this crucial area. Both parents must be careful not to "stir up anger" in their children; in other words, they should avoid actions that exasperate children and make it difficult for them to please their parents. Parents who want to receive obedience and honor must deserve that respect.

In addition, parents are commanded to "bring them up in the training and instruction of the Lord" (Eph. 6:4). The phrase *bring them up* translates a Greek word meaning *to nourish to maturity, to nurture and rear the child.* This process includes every part of the child's life—emotional, spiritual, mental, and physical. The word *training* refers to the discipline needed to bring a child to maturity—primarily the parents' actions and example. Parents train most effectively as they model consistency and discipline in their own lives. However, sometimes children require discipline to awaken them to the importance of obedience. Read in the margin the biblical statements about discipline. The Scriptures certainly do not advocate abusively beating children, but these verses indicate

Meeting Your Spouse's Needs

What a wife needs from her husband:
- For him to be the spiritual leader
- Personal appreciation
- Romance and personal affection
- Intimate conversation
- Honesty and openness
- Home support and stability
- For him to commit to his family first

What a husband needs from his wife:
- Admiration and respect
- Sexual fulfillment
- Home support
- An attractive wife, which flows from inner beauty (see 1 Pet. 3:4)
- For her to be his best friend[18]

How to Demonstrate Love for Your Children

- Enter their world.
- Love your spouse.
- Give them discipline.
- Look them in the eyes.
- Give them physical affection.
- Spend time with them.

- Listen to them.
- Bless them with words.
- Have fun with them.
- Nudge them out of the nest when it is time.
- Admit to them when you're wrong.
- Introduce them to Jesus Christ.[19]

that some situations warrant properly administered discipline. Such discipline is an expression of love—concern for a child's ultimate welfare.

The word *instruction* refers to training and teaching by word as opposed to actions. This kind of teaching includes words of encouragement and guidance. The qualifying phrase *of the Lord* shows that the parents' words and example are to be those that are approved by the Lord.

In summary, Paul called on parents to love their children, discipline them by correction and example, and instruct them. Affirming Paul's letter, *The Baptist Faith and Message* states that "parents are to teach their children spiritual and moral values and to lead them, through consistent lifestyle example and loving discipline, to make choices based on biblical truth."[20]

Read the box "How to Demonstrate Love for Your Children" on this page. Beside each statement rate your demonstration of love by marking it *1–5*, with *1* being *poor* and *5* being *excellent*.

Write a note expressing your love for each of your children. Make time to share it with each child.

Biblical Principles for Children

The Bible also gives children principles of behavior to follow: "Children, obey your parents in the Lord, because this is right. 'Honor your father and mother'—which is the first command-ment with a promise—'that it may go well with you and that you may have a long life in the land' " (Eph. 6:1-3). The word *obey* literally means *to hear under authority* and implies habitual action. Here is another application of the principle of submission: children are to submit to the authority of their parents. And this is to be done "in the Lord." That is, obedience to parents is an act of obedience to God.

TV sitcoms and movies often find humor in a child's disobedience to parents. The Bible describes such behavior in very serious terms. One of the most detailed biblical passages dealing with actions that God condemns is Romans 1:26-32, which identifies sins like murder, greed, wickedness, God-haters, inventors of evil, and malice. In the midst of these evil acts of rebel-lion against God is disobedience to parents! God is serious about children honoring and obeying their parents. Remember that the requirement to honor parents is one of the Ten Commandments.

Parents have a responsibility to practice principles of Christian love and obedience in the home, but the child also has the responsibility of contributing to the Christian atmosphere of the home. *Honor* means *to estimate and fix value.* It refers to evaluating someone accurately and honestly and treating that person with the respect, courtesy, and obedience that his position or character demands. Honor is the disposition from which obedience flows. The way a child honors his parents is to obey them, respect them, and value them highly.

Notice the reason given for such honor: "that it may go well with you and that you may have a long life in the land" (Eph. 6:3). Obedience and respect for parents produce restraint, diligence, and hard work, which contribute to a conducive atmosphere for long life. The prevalent disregard for authority in this nation results from children's rebellion against their parents.

Guarding the Home

Both parents and children must be alert and on guard against the enemies that are attempting to destroy families. The large number of divorces, along with the breakdown of parent-child relationships, provides convincing evidence that Satan is working overtime to cause the disintegration of wholesome family life. Consider these alarming statistics.

- One million children a year experience their parents' divorces.
- America's current divorce rate is more than double what it was in 1960. Thirty-four percent of unsaved adults and 33 percent of born-again Christians who have been married have experienced a divorce.
- Thirty-five percent of our nation's children live apart from their biological fathers. Fifty percent who do not live with their fathers have never been in their fathers' homes.
- In the past 40 years, out-of-wedlock pregnancies have increased 600 percent.
- In fewer than 40 years, cohabitation by unmarried couples has increased almost 1,000 percent. Most people now live together before they begin first marriages.
- Thirty-two percent of all births in 1995 were out of wedlock.
- Fewer than 40 percent of married people claim to be very happy.[21]

Families must work hard to strengthen their relationships and guard against the forces that threaten their health. Husbands and wives must spend quality time together. Couples must make intentional plans for needed intimacy—times of meaningful communication and fun. Be careful not to let career, hobbies, sporting events, community causes, and other activities replace the time spouses need to spend together.

Parents must deliberately and assertively protect their children from destructive influences. The media—television, movies, computer games, and Internet—are potential minefields if not used wisely. Make certain you know what your children are being exposed to. Take the time to nurture their interest in wholesome, godly pursuits. Help your children choose the right friends. Be involved with your children in their activities and take time to share in their recreation. Plan family activities that build memories that will enrich your children's future.

Check ways Satan invades your home.

☐ Television   ☐ Magazines/newspapers   ☐ Internet   ☐ Movies
☐ Relationships   ☐ Computer games   ☐ Music   ☐ Other: _____

List actions you can take to limit Satan's ability to influence your family in these areas.

_____

_____

Our families and our society need a greater Christian influence. People of faith know that God is still on His throne, and He is constantly at work in His world and among His people. I hope this chapter has given you motivation and ideas for joining God's redemptive work in your family, your society, and your world.

Identify ways you feel the Lord would like you to have a greater Christian influence on your family, your society, and your world. Be specific about what you will commit to do.

_____

_____

---

[1] *Transforming America by Strengthening the Family* (Nashville: The Ethics and Religious Liberty Commission). For resources write to 901 Commerce Street, Suite 550; Nashville, TN 37203; or visit *www.faithandfamily.com.*

[2] Donald A. Atkinson and Charles L. Roesel, *Meeting Needs, Sharing Christ: Ministry Evangelism in Today's New Testament Church* (Nashville: LifeWay Press, 1995), 7.

[3] Ibid., 9.

[4] "About Chuck Colson" [online], [cited 5 September 2003]. Available from the Internet: *www.prisonfellowship.org.*

[5] *The Baptist Faith and Message* (Nashville: LifeWay Christian Resources of the Southern Baptist Convention, 2000), 19.

[6] "World Hunger Funds" [online], [cited 5 September 2003]. Available from the Internet: *www.imb.org.*

[7] *Ten Commandments for Christian Citizens* (Nashville: The Ethics and Religious Liberty Commission).

[8] Skip Heitzig, "The Theology of War," *Decision,* May 2003, 18.

[9] Ibid.

[10] John Stuart Mill, in Bob Kelly, *Worth Repeating: More than Five Thousand Classic and Contemporary Quotes* (Grand Rapids: Kregel Publications, 2003), 362.

[11] *The Baptist Faith and Message,* 20.

[12] Ibid., 21.

[13] Ibid.

[14] "Covenant Marriage Movement" [online], [cited 5 September 2003]. Available from the Internet: *www.covenantmarriage.com.*

[15] *The Baptist Faith and Message,* 21.

[16] Ibid.

[17] Richard Land, *For Faith & Family* (Nashville: Broadman & Holman, 2002), 44.

[18] Danny Akin, conference, Christian Family Weekend, LifeWay Glorieta Conference Center, 25–28 July 2003.

[19] Ibid.

[20] *The Baptist Faith and Message,* 22.

[21] "The American Family in Need of God's Help," *Facts & Trends,* June 2003.

CHAPTER 6

Where Is This World Headed?

Two events are permanently engraved on the memories of many Americans: December 7, 1941, and September 11, 2001. The bombing of Pearl Harbor and the attacks on the Pentagon and the World Trade Center are shocking examples of the existence of a powerful, sinister force at work in this world. A bystander exclaimed as the World Trade Center towers collapsed, "What's this world coming to?" That's a good question.

Identify a world event that had a dramatic impact on your life. _____

How did that event affect your belief that God is in control of everything? _____

_____

In an era of improved education and amazing technological advances, why does humankind continue to commit barbaric acts of destruction? The tragic reality of violence today continues the pattern of war established in the 20th century. While about 49 million people died in wars from the first century until 1900, in the 20th century more than 100 million died because of warfare. This means that more than twice as many people were killed in wars during the past 100 years than in the preceding 1,900 years! Sadly, most of the casualties of wars in the 20th century were not military personnel but civilians. Most of these were innocent victims of the extensive bombing of cities—wholesale massacres of men, women, and children.[1]

International conflicts magnify the breakdown of personal relationships. There are more divorces, more criminals behind bars, and more ethnic and racial hatred than ever. In spite of the best efforts of the best minds, the world is getting worse, not better. So the question remains: where is this world headed?

God has not left us groping in the dark for answers. From Genesis through Revelation, the Bible reveals that God is the sovereign ruler of His creation (see Rev. 11:15). He began human history, and He will conclude it in His time and according to His purpose. In the meantime, He is calling out a special people to be the citizens of His kingdom on earth. This chapter will focus on God's present rule and His plan to bring a glorious conclusion to what He planned from the beginning.

What Do We Believe About the Kingdom of God?

The people of God in both the Old Testament and New Testament eras were very familiar with kings and kingdoms. The Israelites had kings like Saul, David, and Solomon, and the early Christians lived during the reign of King Herod and his descendants. Thus, when the Bible refers to the kingdom of God, its first readers easily understood this concept.

The word *kingdom* isn't used much in everyday conversation today. Check the definition that most accurately reflects the meaning of the term *kingdom of God*.

☐ Believers' authority over unbelievers
☐ God's rule over all
☐ The church's rule over the state
☐ The spiritual realm of angels

> **Kingdom of God:**
> the sovereign rule of God over all creation and for all time and eternity

The kingdom of God is the sovereign rule of God over all creation and for all time and eternity. More specifically, it is "the reign of God through Christ in the lives of persons as evidenced by His activity in, through, and around them. The kingdom was prophesied in the Old Testament, pictured in Israel, proclaimed by John the Baptist, inaugurated by Christ during His public ministry on earth, extended in the lives of believers through the church in the present age, and will be consummated by Christ when He returns to earth to rule with His saints."[2] Let's look at the way the Bible develops the concept of the kingdom of God.

The Kingdom in the Old Testament

Although the Old Testament contains no references to the term *kingdom of God,* it establishes the roots of the kingdom. Verses like those in the margin present God as sovereign King.

The first Old Testament occurrence of the word *kingdom* is also an important revelation of the nature of God's kingdom. The Lord told Moses to give this message to His chosen people: " 'If you will listen to Me and carefully keep My covenant, you will be My own possession out of all the peoples, although all the earth is Mine, and you will be My kingdom of priests and My holy nation' " (Ex. 19:5-6). God selected a special people to be the citizens of His kingdom on earth. These would not only have priests but would be a "kingdom of priests." A priest is a mediator, a go-between, a person whose role is to intercede. God's description of the nation of Israel as a kingdom of priests means that He was calling them to mediate God's Word and work to the entire world—to reveal the truth about God to all nations. This concept of the priesthood of believers is developed more fully in the New Testament, but here are the first indications of this plan for God's people.

"The Lord Most High
is awe-inspiring,
a great King over all
the earth" (Ps. 47:2).

"The Lord has established
His throne in heaven,
and His kingdom rules
over all" (Ps. 103:19).

"The living may know
That the Most High rules
in the kingdom of men,
Gives it to whomever He will,
And sets over it the lowest
of men" (Dan. 4:17, NKJV).

Read the box "The Priesthood of Believers" on this page. Which of the following statements do *not* accurately identify the doctrine? Check all that apply.

☐ Some believers, because of their maturity or position, are more important than others.

☐ Access to God is available through His human representatives.

☐ Believers represent God to people.

☐ Believers can interpret the Scripture any way they want.

These words give further insight into God's reason for choosing Israel to be in His kingdom: " 'You are a holy people belonging to the LORD your God. The LORD your God has chosen you to be His own possession out of all the peoples on the face of the earth. The LORD was devoted to you and chose you, not because you were more numerous than all peoples, for you were the fewest of all peoples. But because the LORD loved you and kept the oath He swore to your fathers, He brought you out with a strong hand and redeemed you from the place of slavery, from the power of Pharaoh king of Egypt' " (Deut. 7:6-8). Notice the term *own possession* in Exodus 19:5 and Deuteronomy 7:6. God chooses kingdom people for a special ministry to the world. He loves and highly values them as essential to His purpose of redeeming fallen humanity.

God gave several Old Testament prophets messages about the future kingdom.

Read Jeremiah 23:5 in the margin on page 117. What is the nature of God's kingdom?

The Priesthood of Believers

The concept of the priesthood of believers encompasses these biblical teachings:
- The equality of all believers before God
- The right of each person to direct access to the Father
- The responsibility of each believer for ministry, according to his gifts

First Peter 2:9-10 teaches that the people of God are "a chosen race" to do His work. A Christian is part of "a royal priesthood," a people who are allowed to come into God's presence with petitions and sacrifices (v. 9). God has called out Christians to form "a holy nation," a nation set apart for God's service (v. 10). And we are "a special people" (Titus 2:14), indicating that God's people are uniquely His to do His will and His work.

Our priesthood means that we represent God to people. Each of us is a bridge builder between God and people as we minister and witness in His name. As priests, we can offer up sacrifices of our lives as we witness, praise, intercede in prayer, give, minister, visit, and help. Our priesthood also means that every believer can come before God on his own, without any other priest or intermediary except Jesus Christ Himself. [3]

God revealed that the nature of His kingdom would be righteousness, a people who reflect the righteous character and conduct of their King.

The visions of Daniel also present a clear promise of the future reign of the Messiah as sovereign ruler over all humankind. For example, the testimony of Daniel reveals God's plan to send His Son as the Son of Man, both divine and human in nature. Read Daniel 7:13-14 in the margin. This God-Man would rule over an everlasting kingdom. The King was coming!

The Old Testament ends with the prophecy of Malachi, through whom the Lord made these significant promises: " 'See, I am going to send My messenger, and he will clear the way before Me' " (Mal. 3:1). " 'Look, I am going to send you Elijah the prophet before the great and awesome Day of the LORD comes' " (Mal. 4:5). These statements indicated that a messenger would prepare the way for the coming of the King. Then the King would appear on earth to inaugurate a new era in the kingdom. However, more than four hundred years of silence passed before this promise was fulfilled.

The Kingdom in the New Testament

The long years of spiritual darkness and silence from God ended when a new light dawned to illumine human history. The New Testament is the written revelation of the coming to earth of the King—the One who boldly claimed to be the King of kings and Lord of lords.

Preparation for the King. The first messenger of the kingdom of God in the New Testament was John the Baptist. Before he was born, an angel visited his father, Zachariah, and declared that John would

> "turn many of the sons of Israel
> to the Lord their God.
> And he will go before Him
> in the spirit and power of Elijah …
> to make ready for the Lord a prepared people" (Luke 1:13-17).

Malachi's prophecies about Elijah were fulfilled in the person of John the Baptist.

John came preaching, " 'Repent, because the kingdom of heaven has come near!' " (Matt. 3:2). This was a call to repent. The Greek word translated *repent* literally means *to change one's mind—to begin thinking in a different way.* John called for his hearers to begin thinking in a new way about their sins. Rather than approve or excuse their sinful acts, they must turn from them, confess them as transgressions against God, and begin living in a manner that was pleasing to God. Why was this so important? John's answer was " 'because the kingdom of heaven has come near.' " Although John's audience knew about the kingdom, they

---

"Behold the days are coming,"
  says the Lord,
"That I will raise to David
  a Branch of righteousness;
A King shall reign and prosper,
And execute judgment and
  righteousness in the earth"
(Jer. 23:5, NKJV).

"I was watching in the night
  visions,
And behold, One like the Son
  of Man,
Coming with the clouds
  of heaven!
He came to the Ancient of Days,
And they brought Him near
  before Him.
Then to Him was given dominion
  and glory and a kingdom,
That all peoples, nations, and
  languages should serve Him.
His dominion is an everlasting
  dominion,
Which shall not pass away,
And His kingdom the one
Which shall not be destroyed"
(Dan. 7:13-14, NKJV).

apparently never imagined that it was imminent. John was saying that the kingdom is not a remote, future occurrence. The kingdom is here! Get ready! He called people to begin thinking of the kingdom of God as a present reality.

What was the role of John the Baptist in relationship to Jesus' ministry?
☐ John was sent to baptize Jesus because, without baptism, Jesus was powerless.
☐ John was sent to prepare the way for Jesus.
☐ John was sent to lead a ministry parallel and equal to Jesus' ministry.

John the Baptist's primary role in his brief ministry was to prepare the way for Jesus. John's baptism of Jesus marked the beginning of His public ministry. Later John introduced Jesus to his own disciples by saying, " 'Here is the Lamb of God, who takes away the sin of the world! This is the One I told you about: "After me comes a man who has surpassed me, because He existed before me." I didn't know Him, but I came baptizing with water so He might be revealed to Israel' " (John 1:29-31). By the time John was arrested and later beheaded, he had already fulfilled his mission of paving the way for the King.

The King appears. The next phase in the revelation of the kingdom of God began with Jesus' public ministry. The kingdom of God was the central theme of Jesus' teaching (see Mark 1:14-15), and many of Jesus' parables focused on kingdom principles. When the disciples asked Jesus why He used parables, He answered, " 'To know the secrets of the kingdom of heaven has been granted to you, but to them it has not been granted' " (Matt. 13:11). The Master Teacher made spiritual truth about the kingdom easy to comprehend through simple stories. Matthew 13 contains a series of parables that Jesus used to teach about the kingdom.

> "After John was arrested, Jesus went to Galilee, preaching the good news of God: 'The time is fulfilled, and the kingdom of God has come near. Repent and believe in the good news!' " (Mark 1:14-15).

> "Seek first the kingdom of God and His righteousness, and all these things will be provided for you" (Matt. 6:33).

- The parables of the sower and of the wheat and tares warn against enemies of the kingdom who seek to prevent a fruitful harvest.
- The parables of the mustard seed and of the leaven reveal the way tiny beginnings can have great results in the kingdom.
- The parables of the hidden treasure and of the pearl of great price teach the supreme value of the kingdom.
- The parable of the dragnet reveals truths about the King's final judgment of humanity.

The Sermon on the Mount (see Matt. 5—7), includes eight references to the kingdom of heaven. Among these teachings stands the tall admonition in Matthew 6:33. Read that verse in the margin.

In this verse Jesus gave a clear statement of personal priority. Of all things we might seek, He commands us to seek first the kingdom of God—the sovereign rule of God over our lives. The result will be a life of righteousness, as He is righteous. Paul echoed this idea in his statement "The kingdom of God is not eating and drinking, but righteousness, peace, and joy in the Holy Spirit" (Rom. 14:17). Righteousness refers to a right relationship with God that produces a righteous life—a Christlike

The Beatitudes: A Prescription for Kingdom Living

"The eight Beatitudes [see Matt. 5:3-10] describe a whole person blessed by God, living as God intended. ... The first four Beatitudes demonstrate need. The poor in spirit need God. The mourners need the Holy Spirit of God. ... The meek need others. The hungry for righteousness need spiritual food. ... The second four Beatitudes focus on giving. The merciful give God's grace to the world. The pure in heart give holiness to the world. The peacemakers give wholeness. The persecuted give themselves.

"The two halves of the Beatitudes are in balance. God gives of Himself because of our desperate need. The greater the need, the more abundant His giving. After receiving Christ, we move into the area of self-giving (the second four). We often cycle through these two sides so God can continue to grow and develop our character for greater service.

"The first four Beatitudes—poor in spirit, mourning (brokenness), meekness, and hungry for righteousness—are the keys to God's heart. God loves the needy. Persons who meet these conditions are more receptive than persons who do not. Our need and consequent receiving in the first four Beatitudes prepare our character for something greater.

"The second four Beatitudes—mercy, pure, peacemakers, and persecuted—are the keys to Christ's character. Because we needed God, He gave us Himself, and we are becoming like Christ. These second four qualities are Christlike. In them, we practice perfect giving because we have so much of God."[4]

life. In His Sermon on the Mount Jesus gave specific applications of the way a righteous person relates to various life situations, such as persecution, adultery, divorce, loving enemies, giving alms, praying, fasting, anxiety, judging others, and more. Each principle of kingdom living stands in sharp contrast to the values and behavior of this world. A kingdom person lives a distinctive lifestyle that brings salt and light to our society, serves God and others, and brings pleasure and glory to the King.

Righteousness: a right relationship with God that produces a righteous life—a Christlike life

Jesus conveyed kingdom truths in ways other than teaching. He worked miracles, healed the sick, raised the dead, and cast out demons. By exercising His authority over nature, disease, and the powers of evil, Jesus expressed His sovereignty as King of kings and Lord of lords.

Entering the Kingdom

Jesus made it clear how a person enters the kingdom of God. Most Jews assumed that because they were God's chosen people, they were already a part of His kingdom; they thought that their natural, physical birth guaranteed their citizenship in the kingdom. Jesus corrected this erroneous belief in His conversation with a rich young ruler. This man came to Jesus and asked, " 'Good Teacher, what must I do to inherit eternal life?' " Jesus replied by reminding him of the importance of keeping the Ten Commandments. He did this because this man assumed that he could earn his way into God's favor by his good deeds. In fact, he told Jesus he had kept all the commandments since he was a youth. However, this man loved wealth. Recognizing his covetousness, Jesus told him to sell everything he had, give the money to the poor, and follow Him. When the man turned away, Jesus said to His disciples, " 'How hard it is for those who have wealth to enter the kingdom of God. … It is easier for a camel to go through the eye of a needle than for a rich person to enter the kingdom of God' " (Mark 10:23-25). Jesus' point was that no one can enter the kingdom of God by good deeds. How, then, can a person gain entrance to the kingdom?

Describe how you think someone enters the kingdom of God. Then check your answer as you read.

Jesus chose Nicodemus to be the first to hear about the new birth. Nicodemus was a Pharisee, the most devout of the Jewish religious parties. He was a "ruler of the Jews," which means he belonged to the Sanhedrin, the Jewish ruling council (John 3:1). As a "teacher of Israel" (v. 10), Nicodemus was one of the most religious men of his time. He came to Jesus with sincere commendation: " 'Rabbi, we know that You have come from God as a teacher, for no one could perform these signs You do unless God were with him' " (v. 2). Nicodemus was an honest seeker who was drawn to Jesus by the obvious manifestation of supernatural power. He was sincere in his quest to learn from this heaven-sent Teacher.

Jesus responded by speaking to the deepest need of this religious man: " 'Unless someone is born again, he cannot see the kingdom of God' " (v. 3). Nicodemus then became the first person to hear the good news of John 3:16, which clearly reveals the terms for entering the kingdom of God: " 'Everyone who believes in [Jesus] will not perish but have eternal life.' "

"The kingdom of God is not coming with something observable; no one will say, 'Look here!' or 'There!' For you see, the kingdom of God is among you" (Luke 17:20-21).

Kingdom citizenship is not something a person achieves by good deeds; rather, a person receives this gift by faith. Eternal life—kingdom life—is the gift of God, made possible through the sacrifice of Jesus. Because He died, we who believe in Him will live eternally with Him in His kingdom forever.

The Nature of the Kingdom

Many of Jesus' hearers thought of the kingdom of God as a future reality—a time when God would reestablish His earthly reign as was true during the golden years when Saul, David, and Solomon ruled. These expectations missed the fact that God's rule is a present reality, manifested in His general rule over all creation and His spiritual rule in the hearts of His people (see Luke 17:20-21). *The Baptist Faith and Message* captures both aspects of the kingdom in this statement: "The kingdom of God includes both His general sovereignty over the universe and His particular kingship over men who willfully acknowledge Him as King. Particularly the Kingdom is the realm of salvation into which men enter by trustful, childlike commitment to Jesus Christ. Christians ought to pray and to labor that the Kingdom may come and God's will be done on earth. The full consummation of the Kingdom awaits the return of Jesus Christ and the end of this age."[5]

God's general rule over creation. God always has been and always will be the sovereign Ruler over all creation. He is the King of all kings. Therefore, the kingdom of God is not either a present or future reality but a timeless, eternal kingdom. The presence of evil powers, which cause much destruction and grief, do not threaten God's control. For His own reasons that are beyond our comprehension, God allows the Devil and his demons to create disorder and chaos in the midst of His good and perfect creation. However, the ultimate fate of God's enemies is sealed by His sovereign edict (see Rev. 11:15).

> "The kingdom of the world has become the kingdom of our Lord and of His Messiah, and He will reign forever and ever!" (Rev. 11:15).

Paul spoke of our Lord as the "only Sovereign, the King of kings" and the One who will return "in His own time" (1 Tim. 6:15). The King has absolute and complete control of the consummation of history. Time, as we know it, is in His hands, and His kingdom is beyond the limitations of time. Paul described this final victory: "Then comes the end, when He hands over the kingdom to God the Father, when He abolishes all rule and all authority and power. For He must reign until He puts all His enemies under His feet" (1 Cor. 15:24-25).

God's particular rule in believers. Every person who has ever lived, or will ever live, is subject to God's general sovereignty. God rules over all creation, all nature, all history, and all persons in a general sense. But the particular kingship of God refers to His reign in individuals who choose to acknowledge Christ as their personal Savior and Lord. Only those who bow in submission before Christ, call on Him for salvation, and trust Him for deliverance from the wages of sin enter the kingdom of God. Paul's words in Romans 14:17 describe the nature of the personal, particular kingdom of God in believers: "The kingdom of God is … righteousness, peace, and joy in the Holy Spirit." When King Jesus rules in a believer's heart, that person has the righteousness of God imparted to him, has peace with God, and experiences the joy of God—the joy of salvation.

Indicate the presence of these characteristics in your life. Circle a rating for each characteristic.

Righteousness	NONE	SOME	PLENTY	MAXED OUT
Peace	NONE	SOME	PLENTY	MAXED OUT
Joy	NONE	SOME	PLENTY	MAXED OUT

Being part of the kingdom of God is not static. It is not a matter of having a special position or status in life. Rather, it is dynamic—a living, powerful relationship with God. And it is this aspect of the nature of the kingdom that literally transforms a person's life. Paul was speaking about this kingdom truth when he wrote to the Christians in Colosse about a certain spiritual mystery: "God wanted to make known to those among the Gentiles the glorious wealth of this mystery, which is Christ in you, the hope of glory. ... I labor for this, striving with His strength that works powerfully in me" (Col. 1:27-29). Paul used the word *mystery* to refer not to something strange but to a truth that had been concealed from human understanding until God was ready to reveal it. Jesus Christ died, was buried, arose, and ascended to heaven, where He abides at the right hand of His Father. However, He also dwells, by His Spirit, in the heart of every believer. The presence of "Christ in you" not only identifies us as citizens of the kingdom of God but also empowers us to live the kingdom life (see v. 27). We live every moment in the presence of the King, and He lives in us.

> "It is God who is working among you both the willing and the working for His good purpose" (Phil. 2:13).

> "I labor for this, striving with His strength that works powerfully in me" (Col. 1:29).

> "May the God of peace, who brought up from the dead our Lord Jesus—the great Shepherd of the sheep—with the blood of the everlasting covenant, equip you with all that is good to do His will, working in us what is pleasing in His sight, through Jesus Christ, to whom be glory forever and ever" (Heb. 13:20-21).

God at work in believers. Jesus is not just present with us and living in us, but He is also actively at work in us. Dwelling in us by His Spirit, He faithfully works to make us more like Himself and to fulfill His purposes through us. Read the three Scriptures in the margin.

In *Experiencing God* authors Henry Blackaby and Claude King wrote, "As God's obedient child, you are in a love relationship with Him. He loves you and wants to involve you in His work. When He is ready, He will show you where He is working so you can join Him."[6] God invites you to join Him in doing His work. As kingdom citizens, we must identify where God is working and make ourselves available to join Him. This is the nature of the particular kingdom of God: Jesus is the sovereign King, we are His willing subjects who have been redeemed by His blood, and He works in us and through us to extend His kingdom.

Our Lord's Model Prayer expresses this understanding of the kingdom of God. When we pray for God's will to be " 'done on earth as it is in heaven' " (Matt. 6:11), we reflect God's rule in our hearts. We know Him as Father, honor His name, and desire His will to be done in and through us here and now. Being a kingdom citizen means that every believer is God's chosen vessel to become all He intended His children to be. This includes not only having character and conduct like Jesus but also being a witness to this world about the way others can share kingdom life. Our Lord declared that He came " 'to seek and to save the lost' " (Luke 19:10). To be like Him, we must be passionate about reaching the unsaved and thereby expanding His kingdom.

Being a kingdom citizen means being passionate about reaching unsaved people. If your church's evangelistic fervor mirrored your personal passion for reaching the lost, how would you describe the evangelistic condition of your church?

_____

_____

You and the Kingdom

Teachings on the kingdom of God have implications for an individual believer. Let me ask a series of questions to help you apply your understanding of the kingdom to your Christian life.

Have you entered the kingdom? Beware of assuming that because you believe in God and consider yourself to be a religious person, you are also a part of God's kingdom family. As Jesus told Nicodemus, one of the most righteous men of his day, " 'Unless someone is born again, he cannot see the kingdom of God' " (John 3:3). Make certain that you have turned to Jesus by faith as your only hope of salvation. Receive Him by calling on Him to come into your heart and be your Savior and Lord. John said, "God has given us eternal life, and this life is in His Son. The one who has the Son has life. The one who doesn't have the Son of God does not have life" (1 John 5:11-12). Have you bowed down to God's Son as the King of your life?

If you have not entered the kingdom, read "How to Be Saved" on page 41. If you are already saved, describe the time you entered the kingdom of God.

Are you a true worshiper of the King? The prophet Isaiah shared a remarkable, personal experience of seeing the Lord seated on His throne in heaven. Realizing the Lord's holiness deeply moved him and caused him to sense his sinfulness. Read his reaction in the margin.

This unusual worship experience not only convicted the prophet and led him to confess his sin, but through it the Lord also called him to " 'go, and tell this people' " (Isa. 6:9, NKJV). And Isaiah went. This is authentic worship—the offering of ourselves as servants of the Most High God. Does this describe your worship of God? Does your worship lead you to say with Isaiah, " 'Here am I! Send me' " (Isa. 6:8, NKJV)?

"Woe is me, for I am undone!
  Because I am a man
    of unclean lips,
  And I dwell in the midst
    of a people of unclean lips;
  For my eyes have seen the King,
  The LORD of hosts"
(Isa. 6:5, NKJV).

Assess your willingness to offer yourself as a servant of the King.
- ☐ I'm ready to obey and go where He leads.
- ☐ I'll do what He wants as long as I don't have to make sacrifices.
- ☐ I'm afraid I'm still holding on to control of my life.

Pray that your worship of the King will lead to greater commitment and obedience as His servant.

Are you secure in His sovereignty? Besides the planes that crashed into the Pentagon and the World Trade Center on September 11, 2001, a fourth plane, United Flight 93, was hijacked. The hijackers probably intended to crash into the nation's capitol building or the White House. However, before they could complete their mission, some passengers attacked the terrorists, forcing the plane to crash in an open field in Pennsylvania. One passenger was a young father named Todd Beamer—the man whose voice was heard on a cell phone saying, "Let's roll!"

Early in November, following the crash that killed everyone on board, Todd's wife, Lisa, was asked to speak to a women's conference. This widow, with two young children and a third on the way, stood before 25,000 women and said, "I've chosen to live in hope. ... Hope comes from knowing who is in control. Hope comes from knowing that we have a sovereign, loving God who is in control of every event of our lives. ... I hope for you that you can cling to the one who has all the power, and all the love, and all the care, because he's the one who's really in charge."[7] Do you live with this kind of confidence? Do you experience the peace that comes from knowing that King Jesus is working His good will on your behalf?

Identify the source of your security.

☐ My job ☐ My spouse and/or family ☐ God's sovereignty ☐ My wealth
☐ My routine ☐ My physical health ☐ My abilities

Pray and confess your need for the security and peace that only God can provide.

The next section of this chapter explores kingdom truths about Last Things. You will learn how the King of kings and Lord of lords will bring history to its conclusion in His own time and in His own way.

What Do We Believe About Last Things?

Genesis and Revelation are like two bookends. Genesis is the book of beginnings, which is the meaning of the word *genesis*. All created things, as well as social institutions, government, religion, good, and evil, find their roots in this Bible book. The other bookend is the Book of Revelation. As the word suggests, Revelation reveals the way God will bring all history to His intended conclusion.

"The Son of Man is going to come with His angels in the glory of His Father, and then He will reward each according to what he has done" (Matt. 16:27).

The study of Last Things is called *eschatology,* a term that comes from the Greek word *eschatos,* meaning *last* or *final.* Although Baptists disagree on various details of the order of these events, they agree with the biblical revelation of certain events that will occur at the end of time. Let's look at these events in detail.

The End of the World

The Bible depicts time as having a beginning and an end. When Jesus was asked, " 'What is the sign of Your coming and of the end of the age?' " He replied, " 'This good news of the kingdom will be proclaimed in all the world as a testimony to all nations. And then the end will come' " (Matt. 24:3,14). Jesus said that end of the world would definitely come someday.

When will the end come? Throughout history people have wondered when the end of the world would be. Jesus made it clear that the end of the world would be inaugurated by His return (see Matt. 16:27). But when questioned about the timing of His return, He replied,

" 'Now concerning that day or hour no one knows—neither the angels in heaven, nor the Son—except the Father' " (Mark 13:32). We do not know the exact day and hour of Jesus' return.

In spite of Jesus' statement, through the years many people have tried to predict the time of His return. William Miller, a Baptist preacher, set the date as 1843. When the Lord did not appear, Miller said that he miscalculated slightly and the date was 1844! After Miller died, his followers were led by Ellen White. She reported that Miller was right; the Lord came in 1843, but no one saw Him. This was the beginning of the Seventh-Day Adventist movement.

During the 20th century the leaders of the Jehovah's Witnesses, Charles Taze Russell and Joseph Rutherford, set a number of dates for the Lord's return. The first was 1914, followed by several other guesses, the last being 1975. Another religious group near Waco, Texas, was so certain about the time of the Lord's return that members sold all of their possessions, put on white robes, and waited on a hillside for Jesus' return.

What should be your response to someone who claims to know when Jesus will return?
- [ ] Pack and get ready.
- [ ] Verify the date with several other people.
- [ ] Be doubtful but prepared just in case.
- [ ] Be ready every day because no one knows when Jesus will return.

Remember that Jesus clearly stated that no one would know the time of the end of the age and His return. But He said that the Father knows. As Paul challenged his readers, "I charge you to keep the commandment without spot or blame until the appearing of our Lord Jesus Christ, which God will bring about in His own time" (1 Tim. 6:13-14).

Think about the results if we knew the date of Jesus' return. We would probably be less diligent about our service for Christ until just before His appearance. Knowing the certainty of His coming without knowing the time is a blessing. The fact that Jesus may return at any moment gives us a greater sense of urgency about reaching out to the lost with His message of life everlasting. God has His reasons for not revealing the time to us, but we can be sure that when He brings the end of the world, His timing will be absolutely right.

The return of Christ and the judgment. Although the time of Christ's return is unknown, Jesus assured His disciples that He would return. Shortly before He ascended, He promised, " 'I am going away to prepare a place for you. If I go away and prepare a place for you, I will come back and receive you to Myself, so that where I am you may be also' " (John 14:2-3). When Jesus ascended back to heaven, two angels affirmed His return: " 'Men of Galilee, why do you stand looking up into heaven? This Jesus, who has been taken from you into heaven, will come in the same way that you have seen Him going into heaven' " (Acts 1:11). Some interpreters have stated that Jesus' return will be secret and spiritual. But the angels' words clearly indicate that Jesus' return will be personal and visible. Paul echoed this same truth when he wrote, "The Lord Himself will descend from heaven with a shout, with the archangel's voice, and with the trumpet of God" (1 Thess. 4:16).

When Jesus comes, He will bring judgment, holding all people accountable for their sin. Jesus said, " 'God did not send His Son into the world that He might judge the world, but that the world might be saved through Him. Anyone who believes in Him is not judged, but anyone who does not believe is already judged, because he has not believed in the name of the One and Only Son of God. This, then, is the judgment: the light has come into the world, and people loved darkness rather than the light because their deeds were evil' " (John 3:17-19). This judgment, based on acceptance or rejection of Christ during a person's life, determines who goes to heaven and who goes to hell. All who rejected Jesus must face the consequence of their sin— eternal condemnation—while those who accepted Christ will spend eternity with Him in heaven. Paul's words in the margin confirm the fact of a future Judgment Day.

"God now commands all people everywhere to repent, because He has set a day on which He is going to judge the world in righteousness by the Man He has appointed" (Acts 17:30-31).

Believers will also be judged to determine their rewards, depending on their faithfulness as servants of Christ. First Corinthians 3:11-15 teaches that the Christian life is built on Jesus Christ. Some Christian lives are self-seeking, wrongly directed, and produced by human effort. Paul compared these lives to wood, hay, and stubble, which will burn up when tried by fire at the judgment seat of Christ. Although their rewards will be lost, these believers will still be saved. Other Christians serve Christ with pure motives, humility, and spiritual priorities. These believers' works are compared to gold, silver, and costly stones, which will survive testing at the judgment seat of Christ. These Christians will be rewarded for the lives they have led.

Satan and all other fallen angels will also be judged at the end of time. The end of their deceitful and destructive work will come when they are all cast into the lake of fire (see Rev. 20:10). This event marks the final triumph of truth and righteousness over evil.

Be ready. How should the fact of Jesus' return and His judgment of all people affect us today? Consider this unusual account of how some people once anticipated the Lord's return. On May 15, 1780, an uncanny darkness settled over New England. Cows came in from the fields, and birds roosted as if it were evening. Thinking that Judgment Day had come, some people began to panic, and many cried out to God in repentance. In the state council in Hartford, Connecticut, one legislator moved that they dismiss the session and prepare to meet God. Abraham Davenport stood and said, "I strongly object to this motion. If it is Judgment Day or not, I want to be found at my post of duty. I move that we bring in candles and be about the business at hand."[8] These believers had read Jesus' words:

"In those days, after that tribulation,
    The sun will be darkened,
    and the moon will not shed her light;
    the stars will be falling from the sky,
    and the celestial powers will be shaken.
Then they will see the Son of Man coming in clouds
with great power and glory" (Mark 13:24-25).

These New Englanders wanted to be ready when Jesus came. We too should be prepared. Jesus stated, " 'Be alert, since you don't know what day your Lord is coming. This is why you also should get ready, because the Son of Man is coming at an hour you do not expect' " (Matt. 24:42,44). Think about ways you can get ready for His return and the judgment.

> "Scoffers will come in the last days to scoff, following their own lusts, saying, 'Where is the promise of His coming? For ever since the fathers fell asleep, all things continue as they have been since the beginning of creation.' They willfully ignore this: long ago the heavens and the earth existed out of water and through water by the word of God. Through these the world of that time perished when it was flooded by water. But by the same word the present heavens and earth are held in store for fire, being kept until the day of judgment and destruction of ungodly men" (2 Pet. 3:3-7).

- *Anticipate Jesus' return.* If you took a poll asking people if they expect the Lord to come at any time, most would answer no. Read Peter's timely warning in the margin. As surely as Jesus came the first time, He will return, and we should remain aware that this could happen at any moment. We should begin every day by praying that He will prepare us to meet Him—even if He comes today!

- *Be serious about holy living.* Suppose that a very important person announced that he was coming to visit you in your home, but he didn't say when. What would you do? My guess is that you would make sure both the outside and inside of your house looked as good as possible. And you would want your own appearance to be the best. Paul urged Titus to prepare to meet Jesus by making sure his character and conduct were what they should be. He wrote, "The grace of God has appeared, with salvation for all people, instructing us to deny godlessness and worldly lusts and to live in a sensible, righteous, and godly way in the present age, while we wait for the blessed hope and the appearing of the glory of our great God and Savior, Jesus Christ" (Titus 2:11-13). The Apostle John made this same appeal for godly living: "Dear friends, we are God's children now, and what we will be has not yet been revealed. We know that when He appears, we will be like Him, because we will see Him as He is. And everyone who has this hope in Him purifies himself just as He is pure" (1 John 3:2-3). The blessed hope of seeing Jesus has a definite purifying effect on all who love Him. What about you? Is your house in order?

- *Help others be ready.* One of the strongest motivators for evangelism is the certainty of Jesus' return. Everyone we know—all of our family members, friends, and acquaintances—along with everyone else must stand before the Lord. Those who are not prepared will hear these sad words from our Savior: " 'I never knew you! Depart from Me, you lawbreakers!' " (Matt. 7:23). Do we care enough to reach out to these with the good news that Jesus saves from sin and offers eternal life? All believers are "ambassadors for Christ" who have been given the "message of reconciliation" (2 Cor. 5:19-20). This is one reason the Lord does not take us to heaven as soon as we are saved; He leaves us to lead others to know Him and be ready to meet Him.

The Millennium

The word *millennium*, which comes from two Latin words meaning *a thousand years,* refers to the thousand-year reign of Christ on earth (see Rev. 20:1-7). This single Bible passage has probably produced more controversy over end-time events than any other. Evangelical Christians usually hold one of three major viewpoints about the order of events connected to the thousand-year reign of Christ.

Postmillennialism. The prefix *post* means *after.* Adherents maintain that Christ will come after a thousand-year binding of Satan (see Rev. 20:1-3). Prior to Jesus' return, world conditions will progressively improve through the spread of Christianity. Eventually, principles of righteousness will rule the world for one thousand years. Then Christ will return to bring the resurrection of all the dead and the final judgment.

Amillennialism. This view does not interpret the millennium to be a literal thousand years, so the prefix *a* (*no*) precedes the word *millennium.* Christ's reign is in the hearts of His people; Satan is presently a defeated enemy. Amillennialists believe that the present church age is a time of indefinite length during which the struggle between good and evil will continue until Christ's return. His return will bring a general resurrection of the dead, the judgment, and the beginning of the eternal state.

Premillennialism. This is the position I believe best interprets Scripture on this subject. Those who accept this view believe that Christ will return before (*pre*) His thousand-year reign on earth. His next appearance will be His coming in the clouds to take believers out of the earth to join Him and the saints already in heaven. This event is called the rapture, from a Latin translation of *caught up* in 1 Thessalonians 4:17.

The "great tribulation" Jesus referred to in Matthew 24:21 plays an important role in the premillennial view (also see Rev. 7:14). Premillennialists disagree about the relative timing of the rapture to the tribulation. Thus, pretribulationalists, midtribulationalists, and posttribulationalists position the rapture as before, during, or following the tribulation. I believe the pretribulation-rapture view is the most consistent with Scripture.

- Dispensational premillennialism holds to a literal one-thousand-year reign of Christ on earth following a seven-year period of great tribulation. During the millennium Satan will be bound, and all the saints will rule with Christ on earth. After this period Satan will be loosed for a short time, then cast into the lake of fire. The final judgment will occur at this time.
- Historic premillennialists accept the literal reign of Christ and His people on earth, during which time Satan is bound. This group expects Christ's return to occur between the tribulation and the millennium. Some proponents of this view see the millennium as symbolic and do not insist on a literal thousand-year reign of Christ.

How does your life reflect your anticipation of Jesus' return? _____

_____

How does your life give evidence of your seriousness about holy living? _____

_____

How are you helping others be ready for Christ's return? _____

_____

Life After Death

We have all been to funerals where we gazed into a casket at the physical remains of a loved one or friend. From all outward appearances this is the end of the person. But is this all there is to life? Some people believe that human souls cease to exist after death. This position is called annihilationism. In contrast, the Bible teaches that God creates all humans as immortal persons. The Genesis account states, "The LORD God formed the man out of the dust from the ground and breathed the breath of life into his nostrils, and the man became a living being [soul]" (Gen. 2:7). The term *soul* refers to the entire human being—body, mind, emotions, and spirit. Greek philosophers thought of a person as a soul living temporarily in a physical body. However, the biblical view is that a human being exists as a whole person for eternity. God created us as whole persons from the beginning, and we remain that way forever. What happens after a person's physical death?

The intermediate state. At death the bodies of both the saved and the unsaved are put aside to go back to the earth, and their souls enter an intermediate state. Believers are promised new, resurrection bodies at the end of time (see 1 Cor. 15:35-58), but in the meantime Scripture describes believers as being "at home" with the Lord (see 2 Cor. 5:6,8), or in paradise (see Luke 23:43). *Paradise,* from a Persian word meaning *a beautiful park or garden,* refers to the presence of God. When the righteous die, they immediately go to be with God in a state of blessedness, rest, and joy. Paradise is a conscious state in God's presence. By now the person's response to God's offer of salvation has already determined his destiny, so he has no second chance such as purgatory. Paradise is also an incomplete state. Because we are body as well as spirit, redemption will be complete only when our bodies are resurrected at the end of time.

At death unbelievers spend the intermediate state in hades, the realm of the dead, to await their final judgment and punishment. However, hades is also a state of punishment, as described in the account Jesus gave of the rich man and Lazarus in Luke 16:19-31. As shown in this passage, hades is a place of torment and agony where unbelievers are conscious of their suffering and the fact that they cannot escape. Here the condemned suffer until the time of the resurrection, the judgment, and their consignment to hell.[9]

The resurrection of the body. The Bible teaches the resurrection of the dead. Read Jesus' words in the margin. Those who are in paradise and those who are in hades will not spend eternity in this intermediate state. The resurrection awaits all of the dead.

"An hour is coming, and is now here, when the dead will hear the voice of the Son of God, and those who hear will live. A time is coming when all who are in the graves will hear His voice and come out—those who have done good things, to the resurrection of life, but those who have done wicked things, to the resurrection of judgment" (John 5:25,28-29).

Paul explored the meaning of the resurrection in 1 Corinthians 15. He stated that Christ's resurrection is the basis of the believer's hope to be raised from death (see vv. 20-22). But if the body decays and goes back to the earth, how can it be raised? Paul explained that we will not have the same flesh-and-blood bodies we have on earth (see vv. 35-44). God will shape a resurrection body for each believer that is perfectly suited to eternal life with Him. We will not be disembodied spirits. We will be real persons with real identities and personalities. And the resurrection body will not succumb to aging, decay, and death (see vv. 53-54).

The resurrection will take place when Jesus returns. Read in the margin Paul's description of this event. When the believers who have died are resurrected and those who are alive when Jesus returns are transformed, all of God's people will have imperishable and immortal bodies.

The Bible also teaches that the unsaved dead will be resurrected to face their final judgment (see John 5:25-29; Acts 24:15; Rev. 20:13).[10] After the judgment everyone will spend eternity in heaven or hell, depending on the person's response to Jesus' offer of salvation.

"We will not all fall asleep, but we will all be changed, in a moment, in the twinkling of an eye, at the last trumpet. For the trumpet will sound, and the dead will be raised incorruptible, and we will be changed" (1 Cor. 15:51-52).

Hell: a place of punishment. Three New Testament words are used to describe hell. *Hades,* the equivalent of the Old Testament word *sheol,* is the place where unsaved persons go when they die to await their resurrection and judgment. *Hades* also refers to a place of punishment that will ultimately be cast into the lake of fire (see Rev. 20:13-14). *Tartaros* is found one time (see 2 Pet. 2:4) to describe a place where certain fallen angels are kept until final judgment. *Gehenna* was a garbage dump outside Jerusalem where fires continuously burned to consume refuse, including dead bodies that were not claimed for burial. Jesus frequently used this word to refer to hell, the place of eternal torment (see Matt. 5:22,29; 10:28).

What is hell? Check one definition. Then verify your answer as you read.
☐ A figurative place believers describe to motivate people to accept Jesus
☐ A real place of eternal torment
☐ The spiritual state of those who refuse to accept Jesus Christ

Jesus said more about hell than about heaven. We get an idea of the horror of this place from the description of hades in Luke 16:19-31. From Jesus' account of the rich man and Lazarus we learn the following truths.

- *Hell is a rational place.* The man in hell was conscious of his surroundings, he remembered, he pleaded with Abraham, he suffered in flames, and he called his abode a "place of torment" (v. 28).
- *Hell is a separated place.* The rich man was separated from Abraham and those in heaven, he was separated from his family members on earth, and he was told that a great chasm that could not be crossed was fixed between him and those in heaven.
- *Hell is a place of torment.* There is no hope of escape. The suffering of those in hell is compounded by memories of opportunities refused and an awareness that they cannot influence those left behind who might be headed there. The man in hell asked for help to be sent to his brothers to prevent them from coming there, but his request was denied. Other New Testament passages describe hell as a place of wailing and gnashing of teeth, a lake of fire, outer darkness, and a place of suffering.
- *Hell is an eternal place.* Jesus spoke of eternal punishment and eternal life in the same sentence (see Matt. 25:46). The fire of hell is called an "eternal fire" (Jude 7).
- *Hell is a logical place.* When we look at the violence, hatred, murder, immorality, injustice, ungodliness, and wickedness on earth, we know there has to be a place to punish evildoers. What kind of place would heaven be if evil people went there? The rich man in hell was reminded that in his former life he lived in luxury while Lazarus begged at his gate. The time had come to settle the score. Hell makes sense.

Heaven: a place of perfection. The Bible also describes heaven as a real place.

Read Jesus' words in the margin and underline each time He used the word *place* or *places*.

Jesus used the word *place(s)* three times in this passage. Jesus came from heaven, has gone back to heaven, and knows heaven to be a real place.

What is this place like? The Book of Revelation refers to heaven more than any other book of the Bible. The most elaborate description of heaven is found in Revelation 21—22. John wrote, "I saw a new heaven and a new earth, for the first heaven and the first earth had passed away" (Rev. 21:1). Notice what will not be there:

"In My Father's house are many dwelling places; if not, I would have told you. I am going away to prepare a place for you. If I go away and prepare a place for you, I will come back and receive you to Myself, so that where I am you may be also" (John 14:2-3).

- No sun or moon and yet no darkness, for God's glory illuminates it.
- No temple or place of worship and yet continuous worship, for the Lord is its sanctuary.
- No evildoers, such as murderers, sexually immoral, sorcerers, idolaters, and liars, for only redeemed saints whose names are written in the Lamb's book of life will be admitted.
- No crying, tears, grief, pain, suffering, or death, for all unpleasant, grievous experiences of life on earth will have passed away.
- No more separation from fellow believers, no disappointments, and no temptations, for Satan and all his evil hosts will have been cast into the lake of fire.

From the previous characteristics of heaven, which is most encouraging to you? Why?

_____

What will be in heaven? Heaven is a place of beauty beyond description, joy beyond compare, and fellowship with God beyond imagination. A heavenly city called New Jerusalem is described as being made of pure gold, with high walls standing on 12 foundations made of precious stones and with 12 gates that never close, each made of a single pearl. A beautiful river of crystal water flows from the throne of God down the middle street of the city. And on each side of the river stands the tree of life bearing 12 kinds of fruit with leaves for the healing of the nations.

Who will be in heaven? Heaven has always been the home of God. Jesus called it " 'My Father's house' " (John 14:2). Jesus, the Lamb of God, will be there. The Holy Spirit will be present there. And the bride of Christ, the church—composed of all saved persons throughout all ages—will permanently reside in heaven. Also, an innumerable host of angels will be there.

Perfected in Glory

"One of our greatest joys in eternity future will be our total conformity to the image of Christ. That will inevitably bring many perfections that are now inconceivable.

• *"A perfect environment.* Our Christlikeness is presently frustrated by evil. ... But in heaven we will have a perfect environment. The physical (if that is the appropriate word) ... will show God's glory on every hand. Those around us will help and never hinder.

• *"Perfect relationships.* All relationships will derive from our primary love for God. His supremacy in all points will unite us in a bond never experienced on earth.

• *"Perfect bodies.* No allergy, imperfection, or physical defect will be possible in Christ's unrestricted presence. Our faculties and senses will always respond appropriately to every opportunity.

• *"Perfect minds.* In this life we find it quite difficult to maintain a consistently godly direction of thought. In eternity future our mind will be integrated— in tune with God, ever at peace with itself.

• *"Perfect beauty.* At long last we will enjoy the beauty of holiness—perfect beauty. As glorious as our new environment will be, the outer glories will pale in comparison with our new appreciation of

the inner, perfected attributes.

• *"Perfect communication.* On earth many fights and quarrels originate in our failure to communicate properly. In eternity not only will we say it right, but our fellow royals will also hear what we say. All faculties will function in a totality not now known.

• *"Perfect consciousness.* At rare times in prayer we now become conscious of the unhindered presence of God. We have begun to yearn for more consciousness. In eternity future we will have perfect consciousness. Perfect consciousness is that which faultlessly perceives God."[11]

Revelation 4—5 describes a scene in which the saints are joined by angels and celestial creatures to worship the Lord on His throne. The number of angels is given as "countless thousands, plus thousands of thousands" (Rev. 5:11).

What will we do in heaven? Worship will be foremost. John wrote, "I heard every creature in heaven, on earth, under the earth, on the sea, and everything in them say:

> "Blessing and honor and glory and dominion
> to the One seated on the throne,
> and to the Lamb, forever and ever!" (Rev. 5:13).

All the redeemed of all the ages will unite in singing God's praises, assisted by all the heavenly hosts. What a glorious experience that will be—and there will be no end to it! But heaven is more than worship; authentic worship always leads to service. In one of his visions of heaven, John saw a multitude of Christians who served God "day and night in His sanctuary" (Rev. 7:15). Worship and service will be the occupations of all the redeemed. Our worship and service will be perfect because only in heaven will we have a complete understanding of God and His mysterious ways. Only then will we know the full depth of Christ's love for us. And only in heaven will we know the motives of those we knew on earth and the depth of their love for us and for the Lord.

"The one who believes in the Son has eternal life, but the one who refuses to believe in the Son will not see life; instead, the wrath of God remains on him" (John 3:36).

Although hell makes sense, heaven doesn't. No sinner deserves a place of perfect provision and happiness for eternity. Justice would conclude that we all should be punished for our transgressions against God. This is why the gospel is such good news. God loved all humankind so much that He sent His Son, the only One good enough to die in our place, so that we could be delivered from the consequences of sin (see John 3:36) and live with Him forever. The best thing about heaven is found in Jesus' words " 'I will come back and receive you to Myself, so that where I am you may be also' " (John 14:3). Heaven is being with Jesus!

The Final Victory

Believers look forward to the consummation of history, when the world passes away and a new heaven and earth are created (see Rev. 21:1-3). We are told to wait for this time expectantly (see 2 Pet. 3:13). Paul described the coming event in 1 Corinthians 15:24-28. At that time Jesus will defeat every enemy, including death. The One who established the kingdom and presently rules it from His throne in heaven will deliver it to His Father. The perfect society Jesus taught in the Sermon on the Mount and in other teachings will be realized, for only the redeemed will be there, and God will be its light (see Rev. 21:23).[12]

Christian scholars disagree on the timing and sequence of events during the final period of human history. We must not make a specific view a test of orthodoxy or fellowship. However, we can agree on the clear biblical truths summarized in *The Baptist Faith and Message:* "God, in His own time and in His own way, will bring the world to its appropriate end. According to His promise, Jesus Christ will return personally and visibly in glory to the earth; the dead will be raised; and Christ will judge all men in righteousness. The unrighteous will be consigned to Hell, the place of everlasting punishment. The righteous in their resurrected and glorified bodies will receive their reward and will dwell forever in Heaven with the Lord."[13]

Those who are in Christ know for certain where this world is headed!

What have you learned in this chapter that would help you respond to someone who has been affected by a tragic personal, national, or international situation?

_____

_____

_____

_____

_____

_____

[1]William Eckhardt, "War-Related Deaths Since 3000 B.C.," *Bulletin for Peace Proposals* (Dec. 1991), in George Hunsinger, *Disruptive Grace: Studies in the Theology of Karl Barth* (Grand Rapids: William B. Eerdmans Publishing Company, 2000), 6–7.

[2]Gene Mims, *Thine Is the Kingdom* (Nashville: LifeWay Press, 1997), 18.

[3]Adapted from Roy T. Edgemon, *The Doctrines Baptists Believe* (Nashville: Convention Press, 1988), 89–91.

[4]T. W. Hunt and Claude V. King, *The Mind of Christ* (Nashville: LifeWay Press, 1994), 112–13.

[5]*The Baptist Faith and Message* (Nashville: LifeWay Christian Resources of the Southern Baptist Convention, 2000), 15.

[6]Henry Blackaby and Claude King, *Experiencing God* (Nashville: Broadman & Holman, 1994), 74.

[7]Lisa Beamer and Ken Abraham, *Let's Roll* (Carol Stream, IL: Tyndale House, 2002), 276–77.

[8]Newsletter; First Baptist Church; Lubbock, TX; 15 September 1988.

[9]Adapted from Edgemon, *The Doctrines Baptists Believe,* 127–30.

[10]Ibid., 130–32.

[11]T. W. Hunt and Melana Hunt Monroe, *From Heaven's View* (Nashville: LifeWay Press, 2002), 160–61.

[12]Adapted from Edgemon, *The Doctrines Baptists Believe,* 137–38.

[13]*The Baptist Faith and Message,* 15.

CHAPTER 7

How Can We Participate in God's Plan?

At heart I'm a city boy. I have found my most fruitful ministry among thousands of people. But I love the country, and over the years I've spent time there as often as I can. Several years ago one of my best friends bought a ranch about 50 miles west of Fort Worth, and I often stay there. I have to admit that life on the ranch isn't really roughing it. The double-wide trailer is complete with comfortable beds; hot, running water; a modern kitchen; a computer; and, of course, satellite TV!

During one bitterly cold Christmas season I spent several days at the ranch with my friend. A number of cows were getting ready to have calves, so around 10:00 p.m. my friend decided to go out and check on them. Soon he came back and said, "Come on! You've got to help me pull a calf!" We rushed to the barn, where a cow was struggling to have her calf. She never would have made it without us. We finally had to reach in and tie a rope around the calf's feet and pull the calf out. About three hours later we had to do the same thing with another calf.

It took two of us to do that job. The difficult births of those two calves required four hands and separate assignments for each of us. Without both of us, the calves and probably the cows would have died. I learned again that night that some things can't be done by yourself. It took the cooperation of two persons to accomplish that task.

In the kingdom of God it takes the cooperation of His people to accomplish the tasks God has set before us. Lone Ranger Christianity is not biblical Christianity. The church of our Lord requires all of us working together. The New Testament consistently emphasizes the idea of one another. We are to help one another, encourage one another, pray for one another, love one another, and serve one another. To accomplish the assignment God has given us, we must first realize that we are part of a larger body of believers.

The final chapter in our study explores how we can make a significant difference in our world by cooperating with the other citizens of God's kingdom. Such efforts can be built only on a foundational understanding and acceptance of our role as Jesus' disciple.

Make a Difference as Jesus' Disciple

Sometimes I have wondered, *What difference does it make if I do this? After all, I am just one person in a very big world.* I once read a story that helps answer that question. John Warr was an apprentice shoemaker in England during the 18th century. He wanted to be a faithful witness for Christ but had limited opportunities. One day a new apprentice was hired, and John began talking with him about spiritual matters. The new man was not interested until he was caught stealing from his employer. He then asked John to help him and pray for him. As the result of John's influence, this thief became a Christian. As the two men studied and prayed together, they matured in their relationships with the Lord. This shoemaker, whose name was William Carey, later became a missionary to India, where he influenced thousands of people for Christ and became known as the father of modern missions.[1]

This story could be repeated about thousands of ordinary people whom the Lord has used to make a significant difference in the world. How does this happen? Where do we begin? Our Lord Jesus began making a difference through men He chose to be His disciples. Today Jesus is also searching for disciples who will faithfully follow and serve Him. We must understand certain facts about being a disciple whom Jesus can use to make a difference.

Disciples Are Called by the Master

Jesus chose and called the first twelve disciples, beginning with two brothers, Simon Peter and Andrew. As He walked along the Sea of Galilee, Jesus said to these fishermen, " 'Follow Me,' He told them, 'and I will make you fishers of men!' " (Matt. 4:19). Jesus was saying, "You make the choice to follow Me, and I will make the change from fishermen to fishers of men."

Disciple: a learner—someone who is devoted to the teachings of a trusted leader

Jesus' call to discipleship continues today. He says to everyone, " 'If anyone wants to be My follower, he must deny himself, take up his cross, and follow Me. For whoever wants to save his life will lose it, but whoever loses his life because of Me and the gospel will save it' " (Mark 8:34-35). The call to discipleship is a call to die—to die to yourself and live for Christ. The most widely known symbol for Christianity is a cross, not only because Jesus died there but also because He calls us to take up our own crosses—to die to self and to this world.

To what are you most devoted?
☐ Family   ☐ Job or school   ☐ Sports   ☐ Entertainment
☐ Self-fulfillment   ☐ Church activities   ☐ God   ☐ Other: _____

Because God's plan includes a call for us to die, Christianity is not primarily about us—getting what we want or finding happiness and fulfillment—but choosing to deny self and follow the One who gave Himself for the sake of others. If you have accepted Christ as your Savior and Lord, you have answered His call to become His disciple. But although He extends His call to everyone, billions of people haven't heard that they can be Jesus' disciples. Jesus has called

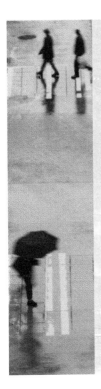

Take Up Your Cross and Follow Me

"A disciple of Christ is a person who makes Christ the Lord of his or her life. ...
A disciple's first commitment is to deny yourself [see Luke 9:23]. That does not mean
to reject your identity but to renounce the self-centered life."[2] To do that, a disciple
of Christ practices the following six disciplines of the Christian life.

1. "*Spend time with the Master.* Growing disciples read their Bibles and pray every day. ...

2. "*Live in the Word.* The Word is the living Word, Jesus Christ, and the written Word,
   the Bible. As you read the Bible, God speaks to you. ...

3. "*Pray in faith.* Prayer is an integral part of a believer's walk with the Lord. Personal
   prayer, in which you talk and listen to God, supports a Christian lifestyle. ...

4. "*Fellowship with believers.* Christians need one another. ... Fellowship provides support,
   leadership, accountability, strength, encouragement, and direction for a unified mission.

5. "*Witness to the world.* ... Witnessing is living in a manner that bears evidence of a strength
   that comes only from the Lord and that draws others to Christ. Witnessing is also
   sharing the good news of Jesus Christ. ...

6. "*Minister to others.* ... Growing disciples minister unselfishly, even to persons who have
   nothing to give in return. You minister because you walk in a relationship with Christ."[3]

you to deny yourself and share the good news so that everyone will have the opportunity
to hear His call.

Read the boxed article above. In which area do you need the most improvement?

_____

What will you do to strengthen this discipline? _____

Disciples Have a Personal Relationship with the Master

Authentic Christianity is not a religion; it is a relationship. Right doctrine is essential as the
framework of our faith, but we must give primary emphasis to an intimate relationship with
Jesus Christ. He is not only our Master but also our Friend (see John 15:13-15).

Healthy relationships require good communication. Bible study and prayer are two basic
ways you communicate with your Lord. When you open His Word, you open the opportunity
for Him to speak directly to you. In chapter 1 you learned that God's Word is reliable, authori-
tative, and "profitable for teaching, for rebuking, for correcting, for training in righteousness"
(2 Tim. 3:16)—for everything you need to be a complete disciple. You can receive God's
personal message when you read God's Word. Each time you open the Bible, pause and offer

this prayer of young Samuel: " 'Speak, LORD, for Your servant hears' " (1 Sam. 3:9-10, NKJV). Pray a similar prayer each time you are involved in a group Bible study, listen to a sermon, or read devotional material. Ask the Lord to speak His truth to your heart, thank Him for faithfully doing so, and listen for what your Master wants to teach you.

You can also share your heart with your best Friend through prayer. Praise Him, declare your love for Him, and admit your dependence on Him as your source and strength. The Lord invites you to share your honest concerns and desires with Him (see Matt. 7:7-8). Although He already knows your thoughts and needs, your prayer of faith enables you to align your heart, mind, and character with His will (see Matt. 6:10). Through prayer you can claim God's promises—His constant presence, power, and guidance.

No other aspect of the Christian experience is as important as getting to know the Lord in a personal way. The time you spend with Jesus prepares you for the service He wants to accomplish through you and cultivates the personal relationship you will enjoy with Him throughout eternity.

A growing disciple of Jesus maintains the discipline of a regular quiet time with Him. I hope that you have already developed this discipline; if not, I urge you to make your time with God a priority. The box "How to Have a Quiet Time" on page 139 will help you get started.

> "Keep asking, and it will be given to you. Keep searching, and you will find. Keep knocking, and the door will be opened to you. For everyone who asks receives, and the one who searches finds, and to the one who knocks, the door will be opened" (Matt. 7:7-8).

> "Your kingdom come.
> Your will be done
> on earth as it is in heaven"
> (Matt. 6:10).

Disciples Are Under the Authority of the Master

Discipleship means lordship—Jesus' lordship over His disciple. On one occasion Jesus asked this probing question of His disciples: " 'Why do you call Me "Lord, Lord," and don't do the things I say?' " (Luke 6:46). If we claim that Jesus is our Lord but do not obey Him, we are guilty of hypocrisy. He does not expect perfection from us; however, He is concerned about direction. Are we committed to doing His will? Are we diligently working to obey His commands?

A common area of pretense in a believer's life is corporate worship. When we join a congregation of believers in singing the great songs of the faith, we sometimes express with our lips surrender and commitment to Jesus as Lord while not practicing such personal devotion in our lives. We can listen to excellent preaching and agree with all that is said without acting on the message. Examine your level of obedience to your Lord. Are you truly attempting to be what you appear to be as a disciple of Jesus? James warned that when you fail to obey God's Word, you deceive yourself about your commitment: "Be doers of the word and not hearers only, deceiving yourselves" (Jas. 1:22).

Reflect on your favorite hymn or chorus. Describe how it expresses your commitment to God.

Another area that reveals your surrender to Jesus' authority is your worldview. Your worldview is the set of beliefs by which you make ethical and moral decisions. In our postmodern society more and more people deny absolute truth and reject reliable, fixed principles that govern life. When only personal preferences guide decision making, the result is ungodly practices like abortion on demand, euthanasia, human cloning, a homosexual lifestyle, and disregard for morality. The writer of Proverbs warned about the result when people choose their own way:

> **Worldview:** the set of assumptions and beliefs that guide your thoughts, attitudes, and actions

There is a way that seems right to a man,
but its end is the way to death (Prov. 14:12).

Name some things in our society that seem right to people but are contrary to God's Word.

Our ultimate authority does not lie in human reason or opinions but in God's truth as revealed in His Word. That Word tells us, "Do not be conformed to this age, but be transformed by the renewing of your mind, so that you may discern what is the good, pleasing, and perfect will of God" (Rom. 12:2). God's Word and the indwelling presence of Christ constitute your authority in life.

I urge you to commit to a biblical worldview. Resolve to determine what is right and what is of intrinsic worth by consulting and obeying God's Word. Be controlled by one supreme truth: Jesus is Lord!

How to Have a Quiet Time

1. Make a personal quiet time the top priority of your day. Select a time to spend with God that fits your schedule. Usually, morning is preferable, but you may want or need to choose another time.

2. Prepare the night before. If your quiet time is in the morning, set your alarm. Select a place where you can be alone. Gather materials, such as your Bible, a notebook, and a pen or a pencil, and put them in the place selected.

3. Develop a balanced plan of Bible reading and prayer. Pray for guidance during your quiet time. Follow a systematic plan to read your Bible. Use a devotional guide if desired. Make notes of what God says to you through His Word. Pray in response to the Scriptures you have read.

4. Be persistent until you are consistent. Strive for consistency rather than for length of time spent. Expect interruptions and plan around them.

5. Focus on the Person you are meeting rather than on the habit of having the quiet time. God created you with a capacity for fellowship with Him, and He saved you to bring about that fellowship.[4]

Disciples Become like the Master

The most influential person who ever lived was Jesus Christ. Think of the difference you could make if Jesus lived His life in and through you. This is exactly what authentic Christianity is all about! As the Apostle Paul said, "Christ lives in me" (Gal. 2:20). Christ is not only present in every believer but also actively working to bring about an amazing, miraculous transformation into His likeness. Read 2 Corinthians 3:18 in the margin.

> "We all, with unveiled faces, are reflecting the glory of the Lord and are being transformed into the same image from glory to glory; this is from the Lord who is the Spirit" (2 Cor. 3:18).

The word for *transformed* in this verse, which is the root of our English word *metamorphosis,* is used to describe the biological change in form that occurs in insects like butterflies. God is in the process of transforming every believer into the likeness of His Son, Jesus Christ. His will is for us to become progressively more and more like Jesus, and His Spirit is diligently seeking to perfect this glorious transformation. The character of Jesus—love, joy, peace, patience, kindness, goodness, faith, gentleness, and self-control (see Gal. 5:22-23)—should become more and more characteristic of every believer as we grow in Christlikeness.

> "Show family affection to one another with brotherly love" (Rom. 12:10).

Our part in this transformation is to acknowledge our total dependence on the Spirit of Christ to accomplish His work. We must also trust Him to make this change. We should begin every day by praying, "Lord, have Your way with me. Thank You that You will faithfully do Your work of changing me into Your likeness today." We must then be diligent in cooperating with God as He brings change in our mind, character, will, and emotions. We do this by choosing God's ways instead of our ways, by feeding on His Word, by spending time in prayer with Him, and by yielding to the direction of the Holy Spirit in our lives.

> "The one who loves God must also love his brother" (1 John 4:21).

As we become more like Christ, He uses us to influence others. The word *influence* is a combination of two Latin words meaning *in flow.* The power of God's Spirit flows into us and affects the lives of those around us. Jesus called believers " 'the salt of the earth' " and " 'the light of the world' " (Matt. 5:13-14). We are to have a penetrating influence in our world as the power of Jesus' life literally flows into us and out from us.

As you have learned in this study, the most important influence you can have is to communicate to others that Jesus saves from sin and death. Take every opportunity to spread this good news wherever you go—home, work, school, leisure activities, and intentional witnessing visits. You have also learned that you can be a Christian influence in society by becoming involved in social issues, by living an ethical lifestyle, and by ministering to others. In addition, don't underestimate the power of Christlike love to influence others (see Rom. 12:10; 1 John 4:21 in the margin). Let Christ's indwelling presence shine through your character and actions. Allowing Christ to live through you will create many opportunities to influence others for His kingdom.

Disciples Are Willing to Sacrifice for the Master

Jesus endured hardship and discomfort during His earthly life. Why should His disciples expect a life of pleasure and ease? Discipleship carries with it the obligation to risk and sacrifice for the Master. Jesus made no attempt to conceal the unpleasant consequences of following Him. He told His disciples, " 'If they persecuted Me, they will also persecute you' " (John 15:20). The Gospels and the Book of Acts reveal that Jesus' first followers faced many trials and mistreatment simply for identifying with Him.

In spite of this biblical evidence, Christian leaders today rarely warn potential disciples of the likelihood of suffering. Most churches promise peace, joy, and fulfillment for those who accept Christ. Blessings are certainly part of the Christian experience, but so is suffering. Perhaps this is why many believers are surprised when opposition comes. One woman came to her pastor and made this request: "Please pray that God will give me a different job." When the pastor asked the reason for her request, the woman said that she was the only Christian in her workplace, and her coworkers often ridiculed her because of her faith. The pastor wisely asked, "Where are lights installed?" She replied, "In dark places." Her pastor then asked her, "Have you ever considered the possibility that God put you in your job so that you could be a light in the darkness?" Several months later the woman reported to her pastor that she was thankful to be working in the same place. Why the change of heart? Three of her coworkers had become Christians as the result of her witness!

David Watson, an Anglican priest, wrote two sentences that have haunted me for years: "It is widely held that the battle of the century will be between Marxism, Islam, and Third-world Christianity. Western Christianity is considered too weak and ineffective to contribute anything significant to this universal struggle."[5] I've been unable to discredit that sobering accusation. I fear that the church in America has retreated from the battle for souls to pursue comfort. We have recruited disciples for Jesus by promising safety and contentment rather than calling them to the way of the cross.

New Testament discipleship demands self-denial, self-sacrifice, and a willingness to suffer for Jesus' sake. The Apostle Paul was well acquainted with the hardships that accompany obedience to Christ. After telling the Corinthians about his sufferings, he wrote: "He [Christ] said to me, 'My grace is sufficient for you, for power is perfected in weakness.' Therefore, I will most gladly boast all the more about my weaknesses, so that Christ's power may reside in me. So because of Christ, I am pleased in weaknesses, in insults, in catastrophes, in persecutions, and in pressures. For when I am weak, then I am strong" (2 Cor. 12:9-10). Do you understand what Paul meant?

Do you regard pain and suffering as opportunities to allow Christ's power to be revealed through your weakness? ☐ Yes, I regard suffering that way. ☐ No, I don't usually think that way.

Randy Alcorn was the pastor of a growing church of two thousand members in Boring, Oregon. As someone who believed in living, not just discussing, his convictions, Randy was active in prolife causes. After participating in a peaceful demonstration at an abortion clinic, Randy and others were sued by the clinic. The court ordered him to compensate the clinic for lost income during the demonstration. Randy told the judge, "I will pay anyone money I owe them, but I will not write out a check to an abortion clinic, because they'll use it to keep killing babies."

The court then ordered Randy's church to pay a portion of Randy's wages to the abortion clinic. To prevent the church from giving money to the clinic, Randy resigned his pastorate. "It was heartbreaking," Randy said. "I loved being a pastor; I loved my church." Yet from Randy's faithfulness to God emerged a new opportunity for ministry. Randy launched Eternal Perspective Ministries to carry out his new calling of pointing others toward an eternal perspective. His goal is to change minds and hearts through writing, speaking, a newsletter, and a Web site.

Randy receives only minimum wage for his salary so that the court cannot appropriate his income for the abortion clinic. He donates 90 percent of his book royalties to missions and the prolife cause, while 10 percent goes to his nonprofit ministry. Randy is free to continue his prolife involvement without paying a cent to the abortion industry.

Randy looks back on this experience and concludes, "It ended up being a great blessing. … The abortion clinic intended it for evil, but God intended it for good."[6] Randy could testify that if you are living for Christ and boldly speaking out for His sake, you will be despised and rejected by your contemporaries. Yet, as Randy's story proves, Jesus also promised that you would be blessed for being persecuted. Read His words in the margin.

The call to be Jesus' disciple is a call to take up your cross and follow Him. He asks His disciples to sacrifice everything for Him.

> "Blessed are those who are persecuted for righteousness, because the kingdom of heaven is theirs. Blessed are you when they insult you and persecute you, and say every kind of evil against you falsely because of Me. Be glad and rejoice, because your reward is great in heaven. For that is how they persecuted the prophets who were before you" (Matt. 5:10-12).

Are you ready to accept the consequences of Christ's call to be a citizen of the kingdom?
☐ I am not ready to suffer for Jesus' sake.   ☐ I am ready to pay any price to follow Christ.

Make a Difference in and Through Your Church

As a disciple of Jesus Christ, you are called to make a difference in and through your church. When you joined the church of Jesus Christ, you became part of something that has no comparison on earth. In Matthew 16:18 Jesus declared that the church is His and that He is building it. The Book of Acts records the birth and development of the church. Individuals were added to the church as they were saved. Those who were saved were baptized. These believers became a living organism, an extension of the very life of Christ on earth. His Spirit empowers this body, enabling it to carry out the mission of making disciples of all people. The church does not exist primarily for the sake of the members but for the sake of reaching those who are not members. The church is intensely missionary in nature—the people of God on mission.

In Acts 17 the Jews brought this charge against Paul and Silas: " 'These men who have turned the world upside down have come here too. ... They are all acting contrary to Caesar's decrees, saying that there is another king—Jesus!' " (Acts 17:6-7). Turning the world upside down graphically describes the difference Christians can and should make in the world. Paul said, "I am not ashamed of the gospel, because it is God's power for salvation to everyone who believes, first to the Jew, and also to the Greek" (Rom. 1:16). The word translated *power* is the Greek word *dunamis,* from which the term *dynamite* comes.

The gospel is like dynamite in making a difference in humankind. Jesus entrusted His gospel to the local church. This body is charged with the task of sharing the good news of resurrection life with a world that is dead in sin.

Christians who are serious about making a tremendous difference in this world must become actively involved in a local congregation of Christlike believers. No church is perfect; no church does all it could as a steward of the gospel. This is the reason each believer must become involved in making the church a more effective instrument of salvation.

Identify with the People of God

When you became a believer, you became part of the people of God. Read the verses in the margin to understand what this means.

This passage declares that the church is God's special people— recipients of His mercy who are set apart for His purpose. Our job is to proclaim God's praises and to be instruments of His redemptive work in the world. As His priests, we are responsible for showing God to the world and for bringing people into relationships with God through Jesus Christ.

In chapter 3 you studied the following purposes of the church.
- Evangelism—sharing with unbelievers the good news about salvation in Jesus Christ
- Discipleship—equipping believers to grow in Christlikeness and to make disciples of others
- Fellowship—experiencing the friendship and support of believers who are united by Christ
- Ministry—meeting the physical and spiritual needs of others
- Worship—praising God in spirit and truth

"You are a chosen race, a royal priesthood, a holy nation, a people for His possession, so that you may proclaim the praises of the One who called you out of darkness into His marvelous light. Once you were not a people, but now you are God's people; you had not received mercy, but now you have received mercy" (1 Pet. 2:9-10).

Beside each function identify the group or individuals who are primarily responsible for this area of your church's ministry.

Evangelism: _____ Discipleship: _____

Fellowship: _____ Ministry: _____

Worship: _____

Because these are the church's tasks, they are your tasks as well. The church is a community of believers in which each member covenants with God and with other members to live faithfully the church's beliefs, practices, and mission. Embrace the church's mission as your own and commit to do your part to carry out each church function. Remember that you are the church!

Underline the first sentence on this page. Now reevaluate your responses to the previous activity (p. 143) and write your name beside each church function.

Make a Commitment to a Local Church

If you are a Christian, the Lord Jesus has redeemed you to be a vital, functioning member of His church. The Apostle Paul, comparing the church to a human body, wrote, "You are the body of Christ, and individual members of it" (1 Cor. 12:27). Just as you need every part of your physical body to be complete, the church needs you in order to be the complete body of Christ. Paul wrote, "The body is not one part but many" (1 Cor. 12:14). Spectator Christians are disobedient Christians. Every believer needs the instruction, fellowship, support, and nurture of other believers. And if Jesus is truly your Lord, you will want to join Him in building His church through witness and service to others.

Explain in your own words why you need to be a participating member of a local church.

_____

_____

Being the Church Before a Watching World

"Your church is the body of Christ, walking in your community. The world must see the difference He can make today, just as He made a difference in the world when He came in the flesh. ... Jesus desires for every church to live our lives in the midst of a watching world so that they may see Him in us." Here is the progression in God's plan to touch the world:

1. "God purposes to use the church to reveal His wisdom.
2. "All that God purposes was accomplished in Christ Jesus.
3. "The church will demonstrate before a watching world the wisdom of God by the difference that Christ makes in their lives.
4. "God reveals Himself by working among His people through the Holy Spirit, drawing a world to Himself.
5. "God touches a world through the churches and brings glory to Himself."[7]

The first step in becoming part of a local church is to be born again. Make certain that you not only believe the truth about Jesus but have also received Him by faith as your Savior and Lord. The next step is baptism—immersion in water as a public confession of your new life in Jesus.

If for some reason you are not sure you have been saved, read the box "How to Be Saved" on page 41 or talk with someone you know is a believer.

Have you followed Jesus by obeying His command to be baptized? If not, make this commitment now and be sure to follow through.

If you have moved from the church where you were baptized, ask for membership in a church where you now live. This transfer of membership is called *moving your letter*—a term that originated many years ago when a person actually carried a written letter of membership from one church to another. Today a church clerk handles this transfer through the mail.

Church membership, however, is far more than getting your name in a record book. Once you are a member of a local congregation, the responsibility of active involvement is yours.

Be an Active Member of Your Church

Americans are famous for being sports fans, but sometimes this spectator mentality carries over into our attitudes toward the church. It is easy to think of the pastor and other church leaders as the players, while the church members sit in the stadium cheering or booing as the team performs. But as Paul explained in Ephesians 4:11-13, the biblical role of church leaders is to equip believers for service. Church members, not church leaders, are responsible for carrying out the work of ministry.

The commonly used term *inactive church member* does not describe a valid condition. Every member is active, either for or against the church. Those who choose not to attend, not to give, not to pray, and not to be supportive are actually against what the church is seeking to be and do. Hebrews 10:24-25, in the margin, expresses the importance of active church involvement. Some members cannot attend services due to poor health or other legitimate hindrances, but everyone else should be present as often as possible. As a pastor I often taught about the importance of discovering and using spiritual gifts. One Sunday a man said to me, "Preacher, I've been listening to what you say, and I think my gift is the gift of showing up!" He expressed his commitment to his church by always being present.

In chapter 4 you learned the importance of discovering and using your spiritual gift(s) to build up the church through obedient service to Christ. If you have not yet discovered your spiritual gift(s), consider taking a course that will guide you to explore and utilize them. Every believer

"He personally gave some to be apostles, some prophets, some evangelists, some pastors and teachers, for the training of the saints in the work of ministry, to build up the body of Christ, until we all reach unity in the faith and in the knowledge of God's Son, growing into a mature man with a stature measured by Christ's fullness" (Eph. 4:11-13).

"Let us be concerned about one another in order to promote love and good works, not staying away from our meetings, as some habitually do, but encouraging each other, and all the more as you see the day drawing near" (Heb. 10:24-25).

has one or more gifts, and every believer is responsible for being a good steward of the gifts and abilities God has bestowed.

In addition to exercising your spiritual gift(s), look for other ways to serve your church. For example, you could be a greeter, an usher, or a helper in a Bible-study class or department. Volunteer to visit the homebound or persons in the hospital. Sing in the choir or maintain the church grounds. Accept your assignments with cheerfulness and gratitude as opportunities to serve the Lord through His church.

Every church member is also responsible for reaching outsiders for salvation and church membership. Be a committed ambassador for Christ in your family, neighborhood, workplace, and other arenas. Ask the Lord to show you someone He wants to reach through you, begin praying for them, and find ways to influence them spiritually. The Lord used someone to influence you to come to church and eventually to Him. Now you have the privilege of reaching someone for Him.

An important ministry every church member can perform is intercessory prayer. Prayer will make a difference in your church and in you. Commit to pray for the ministries of your church. Pray especially for your pastor, church staff, and other church leaders. Ask God to bring spiritual awakening worldwide. Pray for lost persons by name. The ideas in "Praying for Your Church" will help you pray for your church and other believers.

Praying for Your Church

Whom to Pray For
- Church members
- Lay leaders
- Pastor
- Church staff
- Denominational leaders
- Missionaries
- The larger body of Christ— other churches, denominations, and believers in all parts of the world

What to Pray For
- Assurance
- Bold witnessing
- Calling of workers
- Christian fruit
- Christian unity
- Conviction of sin
- Deliverance
- Endurance
- Faith
- Faithfulness
- Filling of the Spirit
- Forgiveness
- Generosity
- Guidance, God's will
- Healing—spiritual, emotional, physical
- Holiness
- Hope
- Humility
- Integrity
- Joy
- Judgment
- Justice
- Knowledge
- Love
- Loyalty
- Mercy
- Obedience
- Patience
- Peace
- Preservation
- Provision of needs
- Purity
- Reconciliation
- Repentance and revival among God's people
- Right conduct
- Right motives
- Spirit of servanthood
- Spiritual awakening and conversion of the lost
- Spiritual cleansing
- Spiritual growth and discipleship
- Stewardship
- Surrender and submission to Christ
- Understanding
- Wisdom[8]

Another crucial area of church participation is giving money for kingdom causes. This discipline is essential not only for your church but also for your development as a steward. Obey the Lord and bring the first tenth—the tithe—of your income to His church (see Mal. 3:8-12). When believers obey God's command to tithe, the church has the resources needed to carry out its mission.

You can see that church is not a spectator sport. I encourage you to come down from the bleachers and find your place on the team.

Serve with a Christlike Attitude

Years ago I read a simple rhyme that challenged me: "What kind of a church would my church be if every member were just like me?" We should not demand more of others than we require of ourselves. This is especially true of our attitude toward the church and its leaders. Many churches are hindered from being and doing what God wants because of the negative, critical attitudes of disgruntled members. Use the following points to keep a check on your attitude.

- You cannot change the fact that some people will act in ways that displease you.
- An attitude of faultfinding and criticism has a negative effect on the spirit of a church.
- You have a choice every day about the attitude you express toward others.
- A Christlike attitude is possible because Christ lives in you.
- Allowing the Holy Spirit to control your attitude will build up rather than tear down your church.

Use the previous statements to prepare personal goals in the following areas.

When fellow believers disappoint me, I will _____

_____

When I am tempted to become critical of my church or its leadership, I will _____

_____

When I don't feel like loving certain persons, I will _____

_____

When my attitude conflicts with the Holy Spirit's direction, I will _____

_____

In the passage in the margin, Paul encouraged believers to adopt the attitude of a servant, as Jesus did. Your attitude is your choice. Choose to seek the welfare of others more than your own gain. Choose to focus on the good in others. Choose to be a builder of your church, not a barrier to what God wants to accomplish.

Being a disciple of Jesus and participating in your church are just two ways you can join God's purpose. You and your church can also work together with other believers to make a difference in the world.

> "Make your own attitude
>   that of Christ Jesus,
> who, existing in the form
>   of God,
> did not consider equality
>   with God
> as something to be used
>   for His own advantage.
> Instead He emptied Himself
> by assuming the form of a slave,
> taking on the likeness of men.
> And when He had come as
>   a man in His external form,
> He humbled Himself
> by becoming obedient
>   to the point of death—
> even to death on a cross"
> (Phil. 2:6-8).

Make a Difference in the World

A Christian author wrote these thought-provoking words: "Few things are as encouraging as the realization that things can be different and that we have a role in making them so."[9] The followers of Jesus Christ have the power and calling to change the world. Jesus' final words before His ascension were " 'You will receive power when the Holy Spirit has come upon you, and you will be My witnesses in Jerusalem, in all Judea and Samaria, and to the ends of the earth' " (Acts 1:8).

We live in the world, but we " 'are not of the world' " (John 17:16). Rather than become like the world, we must change the world because Jesus calls us to bring about change. And this change begins with changed hearts—hearts that repent of sin, receive the Lord Jesus, and grow in Christlikeness. Our supreme task is to share the life-changing gospel with all people everywhere.

Work Together

To fulfill Jesus' Great Commission, believers must work together. We can do more through cooperative efforts than we can alone. This is why Jesus established His church; this is why churches work with other churches. We can always do more by combining resources with other believers. The Apostle Paul understood this principle of cooperation. He was determined to make a difference for the suffering Christians in Jerusalem who were enduring persecution and poverty. As Paul traveled on his missionary journeys, he shared the need of Jerusalem's believers with the churches of Asia Minor and southeastern Europe. He wrote this to the Corinthian Christians: "About the collection for the saints [in Jerusalem]: you should do the same as I instructed the Galatian churches" (1 Cor. 16:1).

For many years Baptist churches have answered this appeal to meet human need. *The Baptist Faith and Message* states, "Christ's people should, as occasion requires, organize such associations and conventions as may best secure cooperation for the great objects of the Kingdom of God. Such organizations have no authority over one another or over the churches. They are voluntary and advisory bodies designed to elicit, combine, and direct the energies of our people in the most effective manner. Members of New Testament churches should cooperate with one another in carrying forward the missionary, educational, and benevolent ministries for the extension of Christ's Kingdom. Christian unity in the New Testament sense is spiritual harmony and voluntary cooperation for common ends by various groups of Christ's people. Cooperation is desirable between the various Christian denominations, when the end to be attained is itself justified, and when such cooperation involves no violation of conscience or compromise of loyalty to Christ and His Word as revealed in the New Testament."[10]

What methods does your church use to fulfill the Great Commission? _____

_____

_____

The nature and purpose of cooperation. Christians are, by their very nature, inter-dependent people. We are dependent on one another, and of course, we are dependent on God. We were created in Christ Jesus for fellowship and cooperation in ministry. We were made to enter a relationship of love, trust, and service with other Christians. If we fail to do that, we become emotionally sick, frustrated, and neurotic. Only in fellowship and cooperation can we become what God created us to be. New life in Christ is not just a personal and private relationship with Jesus Christ to be lived in splendid isolation. John Wesley said, "To turn Christianity into a solitary religion is to destroy it."[11] God's purpose is not just to save independent souls but to build a family, a church whose members belong together, need one another, and join hands and hearts to proclaim the gospel. Read in the margin Paul's description of the way believers unite to function together in love.

If we belong to Christ, we also belong to His people. A relationship with God produces a living partnership and ministry with other believers. We cannot faithfully serve the Lord without being in proper relationship and partnership with one another. When Paul warned the Ephesians to put away lying and speak the truth, it was because "we are members of one another" (Eph. 4:25). We were made for cooperation and partnership in ministry.

> "Walk worthy of the calling you have received, with all humility and gentleness, with patience, accepting one another in love, diligently keeping the unity of the Spirit with the peace that binds us. Speaking the truth in love, let us grow in every way into Him who is the Head—Christ. From Him the whole body, fitted and knit together by every supporting ligament, promotes the growth of the body for building up itself in love by the proper working of each individual part" (Eph. 4:1-3,15-16).

Cooperation is the most effective way for believers to accomplish the work God has given us to do. Christians voluntarily cooperate to accomplish more than we could individually.

Southern Baptists and cooperation. Cooperation among churches is a long-standing practice by Southern Baptists. Throughout our history our churches have organized to minister together through associations, state conventions, and the Southern Baptist Convention.

Southern Baptists and the Cooperative Program

Baptists in the South formed the Southern Baptist Convention when messengers from various churches met in Augusta, Georgia, on May 8, 1845. The constitution approved at that time states: "It is the purpose of the Convention to provide a general organization for Baptists in the United States and its territories for the promotion of Christian missions at home and abroad and any other objects such as Christian education, benevolent enterprises, and social services which it may deem proper and advisable for the furtherance of the Kingdom of God."[12]

For many years the Southern Baptist Convention tried various means of soliciting support for its two primary mission agencies. Finally, in 1925 the Cooperative Program was created. This plan of financial cooperation provides the Convention an ongoing, systematic way to enlist and mobilize churches' financial support for all Convention causes. This plan also allows churches to designate a portion of their contributions to the state convention, with the remainder being allocated to Convention-wide needs.

Today the Cooperative Program primarily supports the work of these Southern Baptist agencies: the International Mission Board, the North American Mission Board, six Southern Baptist seminaries, the Convention's Executive Committee, the Ethics and Religious Liberty Commission, the Annuity Board, and the Woman's Missionary Union. The Cooperative Program enables more than 16 million Southern Baptists in more than 42,000 churches, working together under the lordship of Jesus Christ, to make an eternal difference in the world.

Churches usually form associations on the basis of geographical proximity. Sometimes the association includes all of the Southern Baptist churches in a metropolitan area, a county, or even a larger area in less populated states. Each church is allowed a given number of messengers who represent their church in the association and vote on matters of business. Associations start new churches and strengthen existing churches through missions projects, leadership training, and counseling for church leaders about faith and practice.

State conventions are the next level in the organizational structure. All cooperating Southern Baptist churches in a particular state are eligible to send voting messengers to an annual meeting of the state convention. Like associations, states help start new churches. They also help churches strengthen their ministries and programs. State conventions provide ministries that individual churches could not do effectively, such as children's homes, senior-adult facilities, rehabilitation programs, crisis-pregnancy centers, and adoption services. States also operate colleges and academies, coordinate volunteer missions work, and sponsor chaplains.

The Southern Baptist Convention is an annual gathering of local-church messengers who assemble to hear reports and make decisions about Convention issues. The Convention provides Southern Baptists a way to work cooperatively in national and international missions, theological education, stewardship development, and moral and social issues. Following are some ways Southern Baptists voluntarily work together to do God's work.

- *We cooperate to bear witness to the gospel.* Through our Cooperative Program, Southern Baptists maintain more than 10,000 career missionaries in the United States and overseas, plus hundreds of thousands of volunteer, short-term, and special-assignment missionaries. No individual church could support such a massive missionary program.
- *We cooperate to meet human needs.* Southern Baptists support scores of hospitals, ministry agencies and institutions, retirement homes, and ministries to the hungry and lonely. An individual could never effectively feed multitudes of hungry people, but together we can make a significant difference. More than $8 million of the International Mission Board's annual budget goes to alleviate world hunger.
- *We cooperate to train and equip Christian workers.* Southern Baptists support six seminaries with more than 12,000 students, 46 universities with more than 165,000 students, 20 junior colleges, and a number of academies and theological schools with more than 13,000 enrolled. By cooperating with Baptist associations and state conventions, Southern Baptists prepare church leaders for the task of ministry.

Review the three ways Southern Baptists work together. List specific things that churches cannot do alone but can accomplish by working together.

_____   _____

_____   _____

_____   _____

_____   _____

The uniqueness of the Southern Baptist structure among denominations is that no Southern Baptist agencies have authority over one another or over local churches. All cooperation among Southern Baptists is voluntary; all member churches remain autonomous. No individual, church, or denominational entity can force any other individual, church, or denominational entity to conform to something contrary to its understanding of Scripture, to compromise its ethical convictions, or to violate its conscience. No attempt is made to coerce others to cooperate, and no one is condemned for not cooperating. Southern Baptists honor freedom of conscience and freedom of will under the leadership of the Holy Spirit.

Local Baptist churches also cooperate with other non-Baptist organizations to relieve human suffering, take a stand on social and ethical issues, and sponsor evangelistic crusades and other projects that promote kingdom causes.

The hope for bringing about lasting change in this world depends on the cooperative efforts of those who are being transformed by the indwelling life of Christ. We must be laborers together with God and with all His people to have maximal impact on this world.

Working Together

"The greater the purpose, the greater the need for cooperation. Now who has a greater purpose than the Christian church? Our purpose is God-ordained, worldwide, and eternal in scope because we are to preach the gospel to every person. And we can fulfull this purpose only when we are cooperative rather than competitive, supportive rather than suspicious, other-centered rather than self-centered, and kingdom-focused rather than agenda-focused. Then and only then will we bring our resources, creativity, and energy together for the good of others and the glory of God."—Claude Thomas, pastor; First Baptist Church; Euless, Texas

"Cooperative Program giving allows Christians and churches to practice biblical steward-ship in a way that best mobilizes the body of Christ to fulfill the Great Commission in our generation. The success of the Cooperative Program is vital to the spiritual and strategic health of Southern Baptists' work and witness across America and around the world and deserves our prayerful and generous support."—Jack Graham, pastor; Prestonwood Baptist Church; Plano, Texas

Accept the Challenge

A woman sent a Bible to her husband, a soldier who was stationed in Iraq. His unit was respon-sible for guarding Iraqi prisoners of war. One day as this soldier was discussing his faith in Christ with another American, a group of Iraqi prisoners overheard them. After these POWs were released, one of them approached the soldier and said he wanted to know more about "this Jesus." Later the soldier led the Iraqi to faith in Christ. The man immediately wanted to learn more, and the soldier gave him the Bible that his wife had sent. Hearing this story, someone asked the woman whether her husband was a chaplain. She responded, "No, he's just an ordinary soldier."

Postmodernism—a philos-ophy rejecting absolute truth and asserting that truth is an individual determination

Our contemporary culture is a spiritual battlefield that requires Christians to become committed to serve Christ as ordinary soldiers. Unfortunately, only a few informed Christian voices have been prominent in the debate of today's issues. We must all become champions of biblical truth in a day when such truth is not popular. Here are just a few of the challenges believers face in our nation today.

The challenge of postmodernism. Postmodernism is a philosophical movement that rejects any worldview that claims to know and assert the truth. Adherents reject both science and biblical truth as having no objective basis. The implications of such a position are signifi-cant for believers. This philosophy passionately rejects our claim of Christ's uniqueness and our appeal to the authority of God's Word. The values of tolerance and inclusivism are elevated to the greatest level of virtue, while Christ's claim to be " 'the way, the truth, and the life' " (John 14:6) is viewed as intolerant and exclusivist. When people deny objective truth, they also reject any ethical standards, opening the door to behavior and decisions uninformed by decency and morality.

The challenge of immorality. In America we are seeing a tidal wave of godlessness washing across our nation, but few voices from the evangelical camp are being raised in opposition. One Supreme Court decision basically sanctioned homosexual behavior by repealing a sodomy law in Texas. At the time of this writing, courts in several states are on the verge of ruling in favor of same-sex marriage.

The tragedy is that instead of championing biblical morality, American Christianity is abandoning biblical positions, along with centuries of church history, in favor of liberal and inaccurate interpretations of Scripture. The American Episcopal Church's decision to approve the appointment of a homosexual bishop was a major blow to authentic Christianity. Sadly, the church has been absent in the debate of these and other key moral issues such as abortion on demand and state lotteries.

The challenge of assaults on religious liberty. By ordering the removal of a display of the Ten Commandments, a federal judge ruled that the people of Alabama have no right to acknowledge God, even though the state's constitution invokes the favor and guidance of Almighty God as the basis of that state's laws and justice system. Through a series of judicial rulings over the past several decades, the nation's courts have taken prayer out of public schools, legalized abortion, and legalized sodomy. They are close to completely secularizing America by taking away our Constitutional right as a people to acknowledge God.

The challenge of Islam. Islam is actively working toward a goal of dominating the United States and the world. America currently has around 7 million Muslims, and Islam is growing in this country at 6 percent a year. At this rate by the year 2020 every major U.S. city will be predominantly Muslim. Islam is the fastest-growing religion in the world, with 1.2 billion devotees, and it is growing at a rate of 2.75 percent a year. If this rate of growth continues, the number of Muslims will overtake Christians worldwide by the year 2020.

Islam's core mission of the conversion or submission of all non-Muslims is called *jihad*. The Qur'an encourages *jihad* with the sword, calling Muslims to defend Islam from attack or to forcefully establish Islam in foreign lands if Islam is not granted free expression there. In this sense *jihad* may be waged against oppressors, unbelievers, idolaters, and Christians and Jews.

As tragic as the contemporary social and moral landscape of our country is, it is not nearly as disconcerting as the deafening silence coming from Christianity. American Christians have cowered to pop culture in regard to these pivotal issues. We have failed to play a significant role in showing the world the true nature of the kingdom of God. And many Christian soldiers, though armed with biblical truth and the love of Christ, are reluctant to share the gospel of peace, instead embracing political correctness and withdrawing from the battle.

Identify a way you and your church can be better equipped to meet each challenge.

	You	Your Church
Postmodernism	_____	_____
Immorality	_____	_____
Religious liberty	_____	_____
Islam	_____	_____

I challenge you to become proactive as a world changer. This means living as Jesus' disciple—reading and obeying the Word, communicating with God in prayer, growing in Christlikeness, heeding the Holy Spirit's direction, and sacrificially serving the Lord. It means actively working in and through your church to evangelize, make disciples, fellowship with others, minister to people, and worship God. It means working with other believers to make a difference in the world by boldly taking a stand for Jesus Christ, speaking the truth in love, sharing the good news of salvation, and offering biblical solutions to contemporary problems. When Jesus returns, may He find us in the trenches, near the front line, serving as ordinary soldiers!

Think about what you have studied in this chapter. How do you want to see God work—

in your community? _____

in your church? _____

in your family? _____

in your personal life? _____

Pray for God to show you how He wants you to make a difference as His disciple, in and through your church, and in your world.

[1] "Our Daily Bread," Radio Bible Class; Grand Rapids, MI.

[2] Avery T. Willis Jr., *MasterLife 1: The Disciple's Cross* (Nashville: LifeWay Press, 1996), 134.

[3] Avery T. Willis Jr. and J. David Carter, *Day by Day in God's Kingdom: A Discipleship Journal* (Nashville: LifeWay Press, 1997), 6–7.

[4] Adapted from Willis, *MasterLife 1*, 19–20.

[5] David Watson, *Called & Committed: World-Changing Discipleship* (Wheaton, IL: Harold Shaw Publishers, 1982), 1.

[6] Diane Eble, "A Matter of Perspective" [cited 6 October 2003]. Available from the Internet: *http://www.epm.org/alcornpers.html.*

[7] Henry T. Blackaby and Melvin D. Blackaby, *Your Church Experiencing God Together* (Nashville: LifeWay Press, 2003), 176.

[8] T. W. Hunt and Claude V. King, *In God's Presence* (Nashville: LifeWay Press, 1994), 83–84.

[9] Daniel Taylor, as quoted by John Eldredge, *Wild at Heart* (Nashville: Thomas Nelson, 2001), 219.

[10] *The Baptist Faith and Message* (Nashville: LifeWay Christian Resources of the Southern Baptist Convention, 2000), 18.

[11] John Wesley, as quoted by Terry Smith, "Married and Living Together Too" [cited 16 October 2003]. Available from the Internet: *http://www.emconf.ca/Messenger/38_13/editor.htm.*

[12] *Annual of the Southern Baptist Convention 2002* (Nashville: Executive Committee of the Southern Baptist Convention, 2002), 4.

Leader Guide

Session 1

Goals: Members will affirm the authority of Scripture and describe God's nature.

1. Use the contents page (p. 3) and the ideas in the introduction (pp. 5–6) to overview the study.

2. Instruct members to write in their books responses to the question, What is God like (p. 7)? Ask volunteers to share their responses.

3. Direct members to page 9 and ask them to discuss in small groups their responses to the questions in the activity. Call for groups to share their responses.

4. Write on the board *inerrant* and *infallible*. Ask members to define the terms in regard to the Bible.

5. Define the terms on page 10 and emphasize that divine revelation is the basis of our knowledge of truth. Ask members to complete in writing this sentence: I am committed to the authority of the Bible because … Ask volunteers for responses.

6. Ask members to complete: The purpose of the Bible in my life is … List responses on the board.

7. Summarize "The Proof of the Bible," beginning on page 12.

8. Emphasize the triune nature of God. Direct members to page 16. Invite a volunteer to read aloud John 18:37. Ask for responses to the activities.

9. Divide into three groups and assign each group one of the Scriptures in the activity on page 17. Ask groups to follow the directions. Then call for reports.

10. Discuss "The Essential Nature of God" (pp. 18–21).

11. Explain the meanings of *omnipotence, omnipresence,* and *omniscience* (pp. 21–24).

12. Assign three groups the characteristics of holiness, righteousness, and love. Instruct groups to read pages 25–26 and the suggested Scriptures and to share how God reveals these characteristics. Call for responses to the activity on page 25.

13. Ask members to rewrite answers to the question, What is God like (p. 27)? Summarize what members learned about God in this session.

Session 2

Goals: Members will explain how to enter a relationship with God, identify the nature of humanity, list the consequences of sin, and state the meaning of *salvation by grace.*

1. Write on the board, How does someone enter a personal relationship with God? Distribute markers and ask volunteers to write responses.

2. Instruct members to share their responses to the activity on page 29. Emphasize what it means to be made in the image of God (see p. 30).

3. Read Genesis 2:17 and ask: What action did God forbid? What were the consequences of violating God's instructions? What are the consequences today?

4. Ask a volunteer to read aloud Psalm 139:13-16. Affirm the sanctity of human life.

5. Use the activity on page 34 to identify the purpose of salvation.

6. Ask volunteers to share the way they responded to the activity on page 35. Explain that Jesus made atonement for our sin and redeemed us (pp. 34–35).

7. Ask, What does the term *saved by grace* mean? Allow volunteers to respond.

8. Assign each of four small groups one of the terms on pages 36–39. Allow time for discussion; then call on groups to present the meanings.

9. If you do not know members' spiritual conditions, review "How to Be Saved" on page 41. Offer to be available after the session for counsel.

10. Explain the importance of discipleship and lordship. Emphasize on page 43 the ideas for spiritual growth.

11. Using pages 44–46, lead a discussion of election.

12. Identify from 1 John 2:15-16 believers' three enemies. Ask, How are believers attacked in each way? Close by emphasizing the four ways believers can live victoriously (pp. 48–49).

Session 3

Goals: Members will state the purpose of the church, identify their roles in the church, and commit to serve God through their church.

1. Write *ekklesia* on the board. Highlight the meaning, its uses in the New Testament, and the nature of the church as the body of Christ.

2. Give pairs two minutes to identify their criteria for evaluating the quality of their church experience.

3. Present the five functions of the church (pp. 52–56). Ask for examples of ways your church accomplishes each task and ways members support these functions.

4. Present the concept of spiritual gifts and the ideas for gift discovery on page 57. Ask members how they use or will commit to use their gifts in service.

5. Identify the leaders in your church as you discuss the biblical roles of pastor and deacon. Ask for responses to the activity at the bottom of page 58.

6. Write *ordinance* on the board and ask for a definition. Identify the ordinances your church practices.

7. Form three groups and assign each one of the purposes of baptism on page 62. After time for group work, call for reports.

8. As you discuss the meaning of the Lord's Supper (pp. 62–65), display the elements of the supper. Remind members that the elements represent Christ but have no sacred value.

9. Read aloud Genesis 2:2-3. Ask members what the Lord's Day means to them. List responses on the board. Use the activity on page 66 to identify the reasons the observance of the Sabbath shifted from Saturday to Sunday.

10. Draw a continuum on the board with *0%* on the left end and *100%* on the right end. Ask, Based solely on your church attendance, how committed to Christ would someone say you are? Distribute three-by-five-inch cards and ask members to write a numerical value. Collect cards and calculate the average commitment level for the class. Mark the value on the continuum and ask for reactions.

11. Summarize Baptist beliefs about religious liberty. Ask members to give examples of the public debate on the separation of church and state.

12. Ask volunteers to share ways their responses to the activity on page 71 differ from the one on page 50.

Session 4

Goals: Members will identify the biblical purposes of life, describe God's calling in their lives, and commit to serving God through education and stewardship.

1. Direct members to read Romans 8:28 and to identify how that verse relates to their purpose in life.

2. Ask: What is most important in your life? List responses on the board. Then read aloud Matthew 28:19-20 and ask members to identify what Jesus said should be most important. List these priorities in a column beside the first list.

3. Display a placard labeled *What is our purpose in life?* State that we will discuss four important purposes of the Christian life. Beneath it display a placard labeled *Personal evangelism.* Discuss believers' evangelistic responsibility, using the points on page 75.

4. Display a placard labeled *Church involvement.* Ask volunteers to suggest practical steps they can take to improve their church involvement.

5. Display a placard labeled *Spiritual growth.* Emphasize that the measure of spiritual transformation is the degree to which an individual is becoming like Jesus.

6. Display a placard labeled *Global missions.* Point out that more than 5,000 Southern Baptist missionaries serve in 153 countries. Point out the need for every believer to support missions.

7. Ask volunteers to share their paraphrases on page 79.

8. Ask members to identify how their vocations relate to God's calling in their lives. Ask a member to read aloud Proverbs 3:5-6 and discuss the importance of allowing God to direct our path.

9. Summarize the teachings on spiritual gifts (pp. 82–83) and call for volunteers to reveal their gift or gifts with the group. Discuss ways specific gifts can be used in service through your church.

10. Divide into three groups and ask them to summarize the importance of these elements of Christian education: spiritual transformation (pp. 84–85), the role of teaching (pp. 85–86), and the development of a biblical worldview (pp. 86–87). Ask members to name ways they can participate in and support Christian education. List these on the board.

11. Summarize the principles of stewardship and tithing and point out every believer's responsibility to support God's work through the Cooperative Program. Point out the items listed in the activity on page 90. Challenge members to recognize God's ownership of everything they have and to give Him their tithes and offerings.

12. Ask volunteers to share the purpose statements they wrote on page 92.

Session 5

Goals: Members will identify ways believers can influence society, describe a Christian response to war, summarize biblical views of marriage and family, and commit to honor God in society and in their families.

1. Read aloud Romans 12:2. Ask members to give their responses to the related activity on page 94.

2. Ask a volunteer to read aloud Luke 4:16-19. Ask for responses to the activity on page 95.

3. State, A changed world begins with a changed heart. Ask, How does Jesus change hearts? Call for volunteers to share how Jesus changed their hearts.

4. Ask someone from a social-service agency or ministry to speak about meeting needs. Ask volunteers to share their experiences in helping needy people.

5. Read aloud 1 Corinthians 12:13-14 and call for answers to the activity on page 100.

6. Challenge members to stay informed about the issues described on pages 100–102 and to seek God's guidance in making a difference in these areas.

7. Discuss the Ten Commandments for Christian Citizens on page 103.

8. Ask members to name appropriate ways Christians can influence society. List responses on the board.

9. Ask and discuss: How is peace possible? Is war ever justifiable? Under what conditions? How does a believer wage spiritual warfare?

10. Ask members to turn to page 106 and to give their responses to the activity about the family.

11. Read aloud Matthew 19:4-6 and affirm Jesus' high view of marriage as the ideal.

12. Divide into four groups and ask them to summarize biblical teachings for wives, husbands, parents, and children (pp. 107–12). Call attention to the boxes on pages 110–11. Stop and pray for the marriages and families represented in the group.

13. Read the statistics on page 112 and lead the group to develop a covenant of things they will do to guard their homes. Write the covenant on the board.

Session 6

Goals: Members will describe characteristics of the kingdom of God, identify implications of being kingdom citizens, and summarize biblical teachings about Last Things.

1. Ask for responses to the activity on page 114.
2. Define *kingdom of God* and overview how the concept is developed in the Old and New Testaments.
3. To make sure members understand the meaning of *priesthood of believers* (p. 116), ask for their answers to the activity at the top of page 116.
4. Summarize John the Baptist's role in preparing for the King. Emphasize that Jesus presented new kingdom values that contrasted with the values of the world. State how someone enters the kingdom.
5. Assign three groups to define the nature of the kingdom by summarizing the topics on pages 121–22.
6. Point out the sources of security listed in the activity on page 124. State, Only God provides security. Use the ideas in "You and the Kingdom" to identify implications of being kingdom citizens.
7. Ask, When will the end of the world come? Have a volunteer read Mark 13:24-25,32.
8. Summarize biblical teachings about Christ's return and the judgment.
9. Using the material on page 127, guide members to understand the effect the reality of the end of time should have on their daily lives.
10. Read 1 Corinthians 15:51-52. Discuss the intermediate state and the resurrection of the body.
11. List on the board *hades, tartaros,* and *gehenna.* Discuss each term and ask for responses to the activity on page 130.
12. Assign two groups to characterize hell and heaven, using the material on pages 130–33.
13. Ask members to identify ideas in "Perfected in Glory" on page 132 that were new to them.
14. Ask members to share their responses to the activity on page 134.

Session 7

Goals: Members will describe what it means to be a disciple of Jesus and identify ways they can make a difference in and through their church and in the world.

1. As members arrive, ask them to list on the board things to which they are devoted. Discuss responses.
2. Assign five groups the subtopics on pages 136–42 and ask them to describe a disciple according to their subtopics.
3. Remind members that every Christian is responsible for carrying out the purposes of the church listed on page 143.
4. Call for responses to the activity on page 144.
5. Ask, How can you be an active member of your church? List ideas on the board.
6. Call attention to the ideas in "Praying for Your Church" on page 146.
7. Ask for responses to the activity on page 149. Explain the necessity of cooperation among believers. Explain the way associations, state conventions, and the Southern Baptist Convention allow Southern Baptists to cooperate together.
8. Ask someone to state the purpose of the Cooperative Program. Mention the ways it enables Southern Baptists to make a difference (box, p. 150).
9. Ask for responses to the activity on page 151.
10. Summarize the challenges of postmodernism, immorality, the assault on religious liberty, and Islam. Ask for responses to the activity at the top of page 154.
11. Divide members into four groups and assign one portion of the final activity on page 154 to each group. After groups report, challenge members to make a difference as disciples, in and through their church, and in the world. Ask them to pray in their small groups for commitment, wisdom, and strength to live according to biblical beliefs.
12. Thank members for participating in this study.